Sonic Alchemy

Books and Recordings by Joshua Leeds

Books

The Power of Sound: How to Manage Your Personal Soundscape for a Vital, Productive, & Healthy Life (Healing Arts Press, 2001)

Recordings

The Essential Sound Series (8 CDs)
The Sound Health Series (8 CDs)
The Listening Program (8 CD set)
Sound Body Sound Mind: Music for Healing
Eight Meditations for Optimum Health

(See page 298 for complete discography)

Sonic Alchemy

Conversations with Leading Sound Practitioners

Joshua Leeds

InnerSong Press ♦ San Rafael, California

InnerSong Press, Inc.
PO Box 150326, San Rafael, CA 94915 USA
Tel: (415) 482-6095 Fax: (415) 482-6034
Email: Joshua.Leeds@thepowerofsound.com

Cover design by La Porta Design, Ross, CA www.descomstudios.com
Back cover photo by Denise Winters, NY, NY

The purpose of this book is to educate and entertain. This book is not intended to replace expert psychological or medical advice. The author and publisher disclaim any liability or loss, personal or otherwise, resulting from procedures or opinions expressed herein.

Library of Congress Catalog Number: 97-93472
ISBN 0-9657786-0-6

First printing, 1997.
Second printing, revised, 1999.
Third printing, revised, 2002.
Fourth printing, revised, 2005.

Printed in the United States of America by Morris Publishing
3212 East Highway 30 • Kearney, NE 68847 • 1-800-650-7888

Dedicated with love
to the memory of
Dennis Lambert

Contents

Acknowledgments

Heartfelt gratitude to:

Rachel Leeds, mother and dear friend, for enthusiasm, tremendous editing input, insisting I hold the vision, and without whom this project would have never taken flight–countless thanks!

Jeffrey Isbrandtsen, who called upon me to write, Therese Schroeder-Sheker for inspiring the scholar; Dr. Ron and Kate Minson who graciously shared the Tomatis experience; Karyn Kleinman & Laura Moe for re-defining sound partnership; Kiki La Porta of Descom Studios who paints beautifully upon my sound canvas; Morgan Smith for loving eagle eyes; Em Holland for fine design and production; Sanda Jasper for always being there; Benjamin Leeds for patient ears and coveted blessings; Sharon Leeds for wonderful care packaging; Margaret Tucker for pushing me out on the literary limb; and to my precious daughter, Lyric Kaela Grace, for the unexpected words to my love song.

Preface

Music and sound for the enhancement of human function makes a bold claim. As the banner statement of this book, it is designed to catch your attention and appeal to your inquiring mind. Why should you care about the effects of sound? Because it has been proven that sound–in musical or other manifestations–can either *charge* or *discharge* your nervous system. What that means is that you can consciously use sound to enhance your life.

As a composer and record producer, I surround myself with music. I finally understand what inextricably drew me, forty years ago, into that world. From a little boy with a trumpet to a grown man immersed in the music of chamber ensembles, I crave pleasing sounds. They help me feel like nothing else: whole and in tune.

As I research the inner components of sound and the physiology of the ear/brain mechanism, I fall more deeply into my relationship with music. The fervor of my exploration was ignited by the work of Dr. Alfred Tomatis, a French doctor, inventor, and philosopher. His lifetime exploration of the ear and realization that *sound is a nutrient for the nervous system* has set the theoretical foundation for a field with no official name.

Dr. Tomatis has touched off the pursuit of the advancement and study of sonic awareness by an international, eclectic, and visionary group of individuals. As I delved into the study of sound, I found there was no curriculum. So I sought out my own teachers; women and men who think, practice, and dwell in the bedrock of vibration and frequency. The wealth of their ideas is presented in the following dozen interviews.

The intention of *Sonic Alchemy* is to trigger your imagination and encourage further exploration. I believe a quantum leap in the use of subtle energy modalities, including sound, will take place through the synergy and advancement of the methods discussed herein. ✧

Introduction to Soundwork

THE NUTRIENTS OF SOUND

The theoretical construct upon which I build is that sound is a nutrient for the nervous system. The ground-breaking work of sound pioneer Alfred Tomatis reveals the hidden, extraordinary power of the ear. Dr. Tomatis claims the primary purpose of the ear is to recycle sound to recharge our inner batteries. Sound feeds us the electrical impulses that charge the neo-cortex of the brain. *In utero*, the ear's first function is to support the growth of the rest of the physical organism. After birth, sound is to the nervous system what food is to our physical bodies–nourishment for regeneration of energy. How we use the power of sound is a matter of personal choice. It can either strengthen or weaken us.[1]

THE LOST CHORD

Between 1991-1996, I searched for answers to these questions:

- ✦ Is there a deeper harmony?
- ✦ What is healing?
- ✦ Can I heal myself with music?
- ✦ Can I enhance my life with sound?

I journeyed far and wide, seeking people who ask the same questions. From New York to Colorado, Washington to North Carolina, Vermont to Texas, I've met sweet and gentle people committed to *Soundwork*.

MUSIC THERAPY / SOUND THERAPY — A DISTINCTION

Over the last decade, new forms of auditory-based therapeutic practices have gained momentum in our culture. In this book, I refer to sound as *soundwork* when used as a modality for change. Incorporating the ancient wisdom of shamans and medicine people into the high-technology of the Western world, sound becomes a vibrational tool of transformation.

Some call this burgeoning field *Sound Therapy.* The term *therapy* implies healing and/or fixing. The use of sound to effect change goes far beyond fixing. Controlled vibrational interaction can also be transformational and of great value in enhancing what already works in our lives. Therefore, it seems *soundwork* more aptly translates the process.

For more than forty years, music therapists have combined music with psychological/physiological applications in hospitals and private practice. *Music therapy is psychologically-based;* familiarity with musical content creates relaxation, comfort, and fun with rhythm. The success of music therapy has resulted in acceptance of its legitimacy by the arbiters of Western medicine.[2]

However, the upcoming field of Soundwork represents a radically different approach which emphasizes the powerful interaction of the vibrational frequencies within music and sound upon the body and psyche. *Soundwork is neurologically-based;* its effect comes from the entraining impact of external vibration and rhythms upon bone, tissue, and organs. The primary focus of *Sonic Alchemy* is the effect of sound on the nervous system.

TRADING IN THE CURRENCY OF SOUND

While on my quest, I've discovered there are many of us who are seemingly 'called' to do Soundwork. At a 1993 colloquium,entitled *The Healing Nature of Sound*[3] I expected to see twenty-five eccentrics. Instead, I found one hundred and fifty people who had traveled to New Hampshire to find a fellow seeker. University professors, business people, therapists, musicians, doctors, housewives, long-time soundworkers (and a few token certifiable eccentrics) knew each other, not by sight, but rather as fellow travelers independently journeying upon a river of sweet tone. We shared even more questions: *Who* is doing the calling and *what* is the work?

Society has not yet named or affixed a value to this field. Those of us in it barely know one another's research and explorations. However, a common bond lies in the conviction that conscious utilization of sound is a further step in our evolution.

In my travels, I have discovered that a revolutionary sound diet is evolving. This is reflected in the increasing number of audio products that are specifically designed to help us learn faster, relax and de-stress, strengthen our immune systems, heal from disease, meditate more deeply, soothe emotional upset, realign and balance our entire systems. Possibly, a future sonic prescription will be, "Take two CDs and you don't need to call me in the morning."

SOUND SLEUTH

My path of exploration into the deeper values of music and sound came about in a serendipitous manner. In 1986, I was living in Hollywood, an aspiring film and TV composer. One evening, I was invited to a lecture. As I listened to author Louise L. Hay[4] extol the virtues of affirmative thought, I was distracted by the distortion of the background music which she played on a tape cassette player. After her lecture, I requested a Q-Tip and alcohol to clean the tape heads of the offending machine. This was the beginning of a long-time friendship. I went on to compose four of Louise's albums as she became internationally known and respected.

At this time, the AIDS epidemic was spiraling out of control in California. I accompanied Louise to many standing-room-only gatherings of very sick men and women. She encouraged and greatly comforted them, using the music and affirmative chants we'd written together. Observing the profound impact of her *soundwork,* commercial composing thereafter lost its appeal.

As I considered the role of the *healing* music provider, I realized I knew nothing about healing, let alone the role of music in that process. In fact, I wondered if music was merely a placebo.

As fate would have it, I was subsequently asked to write a magazine article about healing music. I declined–three times! Finally, a persistent editor sent me *The Healing Forces of Music*,[5] a book that literally changed my life. I discovered that many people were thinking about the impact of music and sound.

I began writing. One feature article led to another. Soon I was travelling around the country, seeking those who might know the answers to my enthusiastic questions. With tape recorder in hand, each response spawned a dozen new inquiries. I became a veritable sound sleuth–a student obsessed.

SONIC ALCHEMISTS

I found musicians, scientists, dancers and scholars–alchemists all. These women and men do not attempt to turn metal into gold; rather, they create sonic potions for transmutation. Using sound frequency and musical vibration, they shift consciousness, emotional awareness, and physical structure.

As each spoke of explorations and methodologies, I realized they created unique matrixes of sound to encourage and coax the nervous system. At their soundbenches, they mix a little of this with a bit of that, each formula the result of years of diligent exploration.

Of the many delightful people who welcomed me into their sonic workshops, I have selected twelve of their interviews for this book. Their premises certainly vary. It would be a lively table if they were to all sit together. A common thread I found throughout was the deep commitment of each explorer to the field. This absorption was no dalliance, but rather represented a life's devotion.

These musicians had become college professors, authors, therapists, bodyworkers, business people, and doctors of every stripe. They never forgot their love for music and have incorporated it into other disciplines. They know the vibration of sound in their bones and the inherent power it carries.

In addition to interviews, initial chapters explore the rudiments of soundwork; rhythm, resonance, and entrainment. *Demystifying Binaural Beat Frequencies* explains the art of highly-specific frequencies administered through headphones. *The Tomatis Method* reveals the brilliant pioneering work of Dr. Alfred Tomatis. Finally, a resource section and bibliography is included to facilitate further explorations into this ever-widening field of soundwork. ✧

ENDNOTES

1 Alfred A. Tomatis is a scholar, sound researcher, inventor, and creator of an extraordinary sound therapy known as *The Tomatis Method.* He began his explorations into sound in the 1940's as a young Ear, Nose, and Throat surgeon in France. His discoveries have resulted in international respect and honor; he is widely regarded as the 'Einstein of the Ear.' See Chapter Three and Appendix A; *Core Beliefs of Alfred Tomatis.*

2 The American Music Therapy Association. See Appendix C.

3 The Sound Colloquiums are produced by Jeff Volk for Lumina Productions. See Appendix C.

4 Louise L. Hay is the author of many wonderful books and audio tapes based on the power of affirmative thinking. She is best known for *You Can Heal Your Life*, (CA, Hay House, 1986). For an extraordinary catalog of books on health and well-being by Louise and other exceptional authors, call Hay House (800) 654-5126.

5 Randall McClellan Ph.D., *The Healing Forces of Music; History, Theory & Practice* (MA, Element, 1991).

Part One

The Hierarchy of Sound

Part One

THE HIERARCHY OF SOUND

Effective Curative or Age-Old Curiosity?

The entire planet vibrates to the rhythms and sounds of music. From the most primitive enunciation to the highest sophistication of performance, music plays an exclusive and vital role in every country. Music is an inescapable part of life; spiritual ceremonies, social celebrations, armies marching off to war, initiations, funerals, harvests and mother's lullabies.

As a composer, I am drawn to the mix of music and the healing arts. I also pose the question: Is music really an effective curative, or is it simply an age-old curiosity?

Scholars trace the first musical instruments to frame drums played by women in sacred ceremonies thousands of years ago.[1] The chanting and music of the medicine woman or shaman has been a part of healing rituals throughout the ages. Elements of sound and music have been prominent aspects of indigenous, intuitively-based cultures. Yet, in our scientific Western culture, the combination of healing and music is on the fringe.

However, over the last decade, interest has intensified in the search for the answers of the *how* and *why* of music and healing. High-technology instrumentation can track subtleties previously uncharted. Additionally, allopathic medicine, with its emphasis on treatment using pharmaceuticals and surgery, is losing its appeal due to the harmful side effects and high cost. With the increased attractiveness of alternative modalities, the field of therapeutic sound and music takes its place in the pantheon of subtle energy medicines.

So, how do we define *healing* with music? I reject the label *healing properties* in conjunction with music; my concern is that improper labeling will create a fad. I believe this would discourage deeper exploration into the modality. I prefer to think of sound and music that is intentionally created for well-being as *therapeutic* in effect. This infers that the music has been created for a specific purpose. As in any therapeutic application, there are no absolute guarantees. In energy medicine, what works for one person may not work for another. This is especially true within the context of the elusive and subtle nature of sound. However, subtlety must not be confused with weakness. If anything, it is within the subtlety of sound that its power may lie.

One cannot explore the use of therapeutic music without including the entire spectrum of sound. While music is sound, sound is not always musical. The substance of both is *vibration* and *frequency*.

SOUND IS EVERYWHERE

We are vibrated constantly with sound from jet-planes, jackhammers, horns, sirens, and loud music. Additionally, our cells are bombarded by the unheard sounds of modern society; microwaves, electricity, and radar. All atomic matter is affected through the process of *entrainment* and *resonance* by nearby vibrational elements such as soundwaves. One can hypothesize about a possible relationship between frequency overload, increased stress, and disease.

Might there be a beneficial way to utilize aspects of sound and vibration? Answers are evolving in the domain of Soundwork, where the neurological impact of vibration is a major consideration.

When exploring this field, the terms *music, sound, frequency,* and *vibration* may be interchangeable. Differences lie in the form in which they are manifesting. Consider this: Everything on Earth is comprised of atoms.

- All atomic matter vibrates
- Frequency is the rate at which it vibrates
- The frequency of a vibration creates a specific sound (sometimes inaudible)
- Sound can be molded into music

The continuum of sound that results in miraculous music can be traced to the basic atom. Observe the following:

Atomic matter —> Vibration —> Frequency —> Sound —> Music

This is why there is sound in everything. Yet, how does sound over *there* affect me over *here?* The answer lies in the wondrous process of *entrainment.* ✧

ENDNOTES

[1] Layne Redmond, *When the Drummers were Women* (NY, Harmony Books, 1997)

1

ENTRAINMENT

Harnessing Rhythm

While studying the effects of external rhythm on the nervous system, I've discovered that the physical body–the ultimate form of individuality–paradoxically contains an autonomic mechanism that causes it to constantly match the tempos of others. Within a matter of moments, we can be breathing, palpitating, and thinking in tandem with those around us. Usually we are not even aware of it.

Each of us is equipped with a physiological mechanism that reaches out to mimic–or reunite–with a greater pulse than our own. This process is called *entrainment.* Our vital pulses (brainwaves, heart rate, and breath) will speed up or slow down to match an external, periodic pulse. This occurs every minute of every day. Each cell in our bodies is encoded with instructions to do this.

Entrainment is a little-known process.[1] Curiously, while science continuously deals with the concept, psychologists, physiologists, and health-care practitioners consider it insignificant. I believe entrainment is an extraordinary concept of major significance. Used with awareness, this phenomenon holds great promise as a tool for wellness and enhancement. Understanding entrainment provides a new context to view our sense of singularity within the undulating web of life.

In the house of therapeutic music and sound, entrainment is an indispensable theoretical pillar. Through entrainment, our major body pulses synchronize with external periodic rhythms. Our brainwaves will entrain to musical rhythms or the pace of a speaker's presentation.

Sound is quite often the vehicle through which this phenomenon of entrainment takes place.

Entrainment also occurs on an internal to internal basis: our heart rate entrains with our brainwaves and our breath rate.

Rhythm is infectious because of entrainment. Superficially, entrainment causes us to tap our feet and bob our heads to upbeat rhythms. But inside, the human mechanism experiences an even greater impact; external rhythms can actually alter the tempo of our internal pulse systems. Imagine the conscious use of rhythmic entrainment as a device to enhance health, accelerate learning, reduce stress, and increase productivity. While the intentional use of entrainment is just beginning to take place, I'd venture that 99% of the population has no idea about this physiological process that impacts us from the moment of conception to the minute we die.

ENTRAINMENT — ALL ABOARD!

In addition to '...the act of entering a train,' entrainment is generally defined as the process of drawing away with or after oneself. Curiously enough, while tapping into abundant university data-bases, I found little on the effects of resonance and perception of musical meter. This seems strange because we are always surrounded by external rhythms. Physicists long ago ascertained that atomic matter can be impacted by external pulses. Yet, the study of external rhythms upon the nervous system is widely unexplored. While giving scant attention to this particular arena, scientific disciplines do hold a common definition of entrainment: it is the effect of one system upon another.

We know that rhythm effects us; moving us, propelling, exciting or fatiguing us. But why? Can we harness the power of rhythm to fuel us or cool us? How can we use this physiological phenomenon with awareness? For the most part, entrainment is used unconsciously; we put on energetic music in the morning to get us up and going. At night, soothing music is used for relaxation. If we expand these natural inclinations, we will find that external rhythm can be used as a practical adjunct to our daily lives.

When we learn about brainwave states, we can navigate and exert choice as to when we are mildly coherent and when we are extremely focused. Rhythm can wind us down quickly, put us into trance, or lessen the effects of hyper-tension. There are no major secrets here. It simply comes down to awareness of a potent tool that surrounds us.

The conscious understanding of the interplay of inner and outer rhythms is available to everyone. As music and sound for intentional usage surfaces in our culture, the need for conscious awareness of entrainment increases.

RHYTHM — THE PULSE OF LIFE

Rhythm–as an integral part of all activity–has long been considered by physicists, astronomers, athletes, musicians, and the military. Like air or water, however, the pervasiveness of rhythm is rarely noticed by the world-at-large.

It is in the realm of music that rhythm is seriously regarded and avidly studied. *Rhythm, tone,* and *harmony* constitute music's basic components. Yet to regard rhythm only within the context of music's pulse is to minimize its tremendous power.

There is no life without rhythm and periodic movement. Nature can not exist without its interdependent and independent rhythms; self-contained, yet easily changed by adjoining rhythmic forces.

Within the body, *circadian* rhythms are typically strong and steady. Erratic rhythms, big and small, generate anxiety. Arrythmias of the heart, irregularities of global weather patterns, or a planet's irregular rotation is cause for tremendous concern. *Periodic rhythm*–activity which is cyclic–is considered stable and preferred.

In fact, periodic rhythms are everywhere. In water, air, solid matter, and organic life cells, vibrations are twirling, pulsing, pushed and pulled. Periodic vibrations are classified as frequencies. *Light, sound, smell,* and *taste* are the frequencies humans are equipped to perceive. Anything that vibrates is susceptible to the influence of external rhythms around them. This transpires through the process of resonance and entrainment.

RESONANCE AND ENTRAINMENT

The understanding of the interlocking concepts of resonance and entrainment is essential. For through these processes, external sounds and rhythms can either heal or create havoc to glass windows and cement walls, as well as brain waves and organic cells.

Resonance, according to sound researcher Jonathan Goldman, "...may be defined as the frequency at which an object most naturally wants to vibrate."[2] Resonance is also thought of as a structure that vibrates at a frequency that is natural to it and most easily sustained by it.

Tuning forks demonstrate the concept of resonance. A tuning fork in the key of A is tuned to 440 Hz (cycles per second). This fork, actually an inert piece of metal until struck and put into vibration, will only vibrate at 440 Hz. This is known as its *resonant frequency*. I like to think of resonant frequencies as an objects *home* frequency, or its *resident* frequency. An object's resonant frequency is the vibrational speed at which it is the most comfortable. In the case of the tuning fork, the density of the metal will not truly respond to anything but about 440 cycles per second.

If this tuning fork remains unstruck, but another fork within proximity is struck and sends out the 440 Hz sound wave, the first fork begins to vibrate and sound, even though it has not been struck by anything other than sound waves. Because the surrounding waves are similar to its home frequency, this fork will sing along. When two objects have similar vibratory characteristics that allow them to resonate at the same frequency, they form a resonant system. However, if a fork tuned to 300 Hz were struck nearby, the 440 fork wouldn't even bother to notice, let alone sound.

The principle of resonance holds true with people as well. When we find ourselves feeling good around somebody, we actually use the phrase 'good vibes'. And this is the truth; we feel good because they have a similar frequency to our own resonant frequency which causes us to vibrate. We actually resonate with them. However, a major difference between people and tuning forks is that we are not made of metal.

And if someone resonates in a way that 'offends' our frequency rate, we move away from them because we do not want to be affected by their vibrations.

ENTRAINMENT — RESONATING WITH A TWIST

Entrainment is an aspect of resonance with a major twist. With entrainment, a stronger external pulse is not just activating another's pulse, but actually causing it to move from its resonant frequency to match it. Goldman states, "...with entrainment you are changing the natural oscillatory patterns of one object and replacing them with the different oscillatory patterns of another object." He continues, "...You are actively changing the vibrations (the frequency or rhythm) of one object to another rate."[3]

Going back to the tuning fork, one fork cannot entrain another fork. The metal's density will not allow it. But nature, with its innate mutability, is quite entrainable–as are human beings. We pulse, we vibrate, and we have rhythm; we possess the perfect materials for entrainment.

Common examples of entrainment are seen in fireflies blinking together, college roommates with similar menstrual cycles and lovers sharing a synchronized heart beat as they move closer together. Strong communication may cause entrainment of brain waves–sometimes seen between professors and students, preachers and congregations, therapists and clients. Audiences entrain to performers, while marching teams and choir members entrain to their compatriots.

Individually, we entrain to the rhythms around us–be it traffic, music, the periodic sounds of machines, or the all encompassing electromagnetic frequency fields. Unfortunately, ignorance of the effect of external rhythms on our system invites the existence of unhealthy and vitiating sonic environments.

Within our bodies, the heart rate, respiration and brain wave cycles entrain to each other. If we slow the breath, the heart rate and brain waves will follow. Slowing brain waves cause heart rate and respiration to decelerate.

GRANDFATHER CLOCKS OF 1665

The concept of entrainment was first noted in 1665 by Christian Huygens, a Dutch scientist. Observing a roomful of grandfather clocks, he noted that though their pendulums were started at different times, a day later they would swing in unison.

Brain waves, fire flies, grandfather clocks, tuning forks–all disparate elements adhere to the same physics phenomenon. Entrainment, it appears, conserves energy. Goldman states "...It seems that nature finds it more economical in terms of energy to have periodic events that are close enough in frequency occur in phase or in step with each other."[4]

While these entrainment examples are interesting to me, it is the continuous manifestation of entrainment which staggers my imagination. The concept of a sonic environment of choice is quite foreign to most. This pertains especially to music and sound. Unwittingly, we surround ourselves with sounds, rhythms, and resonant elements which enervate rather than energize.

ENTRAINMENT — WHO OWNS IT?

Another venue of entrainment is visual. Historically, the flickering of a fire was effective in putting people in trance states. Sitting in front of a fireplace relaxes. Why? Because a seasoned fire flickers at a periodic rate equivalent to mid-alpha brain waves. Meditators covet this relaxation state.

The perception of light as a way to entrain the brain generated the creation of commercial Light and Sound Machines in the late '70's. Binaural beat frequencies to the ears and flashing lights to the eyes are effective in this multi-sensory entrainment delivery system.

In 1994, however, The FDA closed down a major West Coast manufacturer and distributor of Light and Sound Machines.[5] The complaint: the flashing lights which are viewed through closed eyes could stimulate a rare form of epilepsy.

Legal spokesmen of the companies protested to no avail, though they asserted that there is a higher incidence of visually-triggered epilepsy among children watching Nintendo games. Recently the companies were notified that a major reason for closure was use of the term *entrainment* in their literature. According to the FDA, *entrainment* is considered a medical term. Therefore, these companies were advertising medical product without proper certification.

Setting aside the political implications of this FDA action, we note that entrainment creates a bonafide physiological and/or psychological response. The opportunity for abuse or misuse exists. As in any medium, the key to beneficial application lies in knowledge and awareness. ✧

ENDNOTES

1 One of the few books written on the subject is highly recommended and most likely difficult to find: George Leonard, *The Silent Pulse; A Search for the Perfect Rhythm that Exists is Each of Us* (NY, E.P. Dutton, 1978).

2 Jonathan Goldman "Sonic Entrainment" in *MusicMedicine,* ed. by Ralph Spintge and Roland Droh (MI, MMB Music, 1992), p. 196.

3 Ibid., p. 196.

4 The author owes a debt of thanks for the fine research done on the field of entrainment by Mr. Goldman. See his interview, *The Power of Harmonics,* Chapter 12.

5 See the Michael Stevens interview, *Light/Sound Machines*, Chapter 13.

2

Demystifying Binaural Beat Frequencies

What Are They? How Do They Work?

The brain has been called the final frontier of the human body. While organ transplants become commonplace and genetic engineering develops at quantum pace, the gray matter that occupies central headquarters is our least understood anatomical part. Although there is considerable understanding of the brain's function and physiology, the Western scientific mind humbly says, "We don't know..." to a plethora of questions without answers.

It is not for lack of interest that we don't know. The curiosity of scientists, philosophers, doctors and psychologists has focused on the brain/mind since time immemorial. However, beyond the frustration of not knowing lies a profound respect for the designing hand that created the ultimate personal computer.

The complexity and speed of processing by the brain is staggering. Consider the following: The human brain must process three billion stimuli *per second* for a person to remain conscious and not fall asleep.[1] There are 100 billion neurons in the brain's frontal lobes alone. It is common knowledge that only a small percentage of the brain mass is consciously used. Consequently, it's not surprising that in this digital age of RAM gigabytes and modem baud speed, higher brain efficiency is a state many seek.

What may raise eye-brows, however, is the conduit in which this increased access to brain functioning is pursued: It is through the *ear* that sound alters brainwaves. Currently, sound tools are being developed and used which have wide medical, psychological, and social implications.

With sound as the doorway through which the brain is approached, the work of high-tech wizards falls into two inter-related categories: *Whole-brain Synchronization* and *Sonic Brainwave Entrainment.* Hemi-Sync™, Holodynamics™, Differential Signaling™, Primordial Subconscious Processing™, and Digital Holophonics™ are just a few of the descriptive, yet cryptic titles describing work being done in this field.[2] The trademark symbols next to these terms also reveal the profit potential in these investigations. Rewards for the discovery of full-brain access would be eclipsed only by the modern *Ponce de Leon* who discovers the fountain of youth.

Whole-brain Synchronization and *Sonic Brainwave Entrainment,* along with the combined elements that create them, are the focus of this chapter. Components of this fascinating field include brainwaves, soundwaves, entrainment, sympathetic resonance, binaural beats, and the Frequency Follow Response.

Further exploration of this work cannot take place without bringing the late Robert Monroe into the picture. His impact and contributions to the field of sonic brain enhancement are legendary.

THE MONROE INSTITUTE

Robert Monroe (1915–1995) was a successful radio/TV producer and multiple station owner in the 1950's. Suddenly he began to have spontaneous, often frightening out-of-body experiences. When Monroe eventually accepted *astral travel* as an extraordinary reality–rather than symptomatic of a psychotic break–he began to see the consciousness potential of these journeys.

Surrounded by sub-audio radio and television frequencies prior to his out-of-body experiences, Monroe linked these two phenomena. To understand what was happening to him, Monroe initiated research which focused upon the effect of sound frequencies. The research and development division in his private radio/production business subsequently became the world renowned Monroe Institute.[3] Over the last four decades, Monroe has subjected his investigations to rigorous scientific and anecdotal experimentation. He was a visionary who pioneered and/or improved upon basic technologies used by other sonic enhancement practitioners. Along the way, Monroe made discoveries that will become part of the treasure chest of higher human understanding.

For the last 25 years, the Institute has identified and evaluated the effects of different sound patterns by blending them into complex combinations with proven effects upon mental states. On tape or CD, these sound patterns–mostly inaudible to the human ear–become powerful, non-invasive tools for the exploration, development and maximization of the brain/mind. Under the steady aegis of Bob Monroe, the Institute created tools which permit a person to delve into deep regions of consciousness, each according to their singular needs and objectives.

Whether it be in sleep/dreams, learning and memory, physical or mental health, meditation, physical coordination, creative problem solving, or stress management, the applications of Monroe's sound tools are vast. Desired changes are achieved by sustaining a focused and coherent brain/mind state. This is accomplished with a stereo audio system.

The basis of The Monroe Institute's work is a process known as *Hemi-Sync.*™ When the brain receives a different tone through each ear, it generally responds by *hearing* a third frequency–the difference between the two incoming tones. With the use of stereo headphones, this process brings both hemispheres into a state of unison known as hemispheric synchronization, hence the name *Hemi-Sync.* The net effect is an amplification of brain responsiveness making increased brain power available.

WHOLE BRAIN SYNCHRONY

The *whole-brain* concept is based upon the synchronization of right and left frontal hemispheres of the brain. This bi-lateral hemispheric synchronization is a natural brain state that occurs occasionally, and momentarily, throughout the day. At these moments, coherent brainpower is at its height. This idyllic state of mind is illusive to most for it is not accessible upon command. However, the application of specific binaural (*bi*/two – *aural*/ears) audio tones can provide, at will, access to this prime state of awareness.[4]

What is then achieved with this coveted and fertile mental state is up to each individual. A net result is the ability to navigate–first, with the use of special recordings, and ultimately, without them–through different brainwave states. The potential rewards of mind mastery are incalculable: Enhanced health, improved productivity, and increased creativity are proven and practical applications.

BRAINWAVES

In addition to whole-brain synchronization, applied sound frequencies have the ability to alter brainwave states. The electrochemical activity of the brain produces electromagnetic waveforms known as brainwaves. These wave forms can be objectively measured with sensitive equipment such as an Electroencephalograph (EEG). As long as one is alive, these continuous electrical waves circulate throughout the brain. Lack of brainwave activity is a sign of death, similar to the stopping of the heartbeat.

In *MusicMedicine*,[5] sound researcher Jonathan Goldman states: beta, alpha, theta, and delta waves "...pulsate at particular frequencies that are measured, just like sound waves, in cycles per second". Through a process of *resonance* and *entrainment*, it is possible to consciously adjust one's own brainwave state, as if, metaphorically, changing the channel on a television set.

The questions arise: Why would one want, or need, to exert this level of self mind control? "Our brains emit frequencies that respond to mental and emotional states," answers musicologist and scholar, Dr. Randall McClellan.[6] "Likewise," he continues, "...a feedback loop appears to take place between the brain, the rest of the physical body, and the mind." It is an integrated system, each part inseparable from the other. The body and mind effects the brain, and conversely, the brain effects the body and mind. The questions continue: Who or what drives who? Which element kick-starts the other components into action and then keeps them going?

The research into brainwave states began in the 1920's and has evolved through the use of biofeedback instruments. Researchers have divided the range of brainwave activity into four categories. Each brainwave state has its own recognizable cycle and is associated with different mental and/or emotional characteristics Therefore, the knowledge of what brainwave state is most conducive to an activity–be it peak output (high beta) or a fully relaxed state (low alpha)–allows for maximal accomplishment of the goal. Understanding how to use the brain applies as much to mind focus for accelerated learning and sports coordination as it does to deep subconscious access for health and healing.

Much interest in the power of brainwave entrainment originates from observing the beneficial effects of alpha and theta-level meditators. Western culture values factual input to nourish the brain. We revere game show contestants with fast retrieval-system-minds. In the East however, the goal of the meditative mind is to *slow* down the brainwaves, in order to hear a *higher* mind. McClellan notes that meditators who have learned to slow their brainwaves achieve, "...the maximum efficiency of brain/body, leaving the mind to attend to other things such as healing and universal awareness..."[7] Now, the province of experienced meditators is available to anyone with a set of stereo headphones.

THE FOUR MAJOR BRAINWAVE STATES:[8]

- <u>Beta waves</u> (13-22 Hz) are found in our normal, waking state of consciousness. One is alert with a focus on the everyday activities of the world.
- <u>Alpha waves</u> (8-12 Hz) accompany the state of relaxed wakefulness, such as daydreaming and meditation. Alpha waves are blocked by sensory awareness, conceptual thinking and strong emotions.
- <u>Theta waves</u> (4-7 Hz) are found in states of high creativity, very deep meditation and as one drifts to sleep.
- <u>Delta waves</u> (.5-3.5 Hz) are found in the deepest part of the sleep cycle and in unconsciousness.

SOUNDWAVES

Where there is motion, there is frequency. And whenever there is frequency, there is sound. In other words, sound is a by-product of anything that moves. This includes all atomic matter. Within each atom, electrons buzz around the nucleus at the dizzying speed of 600 miles per second. And inside the nucleus, protons and neutrons are packed so densely that they're caused to move at a rate of 40,000 miles per second! [9]

Inventor/scientist Itzhak Bentov says, "When we disturb the air in any way, we create sound. The slightest motion of our bodies disturbs the air around us." He continues, "When we make periodic movements with our hand, the sound becomes a note." Bentov explains that we cannot hear the note because it is *infrasound*, below the level of human perception. However, we can hear the sound of a fly or mosquito's wings because, "...the rapid flapping produces evenly spaced compressions and rarifications of the air that become audible to us.[10]

There are many kinds of sound waves, most notably the sine, sawtooth, and square wave. Regardless of the type of waveform, soundwaves–like brainwaves–can be measured in cycles per second, known as hertz (Hz). This is a very important connection: By sharing similar measurement systems, it is possible to note the effect of certain frequencies in either slowing down or speeding up the brainwaves. This is done by a process known as entrainment.

THE RULES OF ENTRAINMENT

A significant element in the field of sonic brain enhancement is entrainment. As we explored in the last chapter, this physiological process is a built-in mechanism in the body, whereby internal pulses (breath, circulation, heartbeat, brainwaves) will resonate to a stronger external pulse. Therefore, a predominant external rhythmic pattern will cause internal pulses to speed up or slow down. Resonant entrainment of oscillating systems is a well understood principle within the physical sciences. And since human bodies are oscillators–moving in a periodic, repetitive fashion between two points of rest–the laws of entrainment apply.

F. Holmes Atwater, a scientific investigator, behavioral engineer, and consultant to the Monroe Institute, believes there to be three basic rules of the physics of entrainment:[11]

1. "The Resonant Rule: For one system to entrain another, the second system must be capable of achieving the same vibratory rate." In other words, a human being would not entrain with a rock. But a human would entrain with another.

2. "The Power Rule: For one system to entrain with another, the first must have sufficient power to overcome the second." Therefore, proximity is an important consideration because if one system is too far away, their power is diminished with distance.

3. "The Consistency Rule: For one system to be capable of entraining another, the first must be at a constant frequency or amplitude."

SYMPATHETIC RESONANCE

Think of resonance as the frequency at which an object most naturally wants to vibrate. As with tuning forks, if we were to play an open string on a violin near another untouched violin, the second violin's identical string will vibrate and make sound. A wine glass which is shattered by the voice of a soprano is manifesting the process of entrainment. Matching the natural vibration of the glass and increasing the amplitude, the vocalist literally overcomes the closed atomic structure thereby causing it to shatter.

Jonathan Goldman points out the following distinction between resonance and entrainment: "Resonance is a cooperative phenomenon between two different objects sharing the same frequency."[12] By stimulating the natural vibrations of an object with its own frequency, it is then set into motion. However, Goldman sees entrainment as the imposition of another frequency onto the *weaker* vibration. With entrainment, he says, "...you are actively changing the vibrations (the frequency or rhythm) of one object to another rate." Goldman likens resonance as being passive in nature while entrainment is active.

Sympathetic resonance takes place between two objects that share a *natural* frequency as with the two violins or similar tuning forks. When objects share the same natural frequency, it is very easy to transfer energy. Bentov says, "The air waves generated by the first violin impinge on the second violin. The string that is tuned to the emitted note will absorb the energy of the waves of that frequency preferentially because that energy comes to it at its own natural frequency." The same process takes place between people. There is more substance in the slang term 'good vibes' than meets the eye.

BINAURAL BEATS

In 1839, a phenomenon known as binaural beats was discovered by German experimenter, H.W. Dove. Binaural beats (an actual *wah wah* sounding effect) takes place when separate frequencies are introduced into each ear, i.e. a tone of 100 Hz in the right ear and a tone of 108 Hz in the left. The brain discerns the *difference* and strives to bridge the gap by creating a third tone which is the *actual* difference between the two. In this case, it would be 8 Hz. This third tone is what is referred to as a binaural beat, manufactured and heard *only* inside the brain.

According to Atwater, the sound of the binaural beat can't be recorded by an external device (tape recorder or oscilloscope) and can only be heard with the interaction of both ears. In fact, the binaural beat exists only as a consequence of the interaction of perception within the brain.

This process takes place not only in humans but in other animals as well. As a sound wave passes around the skull, each ear gets a different portion of the wave. When the wave length of a sound signal is longer than the diameter of the skull, the brain *hears* the inputs from the ears as out of phase with each other. Atwater states, "...that it is this innate ability of the brain to detect wave form phase difference which gives rise to binaural beats."

Understanding that the beat frequency is the difference between two separate tones–and that it is not an actual sound, but an electrical signal created by both hemispheres of the brain working together simultaneously–one can see how this natural device becomes a part of the picture of sonic brain enhancement. Let's add one more element and then wrap them all together.

FREQUENCY FOLLOWING RESPONSE

An original patent in the field of altering brain states through sound was issued to Monroe in 1975 for his discovery of the Frequency Following Response (FFR). According to Leslie France, a director of The Monroe Institute, "...when a listener's environment is dominated by sounds of certain frequencies, the listener tends to reproduce those frequencies within his/her own physiology."

The FFR is a form of entrainment perfectly suited to the binaural beat concept. Put a 100 Hz tone in one ear and a 105 Hz tone in the other, and the brain will hear 5 Hz. Because of the FFR, the brain will then come to meet this 5 Hz pace and lower (or raise) the brainwaves to match it.

In other words, the FFR basically leads the brain, following specific externally-created combinations and sequences of sound into targeted arenas of consciousness; be it an alpha state or theta ramping down to delta. The FFR can be changed at will by changing the sound patterns. The Institute has demonstrated that methods to access different states can be learned and then re-created from memory.[13]

CONCLUSION

Scientist Atwater states that the cerebral hemispheres, commonly referred to as the right and left brain, are two separate information processing modules; each complex, cognitive system processes information both independently and in parallel. It has been proven that when the two frontal lobes of the brain are synchronized, the power of the brain is significantly increased.[14] With the combined tools of entrainment, binaural beats, resonance, and frequency follow-through, soundwaves are able to modulate brainwaves. The effect goes beyond the bi-lateral hemispheric synchronization. Now, one can determine that an afternoon spent in high alpha would benefit concentration, or that low theta is best for deep stress reduction. Never before has technology been able to provide this precise level of self-directed access to brainwave states.

Some of the current explorations of this technology are written about in *Hemi-Sync Journal*, a publication of The Monroe Institute's Professional Division.[15] I include these titles to show the wide range of application currently taking place: *Accelerating Corporate Change, Teen Tapes: A Pilot Study, Studying Hemi-Sync on Animals, Hemi-Sync and AIDS, Hemi-Sync and Archetype Emergence in Jungian Psychotherapy, Hemi-Sync uses in the Military,* and *Recapturing the Intuitive in Therapy and Education.*

The versatility and potential for this technology are indeed impressive. But beyond all claims, personal experience is the true arbiter. Over the last eight years, I've used this technology extensively. The technology helps to reduce my stress levels, induces deep rest, and brings me increased concentration and focus. As a daily regimen, time must be allotted (20-45 minutes) to use the tapes. As in any altering mode, the possibility for misuse is prevalent. Intention and integrity are key concepts with the mind as they are with body, heart, and spirit.

I believe sonic brain enhancement–through the use of binaural beat frequencies and other sound techniques– will contribute to the evolution of man and womankind in the twenty-first century. Like any new tool, the use of sound for brain enhancement requires a new discipline: we must think about *how* we think and how we *want* to think. Certainly not to be trivialized as a dial-a-thought process, I believe sonic enhancement is a gold mine for those willing to go the extra synapse. ✧

ENDNOTES

1 Dr. Alfred Tomatis, *About the Tomatis Method,* ed. by T. Gilmor, et al, (Toronto, The Listening Centre Press, 1989), p. 210.

2 Federal trademarks registered to the following organizations: Hemi-Sync™/The Monroe Institute; Holodynamics™/Synchronicity Foundation; Differential Signaling™/ABR; Primordial Subconscious Processing™/Brain/Mind Research; Digital Holophonics™/Valley of the Sun; Walkman™/Sony.

3 The Monroe Institute. P.O. Box 505, Lovingston, VA 22949. Call (800) 541-2488 for a catalog of activities and products.

4 F. Holmes Atwater, *The Monroe Institute's Hemi-Sync Process: A Theoretical Perspective* (VA, The Monroe Institute, 1988).

5 Jonathan Goldman, "Sonic Entrainment" in *MusicMedicine,* ed. by Ralph Spintge and Roland Droh (MI, MMB Music, 1992), p. 197.

6 Randall McClellan, *The Healing Forces of Music* (MA, Element, 1991),

p. 131.

7 Ibid., p. 148.

8 As per Goldman, two other delineations of brainwave activity have been noted: High-Beta (23-33 Hz), associated with hyperactivity and anxiety, and K Complex (33 Hz+), occuring in short bursts, associated with the sudden integration of ideas or experiences.

9 Randal McClellan. p. 22.

10 Itzhak Bentov, *Stalking the Wild Pendulum; On the Mechanics of Consciousness* (Vermont, Destiny, 1988) p. 9.

11 F. Holmes Atwater, *The Monroe Institute's Hemi-Sync Process: A Theoretical Perspective* (Virginia, The Monroe Institute, 1988).

12 Jonathan Goldman "Sonic Entrainment" in *Music: Physician For Times To Come,* ed. by Don Campbell. (London, Quest Books, 1991).

13 Leslie France. "What is Hemi-Sync?" in *Focus* (VA, The Monroe Institute, Fall 1990).

14 Monroe has worked with over 3,000 test subjects in a controlled laboratory setting. Each of these subjects had a minimum of twenty individual tests. This provides the Monroe Institute with a base of over 60,000 controlled test results.

15 Information on Hemi-Sync Journal and Monroe's Professional Division may be obtained by calling the Institute. See Endnote #3 above.

3

THE TOMATIS METHOD

Frequency Medicine for the 21st Century

"Language is what characterizes man and makes him different from other creatures."

— *Alfred A. Tomatis*

Among the most basic of all human needs is the desire to understand others and to be understood by them. Like food, water, and oxygen, communication is a basic necessity; most noticed in its absence. But what happens when we don't have or maintain the skills to interrelate? Losing the desire to communicate begins an unhealthy spiral of psychological withdrawal and isolation. The end result is a diminished life, often resulting in acute or chronic illness for the introverted or jail for the extroverted foolish. Either way, self-exclusion from our human community is a pained and wasteful journey with ramifications that touch all.

Currently, crime and health care are predominant items on the American civic agenda. Our solution: build bigger prisons, hire more police, make attempts at national health insurance. Yet, there is a missing piece to the logic. Why do people lose the motivation required to interweave within the fabric of society? Why is it that some essentially unplug, or never engage to begin with? What is the cause of learning difficulties, poor concentration and memory, psychological depression, chronic fatigue, immune dysfunction? These symptoms are indicative of physio/psychological malfunctions that ultimately spin out of control.

And, according to a French doctor, these maladies often start–and in some cases may be repaired–within the ear.

TURNING THE WORLD ON ITS EAR

It is a common belief that the primary function of the ear is to translate words into neural images and to help us stay balanced when we stand up. But Dr. Alfred A. Tomatis has become accustomed to taking the most well-worn concepts and turning them on *their* proverbial ear. As an ear, nose and throat specialist, surgeon, psychologist, and inventor, Dr. Tomatis has spent the last fifty years redefining the ear's extraordinary significance. Many consider him to be the *Einstein of the Ear.* And like Albert, Tomatis' theories are not only brilliant, but quite controversial.[1]

He believes the initial purpose of the ear is to help *grow* the brain of the unborn child; that the psychological input of the mother's voice is as important as the physiological necessity of the umbilical cord. After birth, the ear's primary function is to charge the neo-cortex of the brain and thereby the entire nervous system. To Dr. Tomatis, sound is a nutrient. When we are not able to assimilate the full spectrum of sound frequency, the ramifications parallel the inability to digest food. The main difference: food fuels the body, whereas soundwaves, *digested* by the ear, provide electrical impulses that charge the brain.

Certainly, we would not die without sound. But the quality of our lives would be markedly different without the vital energy that creates focus, motivation and desire. Remove these elements, and we are fatigued, uninspired, directionless, and ultimately unhealthy. Sound is essentially a mind food. So what is the consequence to the hearing impaired? We are not dependent solely upon the ear for absorption of sound. Dr. Tomatis believes skin perceives sound waves, that we can sing with our bones! It is the middle and inner ear that translates this potential to the brain, and it may arrive through many routes.

The implications of these extraordinary concepts will be felt for many years. Dr. Tomatis is perhaps the leading figure in the field of therapeutic sound and music. His credentials are stellar with a track record covering half a century. Some would call him an ear specialist.

To me, Alfred Tomatis is a frequency doctor, working in the subtle yet powerful domain of vibrational medicine. An example of the health practitioner of the future, Tomatis prescribes sound frequencies in lieu of pharmaceuticals. He administers his medicine by having patients listen to specially reinforced and filtered music and sounds. Most impressive of all, the results from 200+ busy Tomatis Centers around the world are startling.[2]

Dr. Timothy Gilmor is a psychologist and former director of The Listening Centre in Toronto.[3] Since 1979, he has been actively involved in Tomatis research, evaluation and clinical application. In his book, *About the Tomatis Method*,[4] Gilmor states, "This method provides a comprehensive approach to communication, language, and the learning process which is based on listening. Dr. Tomatis defines listening chiefly as a process of focusing the ear."

Why is the focusing of the ear all that important? On the surface, this is a rather benign concept. But in peering deeply, fascinating concepts emerge. For Tomatis, to look beneath the surface actually meant studying the development of the ear *in utero.*

THE EAR IN UTERO

Tomatis discovered that the ear is functioning four and a half months before birth and that listening is the first sense we develop. Intermixed with the organic sounds of a mother's heartbeat, circulation, gastro-intestinal rumblings, and breath, the unborn child distinctly *hears* her voice. Researchers have verified that long before an infant can speak, they recognize sounds heard prenatally.

Gilmor explains: "Tomatis has stated that while in the womb, the higher frequencies of the mother's voice literally nourish the fetus. A pattern establishes itself very early of waiting for this sound and being gratified when it comes, waiting, being gratified and so on, a process Tomatis calls the *uterine dialogue.* It is with this process that listening begins, and carries on into childhood." Gilmor continues, "The development of later communication skills, language acquisition, learning ability and social adjustment in particular, depends on the quality of this early listening. But for a variety of reasons, such listening can be obscured, impaired or shut down altogether. The Tomatis Method presents a means of retrieving the *open* listening which is our birthright."

If we are robbed of the ability to easily communicate, then learning impairment and social adjustment is a consequence. What chance for success do we then have in a tough, competitive society? The answer lies in this disturbing estimate: two-thirds of the American prison population has learning disabilities. Because the methods of detection and correction have not been adequate, is it possible that children from stressed or difficult pregnancies who did not establish the *loop of gratification* fall through the cracks? They become drop-outs, adopt a misfit attitude and are looked upon as miscreants. If indeed the seeds of social behavior begin *in utero,* then is it any wonder, that with the high percentage of disintegrating family units, we have gangs, violence, and illness like never before? What does Dr. Tomatis suggest we do to remedy this?

"I do not *treat* the children who are brought to me," says Tomatis, "I *awaken* them." He believes that it is not a problem of hearing, rather of listening. While there may be physiological causes that prevent the ability to focus on sounds, Tomatis has devised a method that focuses upon the panoply of psychological and social factors that bear on listening. These include the family system and emotional background. According to Gilmor, "...a child with a reading problem very often presents myriad other difficulties such as short attention span, poor concentration, weakness in oral language, poorly articulated speech, poor vocabulary. Such children are also often immature, with a poor self-concept and sense of self-confidence. They have difficulty adjusting socially to their families and peer groups. Many of these problems affect adults as well."

THE TOMATIS METHOD

Again, because Dr. Tomatis believes most of the problems stated above originate prenatally, his method acts on and with the ear, working simultaneously on the functional, emotional, and relational level. Dr. Tomatis believes that from conception forward, *we shut out those frequencies that correspond to traumatic occurrences.* The goal of the program is to retrain the muscles of the inner ear, so as to be able to take in the full spectrum of sound.

Great attention is placed on the fetal and early childhood hearing process. "It is as if by being plunged into one's own past, one were being offered a better way of mastering the future." Dr. Tomatis continues, "By bringing the ear back to its earliest influences, the filtered sound treatment enables it–in this roundabout way–to achieve the most advanced stage of its evolution, that of *human listening.* A particular state of attention and tension of its components produces this, and filtered sound restores it."

The restoration is accomplished by listening to specially filtered tapes of Mozart, and if possible, the recorded sound of the mother's voice. These sounds come through headsets that have been modified to deliver through bone conduction as well as through air (the ear). These tapes, one's own voice, and Gregorian chants are fed, at different times, through a Tomatis invention known as the *Electronic Ear.* It's function–using highly specific filters and gating mechanisms–is to strengthen the muscles of the middle ear, thereby enhancing the process of focusing. Tomatis believes that focused *listening* is a preferred state to passive *hearing.*

Starting with a battery of diagnostic procedures, comprised of listening tests and interviews with certified Tomatis practitioners, a typical model of the Method is as follows:

- Fifteen concurrent days of listening, two hours a day.
- Three weeks off.
- Seven days of listening.
- Four weeks off.
- Seven days of listening.

The program is highly individual and flexible, with the length of each phase determined by the goals and progress of the individual. Both counseling and repeated listening tests chart the change in ear, psyche and body. There are five basic phases to the Method. Three of these are considered passive, the other two are active.

Simplistically put, the passive phases consist of listening to music and sound with increasing amounts of filtering and processing by the

Electronic Ear and then a decreasing of the same process. The purpose of this section is to adjust to the presentation of filtered sound on a gradual basis, develop the focusing response, and stimulate the desire to communicate. Additionally, a *sonic birth* is replicated to simulate the transition from the liquid pre-natal acoustic environment to the post-natal air environment.

In the passive phases, the individual listens to sound. In the active phases, one becomes more involved. The purpose, according to Gilmor, is to introduce spoken language in the prelinguistic and linguistic stage. This is done by humming, singing, reading aloud, and repeating of specific sentences through a microphone into the Electronic Ear before being fed back to the ears via earphones. The tones of the voice are filtered and gated in the same way as the music was in the passive phase. Additionally, increased stimulation is given to the right ear, in order to enhance it's dominance. This is a preferred state for audio-vocal control.

Dr. Tomatis believes that *music and vocal sounds that are rich in high frequencies have an energizing effect which corresponds to the effect of the mother's voice on the development of the fetal nervous system.* The unborn child hears the highest frequencies of the mother's voice and these frequencies literally nourish the fetus. Consequently, high frequencies still impact upon us as adults. This is why filtered tapes are the backbone of the listening training process. Tomatis rolls off all but the high end of sound, producing the effect of listening to the ghost of a musical phrase. In a gradual process, the harmonics of the music are removed leaving only the sounds of sibilants.

Another discovery that Dr. Tomatis made was that if a person's ear is incapable of clearly perceiving higher frequency sounds, they will be unable to reproduce these sounds vocally. This means that *we can only reproduce what we can hear.* Therefore, if I sing off-key or speak in a flat monotone voice, chances are I am unable to hear specific frequency ranges. Dr. Tomatis is fond of saying, "One sings with one's ear."

Additionally, just as there are *charging* sounds that energize the nervous system, there are *discharging* sounds that tend to weaken and fatigue. Dr. Tomatis believes high frequency sounds energize because of a preponderance of specific cells in the inner ear membrane that respond to high tones by sending electrical impulses to the brain. There are far fewer cells that respond to the lower frequencies. Consequently, lower bass tones may actually have the effect of overwhelming the nervous system to the point of overload, causing mental and physical fatigue.

BRAIN/MIND ENHANCEMENT

As can be seen by the description of the program, the Tomatis Method is a highly unorthodox, yet powerfully effective process for change. Learning disabilities, depression and immune disorders are the most common reasons people seek treatment. Yet, as public awareness of the Tomatis concepts grow, many are utilizing this sonic process for reasons other than the curing of maladies. Increasing numbers come to Tomatis for brain/mind enhancement, consciousness exploration, increased musicality, and inner healing.

The effects of deeper internal listening is uncharted and very possibly evolutionary. Is it possible, that by restoring the ability to hear a full spectrum of sound, many problems and disabilities can simply fade away? This sounds too simplistic for our highly educated (and medicated) Western minds. Yet, in this writer's experience of the Tomatis Method, this has been the case.

As we advance along life's path, it is not uncommon to see patterns of behavior that follow us through different locations, relationships and vocations. It seems that as we mature, negative early childhood influences become more cunning and progressive in their impact on our actions. Many of us go through extensive therapies trying to get to the bottom of our 'stuff'. Others travel arduous spiritual roads in search of peace and well-being; often finding they've unconsciously traded one compulsive context for another. The problem is the inability to discard early behavioral patterns and reactions that no longer serve. Therefore, we are not living the potential to which we aspire because there are too many patterns getting in the way!

This has been my experience. Like so many, I have mind-altered, mind-expanded, meditated, therapized, denied, and Twelve Stepped. Even though I have gained deep insights into where I self-sabotage or fall down, the intellectual comprehension does not seem to reach far enough for significant change.

As a musician and composer, I know that what we hear greatly effects us. I am also aware of the difference between *hearing* and *listening*, just as there is a distinction between casually *looking* and really *seeing*. Listening and seeing are *active* focusing processes not passive perception. Dr. Tomatis believes that active focusing is based upon neural-physiological and motivational components. He prescribes sound as a means of strengthening, re-building, and adding of neuronal activity in the brain. This makes so much sense to me that I decided to experience the Tomatis work myself.

DR. RON MINSON — A HEALER FOR THE FUTURE

I was lucky enough to meet Dr. Ron Minson in Denver, Colorado.[5] A board certified psychiatrist, Dr. Minson had spent twenty-five years directing behavioral/therapeutic activities for major medical institutions, consulting mental health organizations, and maintaining a large private practice. But when his adopted daughter became deeply despondent over the burden of learning disabilities and life-long depressions, Minson found his tools unable to quell her rapid and life-threatening decline.

Minson's daughter was suffering from symptoms endemic to adopted children. According to Tomatis, when a baby is separated from it's mother, the vital sound connection between them is severed. While outer nutrition can be supplied elsewhere, this sonic lifeline is a critical biological connection. Sometimes, aural transference to another mother can take place; often times it doesn't. As referenced earlier in this chapter, the 'uterine dialogue' and the post-birth sonic connection between mother and child has a tremendous effect on the psychological outreach of a new-born. These early tendencies to *pull in* rather than *reach out* can then manifest throughout life as autism, learning disabilities, depression, poor self-esteem, or unstable health.

In a quest for effective treatment for his daughter, Dr. Minson came across the Tomatis Method. He and his daughter were simultaneously treated and both experienced dramatic positive results. So much so,

Minson shuttered his practice and ceased all other professional activities. He hurriedly learned French and went to Paris to study directly with Tomatis. Returning to Denver, Minson set up a Tomatis Centre in 1991.

As is the case with alternative therapies, the going was slow in the beginning for the new clinic. But as word spread of the success of their treatment programs, Dr. Minson's Tomatis Centre began to boom. A more gentle and respectful environment would be hard to find. Minson's marriage of traditional western medicine with breakthrough technologies–such as the Tomatis Method–is not only effective, but exemplary.[6]

LETTING SONIC WATERS SOOTHE — A PERSONAL EXPERIENCE WITH THE TOMATIS METHOD

So what was the effect for me when I went through the Tomatis Method with Dr. Minson? I came to the program, ostensibly out of professional curiosity. Truthfully, I was hoping this cutting-edge concept could help me break tired patterns. I was seeking the balancing of all my fairly common hang-ups. After some 75 hours on the Electronic Ear, I came out a changed man. Perhaps not in the way I envisioned, for I still have challenges. But something has inextricably moved.

It is my observation that everybody responds differently to this method. Therefore, these comments should be taken as one man's experience. Greatly increased concentration, better memory, stronger language skills and improved dexterity just begin to scratch the surface. Certainly after mainlining high-frequency matrixes directly into the brain, one would expect greater mental agility. But to me, the real goods lie deeper. It is now three years since the completion of the program, and I am just beginning to fathom the depth to which this work goes. I don't think one finishes the Tomatis work, for this method is actually a re-tooling of the human mechanism.

I believe the Tomatis work to be some of the most powerful I have encountered. It has changed *the way that I listen.* Listening, in the Tomatis context, means how I process sonic nutrients around me and how I hear myself. For me, I've noticed the most profound value is not how I hear the outside world, or even my new-found awareness of the sounds *inside* the notes of music, but most importantly, how I listen to myself. I am not speaking about increased intuition, awareness of long buried feelings, or receptivity to channeled beings from Mars. Rather, and so simply, just how I listen.

My inner and outer ears are now so attuned, that I can *hear* the energy behind words, feelings, and sounds. I have always been sensitive but this is a quantum leap in perception. The power of the subtlety is immense. And the beauty of this process is that the more I *listen* to myself, the easier it is for me to really hear the truth of things. It seems that once we know our truths, we don't have to hold on to those issues any longer. This sonic energy somehow creates a painless detachment. I don't have to process my 'stuff' inside and out. It seems that by hearing a fuller spectrum of sound, I now hear a larger spectrum of my internal engines. The things that used to be terribly painful in my life no longer hold quite the charge.

When I discussed this with Dr. Minson, he relayed to me the commonality of my experience of deeper internal listening. Something he mentioned really stands out: Many people had come to him, he said, hoping to find surcease from the pain of incest recall and other kinds of childhood abuse. As a psychiatrist, he was aware of the bottomless pain and the arduous road so many abuse survivors travel in search of healing. With the Tomatis Method, Dr. Minson marveled at the shared experience of these women and men; they didn't need to talk so much, they didn't seek his gentle guidance. Most spoke of letting the sonic waters cleanse and soothe; quietly, gently... releasing the pain... letting go. In this aural process, one takes in the frequency medicine while painting, drawing, or laying down. The perfection of Mozart and the vibrational alchemy of Tomatis seems to create a silent healing.

VIBRATION, FREQUENCY AND SOUND

By the nature of the modality of vibrational healing, subtle and obvious changes go hand in hand. The use of vibration–which contains both frequency and sound–to restore original innocence is a masterstroke of awareness. All physical matter resonates. Anything that resonates can be impacted by an external vibrational force. Therefore, using sound to reharmonize our systems is both logical and extremely effective.

No exploration into the therapeutic applications of music and sound would be complete without knowledge of the Tomatis work. From this writer's vantage point, Dr. Tomatis has laid the theoretical foundation upon which the emerging field of soundwork builds. His brilliant concepts and theories cause us to reconsider the awe-inspiring power of music and sound. ✧

RESOURCES

Abbey of Solesmes, *Gregorian Chants from the Abbey of Solesmes.* Audio tapes. (Orleans, MA, Paraclete Press). These are the chants most preferred by Dr. Tomatis and used in his clinics.

Gilmor Ph.D, Timothy and Paul Madaule, L.Ps., and Billie Thompson, Ph.D. *About the Tomatis Method.* (Ontario, Canada, The Listening Centre Press, 1989).

Madaule, Paul. *When Listening Comes Alive: A Guide to Effective Learning and Communication.* (Norval, Ontario, Canada, Moulin Publishing, 1993).

Tomatis, Alfred. *The Conscious Ear: My Life of Transformation Through Listening.* (New York, Station Hill Press, 1991).

— *The Ear and Language.* Ed. Billie M. Thompson. (Norval, Ontario, Moulin Publishing, 1996).

— *The Ear is Life (L'Oreille C'est La Vie).* Video interview. (Denver, Center for InnerChange).

Wilson, Tim. *Chant: The Healing Power of Voice and Ear.* Audio tape. (Boulder, Institue for Music, Health, and Education, 1985).

ENDNOTES

1 See Appendix A; *Core Principles of Alfred Tomatis.*

2 For information about Tomatis Centers worldwide: See Appendix C.

3 The Listening Centre, 99 Crowns Lane, Fourth Floor, Toronto, Ontario, Canada M5R 3P4.

4 Timothy M. Gilmor, *About the Tomatis Method*, co-editors Paul Madaule and Billie Thompson (Toronto, The Listening Centre Press, 1989).

5 Ron Minson, M.D., Center for InnerChange. 55 Madison Street, Suite 375, Denver, Colorado 80206. (303) 320-4411 Fax (303) 322-5550.

6 Dr. Minson's Center is administered by his lovely partner and wife, Kate O'Brien-Minson. The gentle, safe environment that she created could be emulated by all practitioners. In their clinic, positive frequencies occur in colors, fabrics and lighting as well as through headphones.

Part Two

The Sonic Alchemist

Part Two

THE SONIC ALCHEMIST

Inner Views

As a research journalist, writing feature columns for a trade magazine,[1] I traveled America from 1991-1996 with tape recorder in hand. I named the column *A Sympathetic Vibration; Music and Sound in the Healing Arts.* Twenty articles into the investigation, I realized that soundwork generates the enhancement of many facets of human function besides healing. The myriad approaches to the utilization of soundwaves represent a wealth of diverse and often divergent theory. While many network their resources, some practitioners simply dismiss contributions of others. Within the field, I found there to be as much ego, politics, and proprietary considerations as in any other venue trod by humans.

Fortunately, I found a unique approach. As a producer and composer, I came with no vested interest or opinion to defend. I brought enthusiasm and eager questions. Therefore, as an advocate of the entire field, I was warmly received and taken into the heart of each worker's labor. Hence, this retrospective of *inner views* are intimate portraits of their life work. I tender my deep appreciation for the trust placed in me. These soundworkers are my teachers.

Inevitably however, I have become a practitioner of soundwork. With answers gleaned from many questions, rich rewards bring me full circle to *psychoacoustic* producing and composing. Beyond music, I now paint with sound. I understand the dynamically subtle and diffusive effects sound and music can visit upon the psyche and nervous system. For me, musical 'product' has now evolved into powerful sonic tools for the enhancement of life's activities.

SNAPSHOTS IN TIME

My list of Sonic Alchemists of necessity is short. Every day new developments occur in the field. Each time I think I have a map of the territory, I learn of some extraordinary new work.

Today, I was told about an osteopathic surgeon who runs a hospital with a piano in every treatment room. An accompanying classical musician seeks the right tempos and styles while the doctor measures the effects on the patient's nervous system through measurement of the cranial-sacral fluid.[2] A few months ago, I visited a clinic in Tiajuana, Mexico, which draws chronically ill patients, many with cancer, from around the world. The primary modality of treatment: sound frequencies through headphones.

Altogether experimental, soundwork is a magnet for exploration. Though research funding is basically non-existent, none seem deterred. Like artists universally, soundworkers *must* do this work.

Within these pages, twelve extraordinary practitioners share their discoveries and the core of their work. Remember, these conversations took place in a given time and place. Subsequently, some soundworkers have expanded to such a degree that their current work bears little resemblance to the sentiments on these pages. I believe, however, there is wealth inside the developmental process of a methodology. I continue to find value each time I read these thought-provoking and enlightening snapshots in time.

LIST OF INTERVIEWS

- **Therese Schroeder-Sheker:** ***Prescriptive Music for the Dying***
  Director, Chalice of Repose Project; Composer; Recording Artist; Academic Dean of the School of Music-Thanatology, St. Patrick Hospital, Missoula, Montana; Associate Professor of Pastoral Ministry, St. Thomas Seminary, Denver; Author, *The Luminous Wound* (forthcoming).

- **Dr. Fred Schwartz:** ***Music as Anesthesia***
  Anesthesiologist, Piedmont Hospital, Atlanta, GA; Founder, Transitions Music.

- **Michael Jones: *Intention and Music***
  Concert Pianist, Recording Artist/Narada Records; Author, *Creating an Imaginative Life* (Conari Press); Consultant.

- **Dr. Jeffrey Thompson: *Bio-Tuning***
  Chiropractor; Composer; Recording Artist; Founder of Brain/Mind Research; Director of Neuroacoustic Research, California Institute for Human Science.

- **Tom Kenyon: *Psychoacoustics***
  Therapist; Founder of Acoustic Brain Research (ABR); Author, *Brain States* and *The Hathor Material*; Musician; Seminar leader; Intuitive.

- **Vickie Dodd: *Awakening the Amnesia of Wellness***
  Sound Therapist; Bodyworker; Recording artist; Author, *Soundprints; A Layer of Unexpressed Emotion* (forthcoming).

- **Arthur Hull: *The Power of the Drum***
  Master percussionist; Group facilitator (specializing in corporations); University Instructor.

- **Janalea Hoffman: *Entrainment***
  Music therapist; Composer; Recording Artist; Owner, Rhythmic Medicine Music; Author, *Rhythmic Medicine.*

- **Jonathan Goldman: *Overtones***
  Sound Researcher; Seminar leader; Founder, Sound Healer's Association; Recording Artist; President, Spirit Music; Author, *Healing Sounds; The Power of Harmonics.*

- **Michael Stevens: *Light & Sound Machines***
  Director, Theta Technologies.

- **Molly Scott, Ed.D.: *Resonance Therapy***
  Psychotherapist; Musician; Teacher; Founder, Creative Resonance Institute.

- **Robert Gass, Ed.D.: *Chantmaster Extraordinaire***
  Recording Artist; Musical Director, *On Wings of Song*; Founder, Spring Hill Music; Business consultant, Author, *Chanting; Discovering Spirit in Sound.* ✧

RESOURCES:

Contact information for the *Sonic Alchemists* listed herein can be found in Appendix B.

ENDNOTES

1 *New Age Retailer* is a trade magazine for retailers of New Age books, music and merchandise. 1300 N. State Sttreet, #105, Bellingham, WA 98225. (360) 676-0789 Fax (360) 676-0932.

2 Dr. Viola Frymann, Osteopathic Center for Children, 4135 54th Place, San Diego, CA 92105.

4

PRESCRIPTIVE MUSIC FOR THE DYING

A conversation with

Therese Schroeder-Sheker

"...I'll stay with you till the faded moon
has ringed our clasp with dew
And weeps to hear this lullaby:
I sing my love to you...
I sing my love to you."

Gartan Mother's Lullaby (Traditional Irish)

These days, as a gentle breeze blows in the rocky canyons of Montana, a young woman sings the purest of morning aires. The bell-tone beauty of voice and harp are eclipsed only by the nobility of her mission: Therese Schroeder-Sheker ministers to the dying. Her medieval chants soothe while they beckon. Quarter notes and sweet tones anoint the mortal coil; music enables the unbinding.

After twenty years of deathbed vigils, diligent research and unwavering faith, Therese has proven the efficacy of music as a modern medical modality. Based at St. Patrick Hospital in Missoula, Therese's *Chalice of Repose Project* offers musical palliative care services and houses a graduate-level school. The neighboring medical services, Oncology and Hospice, have come to respect this work of *musical-sacramental-midwifery*. Daily, caregivers observe the dignity and tranquility brought to this most intimate of passage-death.

Therese has proudly graduated her first class of 18 Chalice workers. She has a large vision: to train enough musical thanatologists to service hospitals and hospices throughout the country and beyond. This grand task taxes every ounce she can muster; as a scholar, music professor, and renowned concert and recording artist. While blazing new ground in the field of thanatology (the study of the effects of approaching death, and of the needs of the terminally ill and their families), Therese pulls heavily from the medieval monastic traditions of sung prayer and infirmary practices for the sick and dying. Her staff of clinicians and faculty includes several Latinists, who translate selected literature dating back 900 years.

The Chalice team has scaled the barriers separating science and art. They've opened the western allopathic model to include *prescriptive music* as a bonafide medical tool. The ramifications are breath-taking. Now it is conceivable that therapeutic music and sound will be embraced from birthing rooms to surgical theatres. The key, according to Ms. Schroeder-Sheker, is the ability to diagnose the specific musical support needed. Be it lowering blood pressure or increasing heart rate, skilled *contemplative musicians*—on a one to one basis—will be given a mainstream platform unequaled in the last three centuries.

Like their medical colleagues, Chalice interns wear beepers and are on-call for clinical rotation. Two and a half years of intensive, on-site internship have trained these students to engage the prescriptive musical deliveries of *binding, loosening, and equilibrium.* This practice requires the ability to diagnostically assess the patient's state of being—emotionally, mentally, physically, and spiritually—and then to administer musical sounds and sequences that help liberate the tether, ease the pain, facilitate *transitus.* A monastery tradition, originating in eleventh century France, resurfaces almost a thousand years later in Montana.

As a trained archival researcher and multi-linguist, Ms. Schroeder-Sheker has zealously pursued the historical and scientific basis so many alternative healing modalities lack. While enthusiasm, golden intentions, and dedication are common in the field of therapeutic soundwork, the artistic/spiritual/scientific marriage forged by *The Chalice Project* sets a new standard to be embraced.

The following interview took place in August, 1994.

MUSIC-THANATOLOGY IN THE MAINSTREAM

JL: So you were wondering what you were going to do with your life?

TSS: (Laughing) I always think, "Thank goodness that this hit when we were young because otherwise I wouldn't have had the energy. But of course, I think the whole thing is about teamwork. There have been so many people who were supportive of this vision, both at the hospital, hospice and at the geriatric homes. We received the kind of administrative, as well as medical support, that we really needed. That's what made the difference. We couldn't have done this if we were only people gathering together with good intentions and a good idea. It is really teamwork.

JL: Nonetheless, you created this team out of your solitary efforts?

TSS: It was twenty-one years. There was time to garner momentum, strength and concentration.

JL: Did you foresee this degree of acceptance?

TSS: Yes.

JL: So you knew it was only a matter of time before you brought this work into the mainstream?

TSS: Yes, for two reasons. The first is that everyone will die. And although there may still be many people who do not want to talk about it, many people do. And if they had their choice, they would wish for themselves, and others, that they could die well and beautifully, peacefully, if at all possible. With some sort of mediation towards pain.

JL: What does that mean, "...mediation towards pain?"

TSS: Not every kind of pain can be completely met. The advances that have taken place in the last 10–15 years with pain medication are most impressive. And many kinds of pain can be really helped. But there are aspects of spiritual pain that hardly any drug in the world is going to touch. Also, there are kinds of physical pain whereby the patients go off the pain scale, even with the morphine.

JL: Therese, your work is dealing with one of the greatest passages that we will ever have. And I see that the world is responding to what you are doing even though it has taken so long.

TSS: Yes, I think our work brings a lot of people hope. Sometimes we receive letters from people all over the world, saying "...Just knowing that this exists gives me strength to do what I have to do now." It gives people ideas of how they can assist somebody whom they love or else even die themselves, quietly and peacefully.

JL: My mother just visited me. I described my excited anticipation of this interview and spoke of your work. When she heard, she said, "Oh yes, absolutely! In the last year, I have instinctively and spontaneously sang to two relatives as they were dying. This makes so much sense. As a matter of fact, if there were a way I could train with Therese, I would love to be able to do that work." You might have this 73-year–old college professor come trotting up from Los Angeles.

TSS: Well, that would be appropriate. In our school, we do not have young kids who are just going off to college. Our students tend to be people with life experience. Although we do have young people in the program, age 30 or so, our senior colleagues are 68 or 70.

THE SCHOOL

JL: Therese, what motivates people to study with you?

TSS: Love and compassion are the motivating factors. They hear about this work and their hearts are pierced. They go straight to a telephone or write a letter saying, "Please, I have to be in this program!" But we have requests and inquiries from many more people than we could ever accept. Also, sometimes the idea of doing this work attracts people who don't really have the stamina for it, or they have an initial impression, "Oh my God, this is so beautiful," but somehow they think that it's all 'sit there and look great and play the harp and be beautiful.' They don't have any idea what is involved in facing this on a daily basis. So we have a very rigorous screening process. We can only accept 25 interns every two years.

JL: What does the application process involve?

TSS: It's divided into three sections. The first is a very thoughtful series of written responses that are very much contemplative, rather than asking for scores of tests, etc. This phase is about why you would want to work with those who are dying and with music. It asks a great deal of thoughtfulness from the applicant. This separates the wheat from the chaff. These applications are very lengthy and when we receive them, they are read and talked about by the entire faculty.

If we think the applicant is coming for substantial reasons, we have a long telephone interview with all the faculty present. Based on that, if it still looks promising, we invite the person to fly out for an on-site visit. We usually have the applicants visit in teams of 8–10. They live and work together a little bit, meet all the faculty and students, make the rounds, and see what that life is like.

JL: What are the musical qualifications?

TSS: Some people come with no musical background, but they have the love and desire to be there for those who are dying. Others have a lot of musical background; some with harp, while others have never even seen a harp! They just know, "I must do this work."

JL: How long does the coursework take?

TSS: The course content takes two years. The internship, writing of a professional paper, and sitting for comprehensive exams extends it. The whole study ends up being about two and a half years.

JL: Are they on-premises with you?

TSS: You bet!

JL: You get to know them very well then, don't you?

TSS: They're ours for a couple of years. We have a Schola Cantorum in the hospital, as well as a harp ensemble. The image of St. Patrick being the only hospital in the world–right now–with twenty harpists is true. It changes everybody.

ST. PATRICK HOSPITAL

JL: What compelled St. Patrick hospital to house and support your project?

TSS: I think these things are prepared way before we are. I think with a great deal of help from unseen…, from the…, well, there is a lot of grace involved. St. Patrick Hospital and the University of Montana together founded the Institute of Medicine and the Humanities.

The way St. Pat's and the University founded their branch came about organically; the health-care providers were sharing at a very deep level and talking about ethical issues. Doctors and nurses had to communicate deeply to meet the complex medical-ethical issues of the day. So brown-bag-lunch dialogues evolved into an institute with full vigor.

The Institute was already several years old and had established many wonderful programs when they invited me to come address the physicians. The interesting thing was that I was to do a concert, Friday evening, at the university. The invitation to address the medical community was secondary on Saturday morning. As it turned out, the entire weekend was about destiny.

I spoke to the physicians and nurses on Saturday. That night, I was to go to a dinner sponsored by the Institute for Medicine and Humanities. I think that I even got there a few minutes late. I walked in and I was shocked and quite shaken. There was a receiving line! A receiving line just like something you have seen in the movies. A formal receiving line where all these people were beautifully dressed. And at the very end was this beaming, smiling man who handed me a wonderful bouquet of roses. Everyone shook my hand.

JL: This was after you had spoken to them?

TSS: Yes. It was a big dinner; I didn't understand that I was a guest of honor. So I wound up sitting at this dinner, next to the president of the hospital. He has a face like gold; light pours off of him. His name is Lawrence L. White, Jr. We were having a wonderful, heartfelt dinner conversation and he turned to me at one point and said, "Therese, what would make you happy?"

JL: Oh, the question that we love…

TSS: I knew that although it was a warm and gracious question, at a lovely dinner party with lots of talk, that I should pay attention and think carefully before I spoke–because whatever I said was going to come true! I knew it was destiny. I took a deep breath. At the time, I had all my students in Denver, so I said, "I want a place for my students (my turtle-doves)."

He looked away from me for many long seconds and then he said, "I think that can be arranged."

JL: What did you do?

TSS: I was so happy. I knew that it was the beginning of everything. Let me tell you, it was just one of those moments.

JL: We don't get too many of those, do we?

TSS: Lately, it occurs to me that we probably have many more opportunities than we hear. But that was one time when I was wide awake. I heard it and I leapt. Larry White remains the president of the hospital and such a supportive source. I have gone to him so many times when I didn't know how to take the next step or what to do. He has been a friend, mentor and advisor. Without him, this project could never have flourished and we would never have founded a school within a hospital.

JL: So not only were you given a home base within a hospital to perform your services, but they've also given you the funding to create a school?

TSS: We have received generous support from St. Pat's and also other organizations; The Fetzer Institute, Englehard Foundation, etc.

JL: What do you think was his motivation for bringing you there?

TSS: Love, without a doubt. He said to me, "Therese, we are proud of what we can offer in terms of technical expertise. But no one can ever give enough love."

It took a lot of risk on his part. At a certain point, when he knew that he really wanted our program at his hospital, he began rallying the forces. Some of the wise physicians were thinking critically and saying, "Look, let's be really frank. What if Therese just has a vocation? Maybe she's a mystic. What if this is just something that only she can do? We really have to be assured that this can be taught and replicated, that her students are capable of doing this... that this isn't just about a special woman."

So Larry got on the phone and said, "Therese, put your brightest and your best, their bodies and their harps on the plane." So I chose five students and we came up to Missoula from Denver. The physicians chose patients from every type of medical condition you can imagine: multiple sclerosis, cancers, you name it. There were varying kinds of problems. But the one thing in common was that they were all experiencing terrible pain.

Literally day and night, those physicians and administrators made the rounds with us while we played for those that were dying. They asked many questions and it was very intense. I was really proud of my students. They did the most beautiful job you can imagine. They gave us patients that I never would have dreamed we could help at all.

JL: These were people that were very close to death?

TSS: Yes. Pain is described in the medical world on a scale of 1 to 10. One special woman had very advanced MS. She was contracted, not quite fetal position, but quite contracted; both legs, arms, face to the chest. She had been described to us as having lived on a pain scale of "45"! Morphine could not reach her. On top of this, there were other family complications. The spouse of this woman had developed a drinking problem and was very abusive, etc. She wanted to die. Her pain had been described as so excruciating that her nurses said, "Therese, it is as though she has an abscessed tooth everywhere throughout her body." I had an abscessed tooth once, and I remembered wanting to cut my head off! I couldn't even imagine what she was going through. I was actually quite worried. I thought, "Surely, wouldn't every kind of music, no matter how gentle and lovingly played, wouldn't it all be stimulating, and therefore increase pain?"

We went and attended her. That was one of the vigils that Larry White came to, with his vice-president and a few others. That woman received the music so deeply. We thought that she died. Her respiratory pattern was almost imperceptible… only about 4 breaths per minute. She received at such a deep level. The amazing thing was that we had been playing for quite a few minutes and then the contraction changed, one limb at a time. First her jaw fell open and relaxed and then her right hand and arm opened, left arm, and then both legs. We were completely in shock. It was dramatic.

I touched her. She was as cold as a refrigerator and I really thought she had died. We tip-toed out. But she hadn't died! She slept for *seven* hours. The nurses said she hadn't done that in months. And with no morphine. Before she died, she dictated a letter to one of the nurses thanking us. She said that she had been ashamed that she couldn't come out of the experience she was in. She went to such a deep place, while we played, that she was walking in heaven. So in her soul, she was already full of movement and free.

It was amazing. The top administrators and physicians attending all these initial musical vigils said, "We've got to get this program here. We don't know how it works, but we should spare no effort at the end of life." When it comes to the final moment in someone's life, nothing is too much.

So after this very intensive week of playing morning, noon and night for these selected patients ended, we went back to Denver. Later they informed me that the Foundation board and the others had voted unanimously to welcome music-thanatology as a medical modality at St. Patrick hospital. I was thrilled again for I knew that it was another history making moment.

JL: Their choice to accept the Chalice of Repose Project as a medical modality was a big step forward?

TSS: A huge step.

JL: Before that, The Chalice was considered as a what?

TSS: A nice idea.

JL: You'd been doing it for how long by this time?

TSS: Nineteen years.

JL: Just you alone?

TSS: Myself and a small band of students.

JL: Harp or Chalice students?

TSS: Chalice, and we were really struggling. I have an academic background, and am a classically trained musician. I chaired the music department at Regis University–a Jesuit school–in Denver. The Jesuit's are really clear thinkers, but there was no medical school at that university. People heard about what we were doing and were very supportive. But because the dying people were elsewhere, it only remained an idea. There was no hospital on campus. It was a concept. They had no concrete way to get in touch with it. It was like reading a synopsis or an abstract. It was on the paper. I would get little notes and letters from the faculty members saying, "Therese, I heard about what you are doing and I think it is just wonderful. God bless you. I don't know how you do it." But still, it was an idea that was remote.

I think that by the late 80's, I knew that there would be no hope for us unless we were in a hospital or in a medical setting. If we stayed in a purely liberal arts setting, we would remain just an idea. Certainly, if there had been an academic situation inside of a hospital, we would have jumped. Ours was a university without a medical school. It happened just the way it was supposed to have happened. I think patience gave a lot of time to observe quietly, a lot of time to become sure of myself, a lot of time to study internal medicine, a lot of time for a musician to learn the language of the physician.

It also gave me the time to develop the language for music-thanatology. This is been as important as developing the insight and the repertoire. The development of the language to describe a new effort is a major part of the creativity.

MISSOULA

JL: You mentioned to me that in the two and a half years that you've been in Missoula, your teams have been through 450 vigils–and that the effects of your work could be seen rippling through the community.

TSS: It is making a major difference. Missoula is a small university town. If your Grandma has some terrible disease and is dying, but suddenly, something is happening where in the last ten days of her life, some other modality or method has been issued that really works for

Grandma, its going to completely change your experience of death. You are going to know, with your feet on the ground, that you did everything you could for Grandma. You're going to feel OK, the doctors and nurses are going to feel OK. You are still going to miss Grandma. But if you are there–especially if the family is there–when Grandma dies, it is unbelievable.

JL: Please describe that for me.

TSS: It is very peaceful, very sweet. With a lot of families, even with those who are not affectionate–physically or verbally–the music opens something up in them. They will hold each other, sit in each other's arms. They will weep quietly, not any kind of hysteria. Hold each other, hold Grandma. Sometimes the physicians and nurses will get on the side of the bed and hold the dying patient. This is true especially when a patient is removed from life support systems.

JL: When this occurs, do they die immediately?

TSS: Not always, but often within twenty to thirty minutes.

JL: In a situation like this, when are you called?

TSS: We are called before. We play for the whole family perhaps a half hour before the physician has spoken to everyone, quietly. "...This is what you will expect, this is what we are going to do." We keep on playing. Everyone goes up and kisses Grandma, holds her hand, strokes her face, says something to her, even if she is in a coma. They are there for the actual moment of the crossing of the threshold where there has been intimacy and peacefulness.

JL: Often times, you will use the example of an old person. But you tend to the dying of people who are not leaving after eighty or ninety years?

TSS: I just use the example of an older person when I am talking to interviewers so they don't get scared. I don't want to say, "...your wife." We are in there with three-week–old babies to hundred-year–olds. Most of the experience we have with people being removed from life support systems is with people who are young. The childhood leukemia patients, SIDs, and life support removal deaths make a deep impression on all of us.

When a young person, a baby, or someone our age dies, it is completely different than saying good-bye to Grandma. It is more difficult. Your heart just breaks. The first death I attended in Missoula, the young man was dying of liver cancer. He was a young guy with a young wife and two young sons. The wife was crying her eyes out and holding his head. He was so far gone. I have hardly ever seen a man so ravaged. And she was saying, "You promised you would never leave us." It was all I could do to keep playing. "You promised, you promised!" I played with the greatest intention that I could possibly muster up. I was playing with all my heart that she be given the strength she needs. And he was in a coma. And he came out of a coma and sat up and reached toward something that none of us could see. And his wife saw this and she looked at me and stopped crying. She said to him, "I'm sorry, I'm sorry. You can go. Go. Go. Go." And he died within moments. This business about permission… He was in so much pain… I could tell that before the cancer had come, he must have been a golden man. He was big and handsome, beautifully molded and strong.

JL: So what was your function in that role there?

TSS: Pain. The doctor called me in because of the pain. The morphine would not help him anymore. He also knew the wife was almost crazy with grief. And the doctor was hoping that it might help her as well as him.

JL: And as you look back on that experience…

TSS: I think that it helped a lot. I think it helped her to give him permission. And the minute he got it, he left. So we do see a lot of young deaths. And it is difficult. But I know that young man saw something or someone. He was holding his arms out to something we could not see.

The Monks of Cluny

JL: Therese, tell me about the comprehensive infirmary practices used by the Cluny monks. This has become the foundation of your work. How have you adapted and integrated these practices for the twenty-first century?

TSS: The Cluniac monks open the Customary[1] by saying, "When a monk knows his time is drawing near..." This very first sentence addresses the relationship of the person who is dying and his relationship to community. The entire document is based on relationship. It places the person who is dying as the primary agent; he is directing his own death. It does not open by saying, "...and now the doctor gives you the diagnosis that you are dying." It opens by saying, "When a monk knows his time is drawing near..." This is knowledge that the person has inside. The very first words are like fire to me. There was a time when it was common knowledge, when people were in touch with something. We have given a certain part of our lives away by waiting for other people to tell us when to come and when to go.

I remember, twenty years ago, talking with my young women friends. They all wanted to have their babies via natural childbirth instead of having the doctor tell them when they would have it. So many of our mothers had a doctor who made an appointment for them to come in and have a Cesarian, whether or not they needed it or not. Twenty years later, all these women said, "...No, my baby is going to come when my baby wants to come; at the right time." This was the same with the dying. I saw that birthing and dying were so closely related in the way they were being handled, where timing occurred at the convenience of providers, not as an aspect of individual biography.

Second of all, I saw that for the monks of Cluny, dying was not an end. They used a feminine language; the Latin word, *Morir*, to die, wasn't the first word. It was *transitus*, the thought of a transition from one place to another. It was the concept of the great walkabout; while Christianized, it is not so far away from the Australian Aboriginal picture. In the Cluniac teachings, I saw many things that were incredibly relevant. I learned that there was a way of caring, with beauty and intimacy and reverence that could easily be translated to anything that we need today.

JL: Was the practice developed by the monks at Cluny, done just within the monastery? Was that philosophy a general frame of mind at that time?

TSS: Scholars debate this. For one thing, it was a monastic practice. And number two, it was very particular. Cluny founded over a thousand daughter houses in a very short amount of time. These were based on the Cluny model.

The Cluniac spirituality tended to place it's monasteries on the pilgrim's routes. For example, between France and Spain, there was a major pilgrimage route on which Christian, Moslems and Jews traveled. A major part of Benedictine spirituality is to give shelter to the stranger, the pilgrim; harbor the wayfaring. And to care for the sick and dying. This was written into Holy Rule. And when you strip away all that stuff about exclusive identity, the motivation was very simple. Love. Love made them do it. It was the ideal. Be there now, when they need you, not just when it is convenient.

JL: So even with a thousand 'daughter houses,' was conscious dying the common practice with the plain country folks?

TSS: No, it was a monastic practice. Sometimes I wince because a lot of uninformed Americans think that the only conscious death and dying practices are Eastern. But this is not true. Within Christianity, a monk or a nun prepares an entire lifetime to die consciously. This impulse to be there, when others are in pain, suffering in sickness or death, that is in the Gospel of St. Matthew. "I was hungry and you gave me to eat, I was thirsty and you gave me to drink, I was in prison and you came and visited me..." That, I think, is one of the most special things. The Buddhists and the Christians stand together in the desire, whether it is love or compassion, to respond. And the Jewish community has a highly developed rubric for a blessed death, involving elaborate rituals. There is a *Hevrah Kaddisha* in most of the large cities.

JL: Where do you think that got lost along the way?

TSS: Many, many factors. An Industrial Revolution, a technological revolution, the fact that we sit separately in our little cocoons with our computers and faxes.

JL: Devoid of a tribe?

TSS: Yes, we are separated from one another. Today, we have to work hard to find our own destiny, and to be an individual and yet responsive to community.

JL: You ended up creating your own community?

TSS: Well, certainly the Chalice staff, students, faculty, and graduates represent diversity: Jewish, Buddhist, Christian, Quaker, Catholic, Protestant, Methodist and Baptist, Sufi, you name it. We are not a religious order but we gather together with a common vision.

JL: What do you think it was about Cluny that brought together two such noble courses of work, being mediation and the commemoration of the dead?

TSS: An abbot with an extraordinary mind that was warmed by the heart. He was permeated with love. And a group of like-minded seekers.

JL: So one man?

TSS: One person makes a difference! Leadership, too, is a spirituality.

JL: Just one person...

TSS: One person can make a huge difference. We know that. Look at Jesus, Buddha, Francis, Hildegard, or Mother Teresa. It has happened many times in history.

THE CHALICE PROCESS

JL: If we fast-forward nine centuries, with the Chalice of Repose being the modern-day equivalent of a Cluny *daughter house,* what is the process when a phone call comes into your office?

TSS: It takes a lot for this to work. To begin, we have a clinical coordinator who receives referrals. We receive a call from either a physician, nurse, chaplain, social worker, friend or family member. On rare occasions, the dying person will self-refer. The doctor or nurse will briefly describe the patient's medical or psycho-social condition. Then we call medical records and get more information.

Pedagogically, we work with the medical model. We have interns and residents. Either of these, with two younger students will go out and attend these vigils. All interns travel with beepers; on the days they're on rotation, they have to be ready to begin a vigil in minutes. Often, they leave their harps in the hospital if they are on duty.

Before they walk into the room, they will have a medical history of the patient. The three of them will go into the room together. One Chalice worker stands on the left side, and another on the right, with the third at the foot of the bed. The patient is surrounded with music; it is sound anointing. During the course of the vigil, the three Chalice workers may rotate between the different positions. But during the vigil, there are always two harpist playing–when music is being played.

The first few moments, they sit in silence and watch the patient very quietly. They will touch the patient's hands, stroke their head. It is an act of tenderness and also, whether they are conscious or comatose, we will say something quietly, "Hello Joshua, Therese here..." We stroke the hand and the head, temples, forehead, neck. What we are actually doing is taking the pulse and checking the respiration and temperature. We are taking note of the patient's condition. We sit there for a minute or two, watching the person. We are very quiet, breathing with them. After we are all certain that we are breathing *with* the patient, the lead intern begins. He or she has the most experience and one idea is to work very quietly with the patient's own breath. It depends what the person is experiencing. *There are many things that we can do musically to suppress or to support either heating or cooling processes.*

JL: Understanding this is a major part of your curriculum, can you share a little about the significance of the heating and cooling?

TSS: One brief example: an acute febrile tendency, or *heating,* can often be brought into balance with highly developed melody. Also, we look at whether or not someone is suffering from physical pain or spiritual pain. It's not that we think that pain is bad. Fever can cleanse. We all know that for most of us, the pain that we've gone through, some of it we'd never wish upon ourselves again, nor upon anyone else. Yet we know that we grew through some of the worst, most painful experiences of our life.

It is never simple; I don't want to give the impression that I think every kind of pain in the world should be irradicated. Nor do I want to give the impression that pain is what we deserve. It is none of those things. The question for me is, can we be of assistance? How can we help?

A lot of the time, we will work with the phenomena of entrainment. If we can slow someone's breathing and respiration down with the music then frequently they can go into a very deep sleep. Something that is happening more and more, as our students become increasingly skilled, is nurse feedback. The tell us, "This particular person has not slept for more than 15 minutes at a time for days and now they have slept for six hours straight, without morphine, etc."

We work with entrainment a great deal, but it is only one facet of our methodology. If the patient is very close to death, we draw the music out more and more with our phrasing and lyricism. We play music for them that is outside of time. That is the Gregorian music. You cannot count it. This really helps them to unbind from qualities of time. So, it is very important, if they are in a great deal of pain, not to play music that will stimulate, but will in fact, help them *unbind*. We want to slow things down and help remove qualities of time—and of course, replace it with eternity.

JL: If I understand you correctly, you are using the ISO principle, whereby you meet the listener where they are. Then you diagnose what they need sonically, via entrainment, to help them let go?

TSS: Yes, entrainment and other tools as well. The language that we use is *prescriptive music*. Let me describe a different scenario for you. Sometimes the doctor calls and says, "We have a patient up on Five North who has a terminal diagnosis but they are not near death yet. They probably have three weeks to go. They are going rapidly and we have terrible problems going on." Then they describe the situation where perhaps, the dying person cannot accept the diagnosis. Or maybe, they are ready to die, but everybody in the family is furious with them, giving them all kinds of guilt trips. Like, "Mom, shame on you. You're giving up! Fight this damn disease." And the mom is saying, "It's *my* time. I don't want to go through anymore chemotherapy, I don't want to have a bone-marrow transplant. It is my time to go!" So there may be a lot of unresolved material. This kind of call is known as a *processing call*. In this situation, we address anger or grief. Frequently, we are playing for the family as much as for the patient. The first kind of referral that I described for you is known as the *imminency call.* This is where they are actively dying, '*go now!*'

There is a lot of processing work with sudden diagnosis. Sometimes a leukemia will take somebody very quickly. It is terrible when it is a child. They can go very quickly. How do you help parents deal with the sudden loss of a child?

We had a young woman with a baby only six weeks old. Beautiful baby boy. The mother was a teenage girl with no husband. Her baby, through no fault of her own, had just died in the crib. (This is known as Sudden Infant Death.) She lived very close to the hospital and she was crazy with grief as you can imagine. She raced the baby to the hospital and they successfully resuscitated, but the baby was brain-dead. And the providers said, "...There is no cortical activity. It's not going to help." So the doctors called us up and said, "...Please come, you've got to help this woman go through her grief processing very quickly. The baby is not going to regain consciousness."

We came and a male nurse explained to this young teenager what was going to happen, what to expect. This male nurse and a female nurse were so tender with her. About thirty teenagers came from all over Missoula to be with her. She held her baby and sobbed and rocked in the chair. Little by little the nurse removed the baby from all the equipment and we watched this girl hold her baby to her breast. Obviously she was lactating. The nurses got a rocking chair and had their arms around her. They were weeping with her. And she held her baby and sobbed and sobbed like I have never heard before in my life.

And we kept on playing and playing. It was one of the hardest deaths that you can ever attend. We all kept playing and watched as the baby slowly turned blue. It was very difficult... but we kept on playing for a long time. At a certain point, she asked all her family members and everyone else to leave. We stayed and played for a little while longer and then eventually she told us that she wanted to be completely alone. She just held the baby for awhile longer.

The music to help the grieving process happens on such a deep level. Without words, things can move and come to the surface. It is the movement there that we are looking for, not the cognitive, linear resolution.

JL: Therese, you speak of the "pulsating silence" that took place with the first man that you tended. Tell me about the "...alternation between contraction and expansion and how it *potentizes* the effectivity of the musical dynamic in its therapeutic applications." What does 'potentize' mean?

TSS: Potentization is a European pharmaceutical term. It speaks to *raising* something to the next highest level in a dynamic transformation process that involves a complete loss of the original substance. In the potentization processes of vegetable and mineral substances, it is curious that the greater the dilution, the stronger the medicine. Something loses its original form and then acquires a new one. I have seen this to be true in music as well. Let's take a starting point... For instance, through heat, solid things become pliant, like wax. And through heat, water is absorbed into the air. Now if you transfer these subtleties, these imaginations, to ways in which prescriptive music can be understood, you begin to understand that prescriptive music is not about a limited, contained body of repertoire but is rather about an intentional contemplative methodology. Interns learn how to *liberate* and *activate* musical processes physiologically and spiritually. As an example, music itself becomes potentized–becomes a more powerful agent of change and therefore healing–when we alternate sound with silence. All the serious composers know this, and share this with us in their memoirs. I even tell my students to sometimes consciously *fast* from sound, from music, for limited periods, in order to purify, in order to hear and receive more sensitively.

Constant music (continual external auditory stimulus) is numbing. It numbs the soul and manipulates unconscious, instinctive aspects of our humanity and physiologic processes, rather than conscious internal or bodily activities. In our school, the motto is "*Attention to Intention.*" Intentionality is very important.

Besides the sacred aspect of attending the patient's death or *transitus*, prescriptive music is based on physiological phenomenology, and for me, comes with two decades of quiet observation. Here is a small window: I have found that major intervals and scales can actually assist processes in the metabolism, while the minor scales and intervals support cooling processes. If you are thinking allopathically, a patient suffering from an acute febrile condition can ingest an analgesic to suppress the symptoms of feverish pain, but, if you are thinking in terms of the new paradigm of holism, and in terms of prescriptive music, you can deliver very particular kinds of highly developed melodies to cool the patient down, and transform the inflammation processes into bodily equilibriumor homeostasis.

Every single one of your readers already knows, intuitively, that rhythm can activate, engage, and stimulate the autonomic nervous system and metabolism in general. It can lift our spirits, give us energy. You can also potentize rhythm, make it stronger yet more subtle, more lyric and refined, by working with repetition or ostinato rather than simple, driving, pulsating rhythms. Yet another example of musical potentization is to work with a poignant minor third interval—which our varied tuning systems prove to be ultra-personal—and invert it, open it up and expand it to a major sixth. It still affects the heart, physically and spiritually, affects respiration and circulation, but is brighter, and for some patients, less threatening than the inward, reflective, soul-searching minor third.

There are specific examples that can assist you in seeing that prescriptive music at the bed-side vigil requires a really dynamic methodology, and is individually tailored to meet each patient where they are. In thinking about the curriculum, better-faster-bigger-better product-oriented musicians won't succeed in mastering the principles involved. That kind of thinking has already become too rigid, too literal, too dependent on a mechanized causality, and has a difficult time with the contemplative, reflective, process-oriented component. If anyone calls us with simple expectations of learning 25 pieces of static repertoire good for relaxing people, and then receiving a degree, those people would be deeply challenged.

If I go back now and return to your question about the 'pulsating silence' that I experienced in the first death 21 years ago, it involved a difficult, loud, frightened death rattle from a man with emphysema. His lungs were filling up, so he was essentially drowning. Nothing more could be done for him medically. I held him and sang prayer quietly till he died in my arms. The silence I speak about became potentized because I witnessed an agonizing sound, filled with fear, resolve into a trusting, peaceful—though shallow and weak breathing—until the end… a clear diminuendo that eventually became a golden silence. What I experienced then was not about failure or emptiness, because the room was filled with his freedom. He was freed from his suffering and on his way, his *transitus.* I knew that what I had been privileged to witness was intimate, sacred, and obviously, that man has blessed the rest of my life.

I learned many things in that hour; that risking is essential, and that birthing and dying are closely related and equally sacred. I learned that there can be deathbed healing without curing, and the sixth century Boethius was right: "*Music is an all pervasive force, streaming through the universe like currents of light and warmth, weaving body, soul, and spirit together.*" The man with the emphysema rested *into* the music (sung prayer) as well as the intentionality and died peacefully. The silence that filled his room was not a void, it was something protected and protecting, like a chalice.

JL: In attending someone whose death is imminent, do you stay with them until they go, no matter how long it takes?

TSS: If they are actively dying, we stay until they go. Typically, we continue playing for a while after they die. In a few cases—where someone dies before we got there—we will go in and play for a few moments anyway, to comfort family and providers, to respect the departed one's life and soul.

JL: How does the process of unbinding, that you often speak about, fit into that?

TSS: We unbind from attachments, and certainly aspects of physical body. For me, I can only let go when I have given something or someone the very best, when that process involved both giving and receiving. Most of us start out knowing how to do one or the other, but not both. For me, life is the great school, the great initiation.

Sometimes it is when we haven't been loved—or haven't been able to receive—that we can't let go, that we are still hungering and yearning. There are a lot of different ways to look at it. I think about the times, in our love affairs, where there was somebody from the past, and we couldn't let go when we should let go. The destruction that can come about... But with some time, you are able to grow and get strong. You realize that if you actually love this person, you will let go.

JL: How does the music assist in that process of unbinding?

TSS: When they are really imminent, we play music without any time. Time is one of the things that binds you so tightly to your physical body. The physical body has so many different rhythms. If we can help unbind some of the many rhythms, especially the brainwaves, heartbeat, respiration, and all these kinds of things, we can help them let go.

JL: Is it essentially a process of reverse entrainment?

TSS: Earth rhythms bind and strengthen; cosmic rhythms liberate.

JL: Is the process to just keep slowing and slowing down until the patient gets to a place of enough peace that they can let go and leave?

TSS: That is one process of several prescriptive deliveries, to get a patient to a place of being very still and peaceful. Also, it is very important that we tell the family members of the dying people, "...Remember, this is not a concert; it is not a performance." In a concert, you expect invigorating energy. Typically, you'll alternate and pace your program with something vivacious and up and then something inward, and then a love song, whatever. With the bedside vigil music, sometimes we repeat a piece many times. Of course, you couldn't do that in a concert. But the quality is to be there for them in a different way–family and patient. All the attention is on the patient. It is not a concert; it is sung prayer. It is sacred, their dying, and we witness an exteriorization of an internal event.

JL: In terms of your repertoire, is it basically chants?

TSS: Mostly Gregorian chant and lullabies with some other material. As an example, listen to *The Gartan Mother's Lullaby.*[2] There is so much love in this song; it is so tender! For some, we sing it over and over.

JL: How does the process of chant repetition serve?

TSS: Often times a chant has many verses, and so the thematic material can be repeated many times, in many ways. Time is replaced with eternity; the patient rests into a place of trust. At that point, we can usually entrain them and support profound relaxation and 'letting go…'

JL: And the musical prescription is based upon your diagnosis as to how they are *unbinding* on a spiritual, mental, physical or emotional level?

TSS: Yes.

JL: Based upon this diagnosis, you pick pieces of music that will have specific effects?

TSS: The music is not chosen prior to the vigil. Prescriptive music equals dynamic responsiveness to the patient at the moment. But here is an interesting point. Sometimes people will get very agitated. They will immediately let you know they do not want this unbinding music. It is extraordinary. We have narrative after narrative about this. Sometimes a person isn't *that* close to dying yet… They are saying to us that they still want to hold on; they are not ready to go. In this situation, we will play processing music for them. Yet two or three days later, they may want the timeless Gregorian. For now, they are ready to go.

JL: So you go back day after day?

TSS: Sometimes we will see someone three or four times before they die. Often times, it is once. In the last six months, we've begun playing at geriatric homes. We have a very special relationship with a company that has four of these elder care facilities. They have been very concerned with the problem of Alzheimer's and dementia. They are really trying to do something of superior quality. So they have us come in and play for the dementia patients. They have patients there with very advanced Alzheimer's who are stuck, who cannot die, who haven't spoken a word in a decade.

JL: What has been your experience with the Alzheimer's patients?

TSS: Our interns played for an autistic Alzheimer elder who had not spoken to her husband in ten years. The poor husband had been visiting her all this time; he really loved her. But she was stuck in the no-movement place. Not a word, just staring. We played for her once and she came out talking to her husband, asking for the music to come back.

Recently, we played for another Alzheimer's patient who was also stuck. After the students had played for about a half hour, the patient started to vomit. The students became quite frightened! They thought, "Oh my God, we are doing all the wrong things." But a nurse, who had been present at many of our vigils intervened. She urged the interns to continue, saying, "This is important! She's just let go of something that was really important!" The nurse was so sensitive; she encouraged the musicians to keep playing, and the woman died quietly. The nurse said, "This patient had been holding onto something for so long." She had finally let go and now she could go. So what we do not know, especially in the case of someone who has been silent for a long time, is what's really going on in their heart and mind.

JL: Where does the music go, that somehow gives them the ability to come back or to finally leave?

TSS: Movement occurs, which is healing–even though it is not curing–and it is somewhat of a mystery. Often, something physical has to happen before a dying person can let go spiritually. At times it is the opposite. It depends on what their issues are.

JL: Have you ever found yourself in the situation where a patient has had a vehement response to the music?

TSS: Never once. One strong reason is that we never go anywhere unless asked. Even when we're requested by the physician to go immediately to a certain room in the hospital, our coordinator checks with the patient and/or the family, to let them know what we are going to do. Therefore, the person is prepared before we come.

JL: So you have not inadvertently received abusive behavior as somebody was working out their issues?

TSS: I have only one painful story. I think it is a good lesson for everybody. It's about a man who was dying of cancer. He had been married and divorced twice in his life. On his deathbed, both of the former wives showed up. The two women became jealous of each other and began competing over who had loved him more. The poor man was passing in and out of a coma and was in a lot of pain. The former wives realized that he was really going to die. They were both really mad and they started fighting over his dying body! They were on the left and the right side of him at the bed and they started pulling him, tugging on him. "He's mine," one cried! "No, he's mine," said the other woman.

It was so vulgar. They suddenly realized that he was actually dying and one of them looked up at me and said, "It's your fault!" I know that this sounds like a really bad movie, but that is what she said. It was the first and only time that I felt–for the good of the patient–I should leave. He was left with these two incredibly selfish people.

This was a situation, in the old days, where we were working outside of a medical context. I couldn't tell the nurse, "Get in there and protect that man!"

JL: Whereas now you could?

TSS: Yes, you bet!

JL: And you have the authority to?

TSS: Not just authority… the spiritual and medical/ethical responsibility! I tell people all of the time, "Please families, let each other go!" It is so selfish to not let your mom, dad or child die if it is their time.

JL: So you become a grief or transitions counselor?

TSS: We are not grief counselors, but midwives to *transitus.* This is why I call our work *musical-sacramental-midwifery.* We are not there to intervene in the moment with the families. We are there with our music. I leave the counseling of the families to the social workers and the chaplains.

The Transition Process

JL: Therese, you speak of three different levels of the transition process with the *Liminal* phase being the most critical. Can we talk about these different phases?

TSS: It is very simple and it is similar in many different cultures. The patient has already had her terminal diagnosis for quite awhile and has been able to proceed with her life. But now, during the *Rites of Separation,* she can no longer hold down her job. She can no longer even do the nice little things in her house, make her bed, make a cake, etc. So she is starting to withdraw and separate from all the things that give her an identity: a working woman, a mother, a wife, whatever. All the things that formally defined her identity. Eventually she is in bed all the time. Then she will stop eating and even drinking water. These are the *Rites of Separation.*

The Liminal stage is when there is no longer energy to spare and the patient is in rapid decline. Typically, she has not yet completed the internal spiritual, mental or emotional work, and the physical process is not yet over. Often times, there is pain… but not always.

The *Rites of Reincorporation* is after the death has occurred. From the spiritual perspective, both Christian and Buddhist, you are being reincorporated into the next community on a different level. From the Christian perspective, you have a Requiem Mass, whereby you get together and pray for the person who has just died. And you are praying for each other; you are praying that you are going to meet your grief, that the family members will be OK. You are sending a lot of love and energy and devotion, attention and intention. In the Buddhist perspective, you have so many different kinds of prayers and mantras depending on your place in the community. In both of these communities, you have a renewal of these kinds of activities at different rhythms; 24 hours later, seven days later, twenty-eight days later, a year later, seven years later. It is a beautiful way to keep the connection of the spiritual and the earth communities.

JL: In your work, the Liminal is the most critical?

TSS: Yes. The liminal stage is the threshold. Victor Turner's work has helped us so much. Rites of passage. We have many liminal rites in our lives, but until someone points it out to us, we don't have a way to look at it. The day your wife went into labor with your baby daughter changed everything for you. You're not the same guy that you were when you were twenty-five, foot-loose and fancy-free. That was a transition point, a liminal stage.

JL: So dying is the big liminal?

TSS: Yes, it is the big one! It's the Olympic liminal!

JL: The Olyminal. You have written that, "...there is a place where medical miracles and miracles of the human spirit intersect." You go on to say that, "...for me, that sanctuary there in the middle has been a completely musical, lyrical field." Tell me about that sanctuary in the middle.

TSS: The first woman that I told you about, with the Multiple Sclerosis, who was so contracted, her physical body was helped. But none of us know why she was able to receive the music so deeply, so extraordinarily. The morphine didn't work. But the music smoothed her out like nothing else could ever before. She dictated a letter to us before she died, "I was walking in the clouds..."

We saw that happening to her physically. But we wouldn't have known what was happening in her inner life if she had not communicated with us. To me, she is a great example of that 'lyrical field.'

Horizons collapse into one another and there is a fusion. It is physiological and it is also spiritual. I am quite convinced that she went into such a deep place. It was like the deepest place of prayer or yoga, the kind we have read about in books.

JL: This 'sanctuary in the middle' is a very holy ground you have to witness.

TSS: It is. That is why I tell people that this work is a contemplative practice with clinical applications. It is as intimate as we can get, to be there at someone's birth or to be there at someone's death. Both of those rites are holy.

JL: It is a holy privilege.

TSS: Yes. But people say, "...but don't you get depressed?" Well, how can you? It is a privilege. I don't want to give the impression of some kind of 'Pollyanna' consciousness. None of this work is romantic. There <u>is</u> struggle. But there are many blessed moments that you feel and witness; they're not all rosy, but it is extraordinary. Everybody's life is unique. And everybody's death is unique.

TWENTY YEARS OF DEATH-BED VIGILS

JL: How has attending twenty years of death-bed vigils impacted you, in terms of your own preparation for letting go?

TSS: I give thanks and I give praise as often as possible. I try and meet people at the deepest level–which does not necessarily mean that we are earnest all of the time. I try and give meetings a higher priority so they are truly encounters instead of meetings. I make every moment count. I try and think before I speak. I never let my husband, Lorenz, leave... or I leave and get on the next plane without turning to him and saying, "Lorenz... I love you."

But my prayer has altered. It is different. I give praise as often as possible, for everything that we have. And for all the windows that we are given. It has renewed a lot of faith. I see how much can occur in an hour. I see how good people can really be–even after a lifetime of bitter competition. I see how teamwork can change the world. The blessed grace comes through, at any moment, if you just make room. It opens your eyes, it opens your ears, it opens your heart.

HOW THE DYING ACCEPT MUSIC

JL: What is the frame of mind, of consciousness, of a dying person? Are they in an altered state? And how do they receive the music?

TSS: I think that the least sensitive thing I can do is make a generalization or present a static model. Everybody's death is different. Our role is to be present, to be clear and grounded, without agenda or preconceived notions or expectations, in order to meet the needs of the patient.

JL: But are people in an altered state of consciousness by the time they are within an hour of their leaving?

TSS: I would describe it differently. I can tell you what I have seen and it is a lot. Everybody has a different combination. There are some things going on bodily, there are some things going on in the realm of the soul, and in the realm of the spirit. Others would want to call it in the realm of the heart or the realm of the mind. I think that some

people receive the music on all three levels, on one level, on two levels… In and out, in and out. But I do know one thing. I have been present at many deaths where they went quietly and peacefully. Especially if they had finished up the hard work of saying good-bye, or the forgiveness issues, or the 'I love you' statements. If they have completed the personal matters, they were able to die quietly.
Many people just drift in and out. Some people absolutely die consciously. Other people drift into a coma. But I would say that the whole process can be described as a *loosening* and a *letting go*. It is difficult to die if we cannot let go. It is pretty scary in one way because we all know that there are plenty of things that we don't let go of in or daily lives.

In our school, where we have people of all different religious identities, it is very important that we respect the freedom of each student. But there is a meditative practice that each of us can do without infringing on freedom.

I look my students straight in the eye and say, "See if you can die to something every day, it will prepare you. It will prepare you for our own deaths and to help see the small ways in which the patient lets go, one thread after another."

There is a wonderful author named Kenneth Paul Kramer who wrote an article entitled, *Dying Awake*,[3] a beautiful piece about conscious dying. He described the little daily deaths: "Every time I change my ideas or beliefs, each time a relationship changes or dies, whenever I discover a better way to accomplish a task, whenever I have to wait in line, I experience little deaths. A portion of ego-consciousness is rearranged, material discarded…" He also described that the little deaths of daily life are not to be confused with the Great Death, *transitus*. But, recognizing those signs in daily life helps each of us prepare in little ways, not the larger-than-life leaps, accomplished by saints and heros. This 'little way' is given to us, quietly, on a silver platter, any day in the week, every place in the world. I also see it as the *little way* that is accomplished by anyone who learns to fine-tune a stringed instrument. One learns to fine-tune gradually, over time, as the interior life becomes more refined and harmonious, more capable of the widened hearing of which Origin, the Hebrews, or Dr. Alfred Tomatis speaks.

JL: So to you, dying is synonymous with letting go?

TSS: Yes. That and more.

JL: And so here, every day of our lives, we wash, examine, tend to our bodies. Ultimately, it is our oldest friend. And at a given point, we have to let go of even our bodies.

TSS: Yes. I'm thinking of things like when people are becoming middle-aged. A woman looks in the mirror and starts to see a different face, different shape. We have to let go of the fact that we don't have an 18-year–old face or the 18-year–old legs. But we do have to let go and when we don't, it is not so graceful.

JL: No it's certainly not. I have not been going through a very graceful mid-lifing myself. This doesn't bode well but I'm working on it.

TSS: It's the pits, ain't it!

The Spiritual Work of Dying

JL: You talk about the spiritual work of dying frequently in your literature. Is this different now than in the past?

TSS: I think almost everyone that you and I meet today… whether we meet at work, home, in our neighborhoods–everybody that you know, deeply or peripherally, has so many stories. The people that we know really intimately… Sometimes aren't you struck and think, '…it's as though this person has lived two or three lifetimes crammed into one biography.' Most of us will have several careers. Sadly, we are married more than once, etc. We stuff a lot into one lifetime. That is really good and also, we have a lot of *distractions* in a lifetime. So, we can get pulled away from the deepest parts of ourselves when we become too deeply engaged in the rat-race, the money, the competition, power, prestige, fame, whatever. For lay people, of any religious orientation or direction–Jewish, Moslem, Christian, Buddhist–we can come from any kind of spiritual practice. But as part of daily life, to remember to take time for reflection and contemplation, and to acknowledge things at a deeper level takes a conscious commitment.

I've been very influenced by a modern day mystic, Simone Weil (1909-1943). She was a Jewish intellectual who died quite young; a mathematician, philosopher and linguist. She wrote extraordinary things before she died, amongst them a piece entitled *Waiting for God*.[4] She redefined something and it works for me. She called prayer, *rapt attention*. That says it all. To me, if I am cooking with particular thoughtfulness and care, or cleaning the floors or toilets or windows, or doing our administrative work, or writing our articles... if I do it with my whole heart and soul, that's a new kind of prayer. It doesn't have to be the formulaic stuff on our knees, although that still speaks to many.

THE CONTEMPLATIVE MUSICIAN

JL: You know, Therese, I have been traveling around for the last few years, researching this field of intentional music and sound. What I have found is that there are many people who are in the nurturing, gestation phase with their work. There are only a few who have truly defined, birthed their work–who have it up and running and working in society. So much of this work is newly hatched. There are only a few things that have their roots in the ground and are growing strong and having a specific, discernible, quantifiable effect with the use of music and sound. The Tomatis work is one method. Yours is another.

In reading *The Conscious Ear*,[5] Tomatis' autobiography, he speaks about reaching "...out towards that to which one listens." This is *ab audire* in Latin, which translates in French as *obeir*, to obey.

TSS: Yes, *hearing* is a much higher principle. Origin (c.185-251) described hearing as "...a sense-of-the-spirit, as an inner readiness of the soul towards God."

JL: As this concept has been traced back in history, Tomatis recounts, "...in Hebrew, to be heard is already to be answered. If God listens to our plea, he answers it. So it is dynamic, to listen is *ipso facto* to obey."

The idea that if you listen deeply enough, you will hear the deepest truth. Therefore, *to obey* is not about bending over in subservience, but you are actually hearing your own deepest self.

TSS: I think a lot about two particular kinds of prayer. I think of *sung prayer* and I think of *silent prayer*. In silent prayer we can really hear and receive; you make room for a divine presence. But also with the sung prayer, we are singing our prayers and chanting, praising. There is a way of singing *from the future* where you are hearing at a higher level. In antiquity, they called it the widened priesthood. Certainly, the Pythagoreans referred to it as the *widened hearers*. You can sing imagining the heavenly host. This is a very different performance practice than what we learned in music schools to receive degrees.

No matter how beautiful and rich and great our teachers are, a young music student with a potential to become a great soloist is primed to 'fill that stage' or 'fill that hall.' I call that projectile singing. This other kind of music making, I have called it *contemplative musicianship*, requires a life of prayer. This does not mean that concert work is bad. It just means that there are many different routes to walk as a serious musician.

Remember that old Joni Mitchell song lyric, "...he was playin' real good for free?" I think that image of somebody playing on the street corner, they almost pluck your heart out of your body, and make you brand new. They play with their whole heart and soul and you hear it. But other times, we pay $40 for a ticket to hear something really great and we come out of the concert and we are not changed.

JL: We haven't been moved; it hasn't touched our hearts. What other formats are there for contemplative musicians?

TSS: I think that there is a tremendous movement for pastoral musicians and liturgists. There is a very important North American Academy of Liturgy. This is composed of Jewish and Christian liturgists. These are the people who prepare the music, words and prayers for all the liturgies for their different congregations. They meet once a year and truly dialogue with each other. From this, I am starting to get a different pulse on a whole dignified renewal of this field. All the different traditions are hungry to make their worship authentic and beautiful. All of them.

INDIAN MEDICINE

JL: Have you studied anthropologically where music and sound is used in transition among indigenous people?

TSS: Oh yes. There is a great deal to be learned there. I have been blessed with very serious relationships with different people of the Native American Indian traditions: Cree, Micmac, Ojibwa, Cheyenne, Chickasaw, Haida, and Blackfeet. That has been very special. They have taught me a great deal. They have also been hurt because they've been exploited. They have very deep medicine.

JL: Have you adapted some of their shamanistic processes into your work?

TSS: No, but I have learned from them enormously. The first thing they taught me was that this is not a smorgasbord, so to speak. They said, "...If you use this music incorrectly, it may never be used again. Respect it so much." What I have learned from them, instead of their sacred music, is about their intimacy, about their strength, about the body of meaning, about lineage, about the Earth/Sky axis. I don't use their Medicine Songs. They told me not to, because then it makes it into a smorgasbord spirituality.

They told me an absolutely extraordinary story about some good-intentioned natives who wanted to recover the old ways from their grandparents. There was one woman, a mother in her fifties or sixties who was furious at her children because they were using the Medicine Songs incorrectly. She said, "See, you're pride, your vanity and ego has caused you to do this. These songs can never be used again. Ever!"

For them, they sing people into existence and sing them out. The songs are considered living beings. When a Medicine Song dies with somebody, it rests with them and travels with them. They let it be silent and rest. Sometimes it will come back into existence thirty or forty years later again. They don't know how... Somebody else in your family line will wake up singing it one day and then they will know, "Uncle Leroy has been here." But I paid really close attention to what they taught me: "Don't do smorgasbord Medicine Songs!" I have honored that. I have learned how to stay in a magnetic field of attention and intention. That is what I learned from them.

CROSS-CULTURAL USE OF MUSIC-THANATOLOGY

JL: Utilizing the concepts you have learned over all these years–being primarily a white, European, Western tradition–with a Black African or on an Indian from Alaska, would this *white man's* method be effective cross-culturally?

TSS: Yes. I have done it all. The phenomenology that I was allowed to observe, during the first eighteen years, is based on physiology. An Indian has a heart, an African has a heart, a middle-class housewife from the 'burbs has a heart. It is based on physiology and phenomenology. After many years of experience, I have been able to get to some universals instead of some particulars. Sometimes people say, "Wouldn't this be offensive for someone Jewish or Islamic?" I have played for everybody and everything. I have played for Buddhists; I have played for the deaths of Buddhist teachers. I've played for many Jewish people. You name it, I've been there. What it comes down to, is not the repertoire, but the intention and methodology. The intention is to serve what they need and want. With this, you will find the prescriptive music out of love, not out of agenda. Love. Love has to be the guiding force there. You or I have never met anybody who couldn't benefit from love.

MUSICAL MIDWIFERY

JL: Do you think there is a value for musical midwifery for birth?

TSS: Yeah! I have recently come across articles, written by female nurses, who did double-blind surveys saying, "...for some women it was true that the music was awful," that the music was a hindrance rather than a help. But what I learned from that was that we can't be too attached to all our theories. What I've also realized is that they did not know how to do prescriptive medicine. I bet if they had been sensitive, and brought in a certain kind of music that was right for *that* woman, it could have helped her.

JL: Is there anyone presently working in this field?

TSS: I think there are. But I don't know that there is a group of music therapists who are working solely on the labor and delivery. I'm sure that music therapists would love to work in this field.

JL: Now that you have established your method as a medical modality, do you think that you will branch out into other areas of music in a therapeutic context, such as birthing, pre-op, post-op, etc.?

TSS: I could because I have a lot of energy. But I won't because death and dying is such a huge field. I would rather have done one thing well before I die than many things sloppily. What I feel is this: If I can work, just like the gospel says, "...with my whole mind and heart and body and soul," to assist this one thing, if I can do it really well, then before I die, we will leave a written legacy (as well as the method), and then many others will come after. They will take what we have learned and apply it in every field of medicine. Death and dying is an area that frightens off a lot of people. So hey, I've got a vocation. Let's stick here!

Harps and Healing Music

JL: Besides the angelic sound, why do you exclusively use the harp?

TSS: Harp strings move in circles rather than being projected. When you play a brass instrument, there is a force, a mechanism, a valve there. And there is a tonal substance that comes out like a stream. The harp strings, lute strings... they move in circles. They don't invade the dying space of the person. And also we are looking for tonal warmth. Many sounds are very high and stimulate the nervous system. This brings you back into your metabolism and ties you to your body.

JL: So you would not use any kind of rhythm or drumming because you are attempting to unbind?

TSS: Yes. And even with beautiful instruments, like the violin, the timbre is such that it is stimulating. I am not saying that harp is superior.

But we look for tonal sounds and timbres that are not stimulating, not adversely stimulating to the nervous system. Our job is not to engage them but to help them let go.

JL: Let's talk about *healing music.* I know that you go to great lengths to address that. You've written, "...We do not, in any way, perceive ourselves as healers. Rather, we think of our service work as clarifying." Do you think that there is any such thing as *healing* music?

TSS: Sure.

JL: But your purpose is not to be creating healing?

TSS: More importantly, I did not want our music to be marketed as healing music. I wanted it to be taken seriously by the medical world. I definitely did not want my own concert career to be locked up with a, "...This key correlates to that chakra," kind of mentality. I'm not behind that.

Meanwhile, I think great music, played beautifully, is healing. But I differentiate between the music for the living and the music for the dying. And we need both kinds of healing music. At the deathbed, we can have healing without curing. And in the other phase of our life–when we are very much living, engaged with the world–we need music that helps bind us to life and to live more richly and more deeply.

JL: What helps us to bind?

TSS: Rhythm. That is one of the most incredible healing things about rock 'n roll in the old days. They had these wonderful rhythms. There was a goodness about a lot of it. It really helped engage us. On a larger context, look at the wonderful thing that has come our way in the last fifteen years with World Music. We have been exposed to new scales and rhythms and colors, the likes of which we didn't even know about. Look at what Peter Gabriel did with the score from *The Last Temptation of Christ.*

It's like some sort of new incredible essay. So of course we need harmony, melody and rhythm for engagement. But many different kinds of things can help engage us. Look at the effect of the Bulgarian women singers *(Le Mystere Des Voix Bulgares).* Those harmonies! I have all kinds of friends who said, "Oh my God! The first time I heard those harmonies, I thought someone put their hands inside my body and twisted my heart!" They heard harmonies like they had never heard before; those really close seconds. They heard intervals and harmonies that weren't being used in our American culture and they were thrilled and moved. We need it all; harmony, melody, rhythm.

JL: Which musicians or composers first come to your mind in the field of therapeutic music and sound?

TSS: I can tell you about great composers. But I don't think great composers need to say they are doing healing music. I want to stress that I don't think a great composer would ever think of themselves as a healer. What they do is great music and great music changes people. But they don't bill themselves as a healing composer. I think that Arvo Part is one of the great composers of the 20th century. I think his music leaves people completely changed.

JL: Do you think that he set out to do that?

TSS: Of course not. He is a man of prayer. He did what was inside of him and it was so absolutely truthful, it took people completely.

JL: Tell me somebody else who stands out for you.

TSS: I could tell you a healing story about someone who has worked very seriously through the years but who also is considered commercially successful: Paul Winter. I think, with my particular background, I had a tendency to take things very seriously. When I heard his mass, *Missa Gaia*, I was thoroughly changed in a heartbeat. That piece of music moved all the furniture inside of me around. That music taught me about the celebratory aspect of prayer. Paul doesn't use the language of theology or prayer. Yet he is an incredibly thoughtful, caring, loving man who knows what praise is... and love. He is a man of very deep feelings. But that is an example of a musician who is considered popular, whose *Earth Mass* greatly enriched, widened, deepened my understanding of prayer. I also grew enormously from the Bulgarian women. They are now considered part of a popular genre; they have sold millions of albums.

THE FUTURE OF THE CHALICE PROJECT

JL: What are your plans for the future of the Chalice project?

TSS: That death will be recognized as one sacred aspect of life and that Chalice workers will be in hospitals, hospices, and geriatric homes.

JL: Do you think the field of music-thanatology will grow quickly?

TSS: We are the only school and we don't have the capacity to graduate that many students. But I think we can have students in most major cities by the turn of the century. Hospitals and hospices are calling and asking. So there is hope. And hope begets hope. It is just like love...

I know that even if there isn't a Chalice worker in your town, for example, if people just get the message... If somebody simply holds the baby or holds the grandma and sings to them, if they are really singing out of love it is going to make a difference.

JL: What plans do you have for your musical career given this quantum leap of the Chalice Project?

TSS: I have continued my concert career, but don't usually discuss it when we're talking about Chalice. I tour Europe with regularity. If I didn't, the music wouldn't be alive. Additionally, I am preparing to record a new album now. A year ago, I went to the island of Patmos, in the Mediterranean. It was where the *Book of Revelation* was written. I lived there for a week in silence and followed a higher prompting inside my heart. From that, an album has been cooking called *Patmos*. I have written a lot of new music and I've also set quite a few of Emily Dickinson's poems to music. I will go into the studio this fall.

JL: Are you writing some of the music used by the Chalice?

TSS: We mostly employ Gregorian chant. But I have written some new threshold pieces. A lot of people are urging us to record the music. That has been a very difficult spiritual question for me. You know, if I do Chalice music on tape, dying people everywhere will be plugged into some earphones. I have struggled and prayed about this repeatedly. That is not what we want. We do not want dying people hooked up to one more machine. We want caring musicians, of which there are countless numbers, to play live music. We want a new kind of army. We want a peaceful, harmonious strength.

MONASTICISM

JL: Therese, you have had the opportunity to look at the dharma of this work for a long time now. Clearly, this is your spiritual work. What is your karmic relationship to all of this?

TSS: Joshua, I have always had a sense of lineage. I have been so incredibly blessed by the beauty that just pours out, specifically, from Western Christian monasticism. It is a most extraordinary wellspring of beauty, of wisdom, of intimacy. And I have never exhausted it.

So many people today would like to attribute every neurosis we have in the world to one church or another. I feel that the mysteries have always been present because churches and synagogues are run by people and people make mistakes. We confuse that fact that our churches are often narrow or hurtful. We blame the church, and abandon the mystery. I feel that there is pure gold in each of the world's religions there for us. I've always benefitted from my relationship with Cistercian monasticism. (Even though I have chosen to be a lay woman and live in the world rather than in a monastery.)

JL: With your love of medieval history, have you spent time in European monasteries?

TSS: Yes! Yes! American monasteries, too. I am a faithful retreatant. Also, when I am on tour, one of my ways of giving back to that spiritual tradition that has given me so much, is by doing concerts for the monasteries. This is something that is a very special privilege. All over America and Europe, I play for monks and nuns, especially our elders.

JL: Do they respond differently to your music than the general public?

TSS: Oh sometimes with unbelievable tears of joy. Not long ago, I played for monks at a Cistercian monastery in Snowmass, Colorado. Afterwards, they were singing one chant after another, one leading to the next. They had tears rolling down their beautiful, rosy monk cheeks. They said, "...we haven't really done this since Vatican II." It had come back up out of them, word for word; they remembered everything. But some of them hadn't sung those songs in twenty years.

JL: You were bringing up sacred and beloved memories for them.

TSS: Yes. Can you imagine having chanted every three hours for your whole monastic life, and then to suddenly stop? This must have been very difficult. It is a kind of deprivation to have the privilege to sing prayer and then be told to be silent. It doesn't go away. It rings inside your body and your soul.

I once played for a very famous, very elderly Benedictine nun. She has accomplished a great deal in her life but is very old now and letting go. I was there on her birthday. The Abbess called all the nuns together and myself. I had the harp and there was great festivity.

Lady Abbess said, "Mother Columba, this is your birthday and all of us are younger women here. You've done this and that and won this award and that award, what great words of wisdom do you have for us younger women on your birthday?" Mother Columba looked both ways, a little like a bird, and said, "Well! I can take a nap! Whenever I want!"

We'd all been waiting with baited breath to hear some incredible words of wisdom and... ✧

Grace Notes

Therese Schroeder-Sheker is currently Director of *The Chalice of Repose Project*, Academic Dean of the School of Music-Thanatology (St. Patrick Hospital, Missoula, Montana) and visiting Associate Professor of Pastoral Ministry (St. Thomas Seminary, Denver).

Adding to these responsibilities, Ms. Schroeder-Sheker is a prolific concert and recording artist and composer. She has four solo recordings, twelve television and film scores, twenty-nine radio documentaries, and numerous guest-artist performances featured on American and European recordings. In 1980, she made her Carnegie Hall debut. Her musical career has been distinguished with numerous awards, grants, and over a dozen fellowships.

Ms. Schroeder-Sheker publishes frequently on medieval music, women mystics, and palliative and monastic medicines. She is currently working on two book projects: *The Luminous Wound,* a text for The Chalice of Repose, and a critical edition of the visions and vision-lieder of the 20th century Swiss mystic, Joa Bolendas.

RESOURCES

Music albums by Therese Schroeder-Sheker currently available:

1. *In Dulci Jublio.* Celestial Harmonies, 1991.
2. *Rosa Mystica.* Celestial Harmonies, 1990.

ENDNOTES

1 Customary is a genre of monastic manuscript. Music-Thanatologists refer to the Cluniac customaries of Bernard & Ulrich, 11th century scribes.

2 Therese Schroeder-Sheker, *Rosa Mystica* (Celestial Harmonies, 1991).

3 Kenneth Paul Kramer, "Dying Awake: The Practice of Spiritual Death," Studies in Formative Spirituality, Vol X, #3, Nov. 1989. p. 311-318.

4 Simone Weil, *Waiting for God* (NY, Harper & Row, 1951).

5 Alfred Tomatis, *The Conscious Ear* (NY, Station Hill Press, 1991).

5

MUSIC AS ANESTHESIA

A conversation with
Fred Schwartz, M.D.

Placenta Music[1] is an odd name for a corporation. But this Atlanta-based record company practices truth in advertising. The music they release is literally using the sounds of the placenta... and not because they couldn't find anything else to sample. Well, actually company founder and anesthesiologist Fred Schwartz had a new sampler and was looking for something to record... and the rest is his story.

YOU WANT TO RECORD MY WHAT?

"Eight years ago, my wife was pregnant," remembers Dr. Schwartz. "You think a lot and have time to worry about things at a time like this. We were in New York and I was looking at synthesizers that would be able to sample sounds and then play them back on the keyboard. After I purchased the instrument, I was looking for something to sample and play back. And my wife was right there, and I thought, 'Oh! She's got some sounds right here. I could sample these. I wonder what could I do with them?'

"So I decided I would record some sounds. I went to one of the obstetricians I work with, borrowed a Doppler stethoscope, and started recording Marilyn's intrauterine sounds and then put it on the keyboard. But it sounded terrible! It was awful."

As awful as it might have sounded, it did not detour this musically-inclined anesthesiologist from a new insight. After observing the positive effects of music in the operating room, Dr. Schwartz knew the right sounds would be equally effective in the birthing process. His wife was about to deliver their first child and he needed something! After years of wheeling around an anesthesia-turned-music cart at Atlanta's Piedmont Hospital, he simply had to have the right sounds. Going back to the drawing board, Schwartz figured he had the right concept but the wrong equipment and not enough expertise in using sampling technology.

"After playing around a lot", says Schwartz, "I hooked up with musicians Joe and Burt Wolfe, who had been doing advertising work, sampling all kinds of things for a long time. They had a big library of sounds. I finally asked them, "How would you like to sample some intrauterine sounds and make some music?" And they said, 'Oh no, we don't want to do that!'"

But one thing led to another and the Wolfe Brothers became intrigued. With a skilled team at hand, Schwartz and Co. started to think about what sounds they could add. They knew that babies would respond to heartbeat, breath and bloodflow sounds; they had been hearing it since they were sixteen weeks in utero. Schwartz knew the mother's voice also gets to the baby through the abdominal wall and amniotic fluid. Since the baby hears a lot of the mother's voice, the more sonic familiarity that could be created, the less stress on the emerging infant.

The musicians used sampled female vocal sounds and played them melodically on the keyboard. This was mixed with intrauterine noise and some other gentle, subtle sounds, mostly to add interest for the adults. According to Dr. Schwartz, womb sounds by themselves are boring. On his recordings, I found the rhythmic pulsation of the bloodflow a relentless whoosh in the treble range. The slower breath sounds reminded me of a distant subway, moving in and out of the tunnel.

"So the Wolfe brothers came up with this recording, *Transitions*," says the Doctor. "It was so beautiful that I decided we had to find a way to get it out to people." Schwartz began an educational program to introduce people to the concept and product. To establish credibility, he hooked up with two neo-natal intensive care nurses whose study proved that this music had a profound effect on premature babies in intensive care units.

Selling through mainstream record outlets and baby stores, Transitions Music[2] sells about 20,000 units annually in America in addition to what is sold around the world. Schwartz, who handles the international sales between doctor duties, is pleased to have supplied 25,000 units to Taiwan alone.

When I queried Dr. Schwartz about the effects of these recordings on adults, he told me about a recent experience.

"I had a middle aged woman come by. I was playing *Transitions* and she didn't know what she was hearing. She said, 'That's terrible. I'm getting a migraine headache. I can't take it!' It turned out that her mother had died the week previous and she hadn't gone to her funeral. I think that there is a connection there.

"We've noted that people that have had terrible birth experiences, or terrible relations with their mothers, have very unpleasant reactions to the music right away. I think that they can use the music, in an intensive kind of therapy, to get in touch with their feelings."

The following interview took place February, 1994.

MUSIC AS ANESTHESIA

JL: What was your personal musical background and how did you arrive at the use of music in medicine?

FS: I went to medical school because I was not a good enough musician to become a professional musician. But I always continued to play music on the side.

JL: What was your instrument?

FS: Saxophone and clarinet. I've always loved music and thought that it had a lot of applications. Starting in medical school, I started using music with some of my patients. But what really affected me profoundly was when I was an intern, working in an intensive care unit.

I had a 17-year–old fellow who had a motorcycle accident. He had become comatose from the head injury and he was in the intensive care unit. I was taking care of him and spending a lot of nights there. He wasn't responding to anything and it had been weeks already. So I started playing flute to him and his eyes would move when I played the music. So I thought, "Gee, he is responding, there is something there." So we kept playing him music. His parents bought him a radio and rock 'n roll was what he liked. He woke up and made a full recovery three weeks later. And he remembered the music. And it turned out that he didn't really like flute music!

JL: That's why he was moving his eyes!

FS: Yeah! He was trying to tell me to stop. He came back from the near dead to tell me, "Let me die in peace, leave me alone!" So that impressed me.

I started using music in the operating rooms. I am an anesthesiologist and I started playing music for my patients. Even during surgery I would play music, partly to sedate and appease the surgeon who can sometimes be very agitated or hard to get along with. So I was using music to control their behavior, but then found that the patients, even while they were asleep, seemed to benefit from the music. So I have been playing music for years to people, while they are awake or asleep, in the operating room.

There have been many studies to show that you can blunt the rise in stress hormones that the body puts out in reaction to the stress in surgery. Even general anesthesia itself does not blunt this rise in stress hormones, such as norepinephrine, epinephrin, or growth hormone. When these things increase, it is not really good for healing. Blood pressure increases from them, increased bleeding. So there are good studies that show that music–played to patients asleep under anesthesia during surgery–will blunt that rise in the stress hormones. That effect continues in the recovery room, even after the music is not playing anymore. This is what we are trying to do with drugs in surgery, and we can do it with music! Surgeons and anesthesiologists are starting to realize that. There is becoming a new age of music in the operating room. I think that is happening now.

JL: You have seen this industry-wide?

FS: In Atlanta, where I practice, all of the major hospitals are installing stereo systems in all their operating rooms. It has mushroomed. It first started because some realized that this was a great thing to do, but then the hospitals decided that in order to compete, they had to offer it as one of their services. I am hoping that it is going to catch on across the country. There are a lot of places around the world that already have this.

JL: Is there any kind of networking going on amongst surgeons, anesthesiologists, and other medical people in relationship to this?

FS: Yes there certainly is. The International Society for Music and Medicine is a good starting point.[3] This is a group of doctors, professionals, music therapists who meet every year or two. There is on-going research, etc. There is also a lot going on through the American Music Therapy Association.[4]

JL: The domino effect of music moving through the professional community is slow, medium, fast?

FS: I would say that we are in the middle of really rapid changes in research. People are doing a lot of physiologic experiments to look at the body to see what kind of effects you can get. Not only in the operating room, but in many areas.

Let me go back to music in the operating rooms. Not only do you get a change in stress hormones, but when you are doing regional anesthesia, whereby the patient is somewhat awake, but numb, from an epidural or block of some kind that numbs the surgical site, you can give less drug sedation. You can actually give less drug to sedate the patient, and get the same effect, when you've got music playing. So a patient that might be laying there awake, and perhaps a little bit anxious, and still being sedated with drugs, you add music, the patient falls asleep. So you can actually give less drug, have less side effects, and get a faster recovery.

JL: What kind of music are you using?

FS: What works best is what the patient chooses. If the patient can connect with past emotions they had when listening to certain music before, he/she can color their environment and bring some of the good emotions into an environment that might otherwise be threatening and anxiety-provoking.

JL: Do you interview the patient before surgery about music?

FS: Yes, I ask them what they like to hear. If it is a mother who is having a C-section, I ask her what kind of music her fetus likes to hear. We play a lot of classical and New Age music, some jazz, country, whatever the patients like. Teen-agers and children seem to like rock 'n roll. That might make me anxious, but they really love it.

RESISTANCE

JL: Have you run into resistance from other people that you work with?

FS: Yes, there are certain types of medical people who are very rigid and really can only look at black and white. They can't seem to see some of the things that are really subtle. The fact that patients have emotions and are human beings is important. I think that it is changing; a lot more people in the profession are opening their eyes up. There are some that will never accept this stuff.

JL: I wonder if the fact that baby-boomers are becoming the majority of practitioners has any effect?

FS: I don't know.

JL: The Boomers come from a time that was more open-minded, with a greater sensitivity to holism than the generations before.

FS: Yes, I do think that is true. There are some people who are fixed in their ways and are not going to change after thirty or forty years of doing things a certain way.

WOMB SOUNDS

JL: Let's talk womb sounds. What was your primary motivation for recording these sounds?

FS: I thought they would soothe the baby. Having a newborn coming into the world, I thought maybe I'd get something I could use for my new baby. And maybe I could help a lot of other babies that are agitated and need soothing.

Just as you have a stress response from an adult patient in a medical situation, with a lot of sympathetic stimulation as far as rising blood pressure, heart rate, consumption of oxygen, and a fast metabolism consuming important things, I thought that you could look at the baby in the same way. Some babies are so agitated that they are actually stressed. We need to de-stress them and their situation.

Perhaps, they don't need to eat anymore, they've had their diapers changed, and the fact is that they are just anxious, that their sympathetic nervous system is activated. They are thrashing around, consuming a lot of calories for nothing. This will help that kind of thing.

JL: You were thinking in terms of normal babies?

FS: Initially, normal healthy babies. But then you realize that these recordings would be really advantageous for a premature baby. They may have low oxygen level in their blood because they are consuming a lot of oxygen from being stressed.

JL: My daughter was born nine weeks premature. She was born on the day that the moving van came to move us from New York City to California. It was a bit of a crisis. We went through four weeks at the Mt. Sinai Neo-Natal Intensive Care Unit and so I have a place in my heart for what you are talking about. I know about the never-ending cacophony of sounds from the monitors and other equipment, from the nurses, the procedures. My daughter's mother is a classically trained opera singer and she spent 15 hours a day at the ICU. She sang to the baby most of the time.

FS: Oh that is wonderful. Its the best thing she could have done.

JL: My baby came out of there in four weeks instead of the possible nine weeks they had suggested it might take for her to gain enough weight, etc.

FS: And your wife's singing is partly why.

JL: The effects of the womb sounds on the baby are because they are familiar. And this causes the relaxation and de-stressing. Is part of this effect from the entrainment that takes place from the rhythm?

FS: I think that is very possible. There is a central effect on the brain as far as womb sounds, especially on a neonate. I think these sounds are essential in the uterine environment for the fetus. There are a number of studies that are showing that the sounds are important to the baby. If you take the baby away from this situation of having this constant heartbeat and other sounds coming through, it will be noticeable. Many think these sounds are vital for the proper development of the brain.

There are people doing work with heartbeat-type rhythms, varying them in subtle ways, to try and increase the intelligence of the baby. They are saying that they can get babies coming out with larger heads, larger brains that are much more developed immediately upon birth. There is evidence that these sounds are necessary for the growth and development of the fetus in utero.

JL: Amongst the intrauterine sounds that you are recording, there is the heartbeat and the breath. What else are you gathering?

FS: *Transitions*, our first album, had the intrauterine sounds from the placenta blood flow from the mother. On *Transitions 2*, we added the breathing, too. This is a much different rate, per minute, than the intrauterine heartbeat. I think that you get accommodated to that in utero. I'm sure that breathing is soothing for the baby just by itself.

WOMB SOUNDS AND ADULTS

JL: What do you think is the effect of these sounds on an adult?

FS: It depends on how open your mind is. Some people can relate to this immediately and there is something very profound there. It allows them to get in touch with some feelings from around the birth experience and from being a baby–or from being a fetus. That can be either pleasant or very unpleasant. I have seen some people have some very strange reactions to it.

JL: Is there any kind of an outreach program to therapists to let them know about this work so they might begin to fold it into their practice?

FS: There are a number of therapists who have been using our tapes. John Bradshaw is one. He does a narrative with the tapes, where he brings people back to the birth period, and gives them healing visualizations. For example, "Imagine your mother saying, 'I love you'". Saying things that maybe weren't said back then. People at these session cry and go through quite a lot. They go through some really intense emotions.

There are a lot of re-birthing type therapists that we are aware of using our products. There are schools using *Transitions* with juvenile delinquents. They play the music in a classroom situation and find that the kids are less disruptive. I think that the use of music and sound to increase learning is a very valid area.

JL: Tell me about any other sub-conscious or emotional impact that these sounds have on adults?

FS: It helps the parents bond with there child. It allows you to get in touch with yourself and your feelings. If you can sit and listen to this music, it will have the effect of slowing your body down. Most of us can use that. The problem is being able to sit in one place and listening to music like that. Most people won't do it.

JL: Imagine taking a half hour each day and doing nothing but listening to music. So many people have trouble carving out a half hour a day to meditate, or relax with music, yet most Americans people spend hours each day sitting in front of the TV set.

FS: Look at me. I love music and I'm so busy that I often don't take the time to listen to any in a day.

WHERE'S IT ALL GOING?

JL: Where do you see music in the healing arts going? What excites you about this field?

FS: People in hospitals are starting to use music. We'll be able to see effects on patients that will actually save money, which is the bottom line these days.

Just as the music therapists are doing a lot of studies on the effects of music with Alzheimers. They show that, again, they can save money and get better results than other treatments. I'm hoping that we will see more studies that will conclusively show that we need to incorporate music into our medical care all over the hospital.

JL: Are the hospitals basically receptive to this?

FS: It takes some time. But there is usually someone around, nurses, whatever, who become very enthusiastic about effective treatment for their patients. This acceptance then goes from one person to the next. Once people see the effects of music...

For example, we now have music in our coronary care unit for heart attack patients. Once they see how the patient does better, has less complications from their heart attack because of the music, it is not hard to convince the cardiologists. If there is a patient who has high blood pressure, the damage to the heart muscle is extending, his real stress has high catecholamine levels, he's consuming oxygen in a critical area of his heart, music can actually make quite a difference there.

I think we are going to see music incorporated for a lot more patients; we are going to see patients do better, have less complications, get out of the hospital faster. It has been shown that premature babies do get out of the hospital faster when music is played. This all saves money for the hospitals.

It's Pretty Loud in There!

JL: When my family was in the Intensive Care Unit, one of the first things I did was purchase a small cassette player. I picked out some Mozart and a few other pieces that I thought would be soothing for my daughter.

When we brought the music in, the nurses were very cooperative with what we wanted to do. But we had one supervisor who told us that although our intentions were good, we had to be very careful with the music. She said that few people realized that the incubators actually served as a speaker cabinet and that because music was not designed for this kind of sensitive listening, we could actually cause reactions that were the opposite of what we desired. She maintained that the dynamics and crescendos in the music were enough to cause additional discomfort and reactions to the premature infants. What do you think of this?

FS: I know that this worries some people but it is pretty unlikely. The sound levels inside the uterus actually get as high as 95 decibels every heartbeat. This is like being on the dance floor of a loud rock club on a Saturday night!

JL: What are normal decibels in a regular conversation like the one we're having?

FS: About 40 decibels. ✧

ENDNOTES

1 Placenta Music has since been renamed. They are now called Transitions Music. For a catalog of womb-sound music, call (800) 492-9885.

2 Transitions™ is a registered trademark of Placenta Music, Inc.

3 The International Society for Music and Medicine. See Appendix C.

4 The American Music Therapy Association. See Appendix C.

6

INTENTION AND MUSIC

A conversation with
Michael Jones

"I was two when my aunt first helped me onto the piano bench to watch her play," says Michael Jones. "I was fascinated by how her fingers disappeared into the keys, and as I listened, I tried to imagine where the sounds came from. One day, I discovered a music book filled with pictures of animals and felt convinced that there were animals residing inside the piano making the music. I realized I wanted to create at the piano. I wanted to dance with the animals."

Michael Jones is a Canadian pianist and composer. Deeply steeped in the classical repertoire, Jones is a fine improvisational player. His inaugural album, *Pianoscapes,* was also Narada Record's first release. Since 1983, both artist and record company have flourished; ten critically acclaimed albums later, Jones has sold well over a million units.[1]

Michael Jones says that he often thinks of himself "...as a communicator and educator first, and a musician after that." If record sales are indicative, audiences like the formula. His music sets the stage for our own internal wanderings; the unique combination of his tones cast us in search of our own illusive feelings. He urges us to go deeper–to find the path into the child's magical kingdom; the place where imagination and creativity reside.[2] A gentle man with gentle music, Mr. Jones invites us all to the dance—and a sweet dance it is.

The following conversation took place at the *First International Colloquium on the Healing Nature of Sound*[3] in New Hampshire, Oct., 1993.

MUSIC, PRISONS AND HOSPICES

JL: We had the privilege of a private house concert at this conference. Do you perform small concerts often?

MJ: From time to time. When possible, I connect with people where I can do a more intimate kind of thing–which really suits the kind of music I like to do. I think of my music as being more of a lower case spontaneous creation rather than a spectacle. It's not on a grand scale, although I have had success doing solo concerts in large concert halls. I really feel that we have lost that kind of intimate sense of where the music came from. I follow my track classically through Mozart, Chopin and Debussy. That music was always performed, not so much in big concert halls, but in parlors. It was a very intimate kind of music; people connected to it that way.

Where I can, I love doing community outreach. What that means is playing in places that don't often have the benefit of live performers. I've played at a Governor's Mansion, in private homes, penitentiaries, schools for emotionally gifted children, and likewise, for severely emotionally disturbed children.

JL: Tell me about that.

MJ: This was quite an experience for me and for the staff of the school. They had not had any experience with anybody coming in and doing music in their facility. They were particularly concerned because these kids are very hyper-active. They are not comfortable being in their bodies because their bodies have really let them down. They are severely limited in what their emotional and physical capacities are. They have a real intelligence but it is more of a kinesthetic intelligence; one that music connects to very readily. But it's not one that is widely known. The staff had about forty kids gathered in the room and said to me, "Look, probably about ten minutes will be enough." They continued, "These kids have a really short attention span. We have a couple of children here that we might have to wheel up very quickly because they can really start to act up. They start screaming and really upset the other children."

I played for about 45 minutes, maybe close to an hour. There wasn't a sound! The staff told me a couple of days later how incredible that was. I hadn't realized the significance of it. I never expected that there would be a lot of noise behind my playing. I didn't know any better. But they said that they had never seen those children be as quiet as they were. Of course, we then left them with a whole bunch of complimentary music. Several of the children, when they put the music on, said, "That really feels good to me."

That was really an education for all of us. When I played at this children's concert, it brought tears to all of our eyes. The woman who was traveling with me was from the record label. We'd been on the road for about a week and were quite tired that morning. But she stood and watched this event and she tells me that this has been her most moving moment ever. She's toured with rock bands and done a lot of stuff in the business. But to be in that room with those children and to hear that quality of silence and attention was something that was deeply moving for all of us.

JL: What about playing in prisons?

MJ: One story that comes to my mind was at Lebanon Penitentiary in Ohio. I didn't know that it was Lebanon when I was initially approached to play. I thought it was a minimum security prison. But that's not what I saw when I pulled up the next day; barbed wire, turrets, guards and guns. I had to sign a form absolving the state of Ohio of any responsibility for my welfare as I was entering into what they considered dangerous territory. And it felt dangerous!

JL: What were you feeling as you drove up and saw those turrets?

MJ: There was a certain amount of terror. There is a little bit of terror playing in front of almost anybody! But there is even more terror playing in front of a maximum security penitentiary audience.

You know, my music has a power. But it is a subtle, gentle power. It is not always that apparent in places that are not tuned to that subtlety. I wasn't sure how it would go in a prison.

I went into the chapel. Even though it was March, the temperature was about 90°. They had a couple of big industrial fans going in there.

So it meant that about 1/3 of my repertoire was out of the question. It was too quiet and they would never have heard it. About 60 guys came in. Fortunately, they were hand-picked. They were all taking a music appreciation course run by a local university that had sponsored my trip in.

It was a wonderful afternoon. The piano was a wreck and I really had to trust that there was some other force at work. Pianos that sound awful when I first play them suddenly start sounding like gold after I've worked with them for a while. Well, this old upright started to glow.

What really threw me took place about five minutes into the concert. This great big guy with tattoos up both of his arms, wearing a dirty T-shirt stands up, slowly starts to walk out of the room. And I say, "Damn, I think I've lost them!" I think that I am not connecting with these guys and he is the first one to leave. They were under no obligation to stay.

So I heard the door slam at the back of the room. I was a bit distracted at this point but I kept playing. Five minutes later he comes back in. He walks slowly all the way up to the piano. He then sets down a glass of water by the ledge, stands beside me for a few moments watching me, and then goes back and sits down. I was so relieved!

JL: This was after signing this waiver that said, "We take no responsibility, this is your choice, pal!"

MJ: Yes. I figured the rest of the guys were going to follow him out, that he was leading the group. My music is thought of as New Age music. I don't think that it was the kind of thing that those guys in that population had much exposure to. I thought that it would be a little too feminine, too flowery, a little too *anything* for what they wanted. I didn't know how long they would hang in with it. I write really sweet music!

Instead, what it invoked was a lot of deep feeling. A lot of stuff started coming up. I made it a point–particularly about two third's of the way through–to stop and ask if there was anything coming up around the music that they wanted to talk about. They started to share some stuff around relationships, around feelings.

I love to use the concerts to get people into a deeper space. I use stories, sometimes questions, before or after the concert. Sometimes, I play a piece that I have not titled yet and will ask the audience what they would name it. It's a way to invite them into the music.

At another small concert–with art patrons at the Ohio Governor's Mansion–a lot of the images stemming from a particular piece were of nature. This was interesting because during the concert, we had a couple of rabbits mating. There were floor to ceiling windows just behind the piano. It was just about dusk but still light and there was a beautiful magnolia tree in bloom with blossoms. And we had a pair of rabbits mating right under the Magnolia tree. And I got a glimpse of it as I was playing. But most of the people could watch, right past the piano, those rabbits. So a lot of images of nature came up for them.

But with the guys in the penitentiary, while feeling into the same piece that I played at the Governor's Mansion, it was all around failed relationships; the pain and despair of things that hadn't worked out. It was really touching for me. I hadn't worked with these guys before, but the depth of feeling and their willingness to be open was really moving for me. They were very close to the truth with their own experience. It surprised me.

JL: This is an amazing image that you are sharing with me: You with this funky upright piano in a maximum security prison, with some big tattooed convict walking up to the piano and you not even knowing what he was going to do.

MJ: With that glass of water, it was so symbolic. He was really considerate; he knew that I would probably be a little dry because it was hot in the room. That he would think of going and getting a glass of water and quietly setting it on the piano was a like a blessing.

JL: It was both permission and blessing.

MJ: Yes.

JL: You mentioned that one of the things you attempt to do with your music–in settings that will permit–is bring about self-disclosure. Tell me more about that.

MJ: In the prison setting, I knew that they were all a part of a music appreciation course. So I trusted that my invitation to talk would have been in keeping with the discussions they'd been having along with their listening to recorded work. It was actually an instinct on my part; sharing a few stories to orient people around pieces that I was playing, which I did here. But I really wanted to open that up into a dialogue with them, to exchange what was happening with them from my music, to give them an opportunity to share as well.

JL: Were you playing the same program of music at the Governor's mansion with a cultured white audience?

MJ: Yes. They were a very professional bunch: Judges, doctors, lawyers.

JL: A higher, blue blooded echelon of society. And then here you were the next morning, playing to imprisoned men. I imagine that most of them were non-white?

MJ: About 2/3's of them were African/American.

JL: And the cultured set was thinking about nature while the inmates were dealing with failed relationships?

MJ: They were really connecting with despair, hope, failed relationships and broken lives. The sadness and grief that they felt around that. They were also connecting with some uplifting feelings of joy and euphoria. I think it was all within the music and they really tuned into that. I think that they tuned into some of the sadness that is in the music when I play it, that other people don't necessarily hear.

JL: Because they are so close to their own sadness?

MJ: Yes. You know, I think that there is another thing that may have gone on for me too. Because I find that when I am playing for groups that are somewhat marginalized in our culture, like the emotionally disturbed kids, for example, and the guys in the penitentiary. They are forgotten people in our success-driven culture. We don't choose to think about them a lot. They are institutionalized and put off to the side. The same way as people in an AIDS hospice are. I've played there as well.

When I play for these groups that are marginalized, the feelings are very close to the surface. The feeling of vulnerability is very close to the surface for them. So it opens a door for me to be more vulnerable with myself. I find that I am more open in those settings because so much of it is present. I think I instinctively allow more to be in the music because I feel safe letting that be there. If there is some sadness that I am feeling, I am more likely perhaps, to let that be in the forefront of the music. When I am playing for a bunch of people whose lives are all together, where that is not as present, in some ways, I may not feel as free to let that be there. At least, not as quickly.

Some of that may have to do with me, in terms of how I approach the music and how I play it. I read and feel an audience. I tend to play to an audience; if I feel that a particular group is closed emotionally, there is less for me to play back or pick up.

JL: It seems that your music–being original, improvisationally based, and the fact that you are a single artist–gives you the space to be a weather vane. You pick up the focus.

MJ: Definitely.

JL: But it's also a loop, isn't it? You're picking up the group sentiment from the crowd while they're picking up the energy from your music.

MJ: Being a single artist, without any other musicians to stay in synch with, has many advantages. I have nobody I might lose when I decide to make a change mid-piece. It allows for me to be much more transparent with an audience because I can, on the moment, switch gears. If I'm picking up something, or feeling something I want to follow, explore, and inquire into more fully, I have the option to do that. This is the wonderful freedom of being a solo artist. But it is also the vulnerability.

With a band or group, you know that on a bad night, you've got somebody else who is having a great night. So it's going to cook one way or the other. On your own, you don't know. Sometimes, I feel great until five minutes before the performance, and then suddenly, I'll get a cold. It's just the unknown. It is both the adventure and the challenge of it. You never know what you are stepping into.

JL: I want to go back to the prison setting just for a moment. People respond to your music and you create a safe space for them to have and express their feelings. How did you close and ground that experience?

MJ: I went into more music. I played two more pieces and then our time was finished. In prisons, they have bedchecks about four times a day. Everybody has to go back to their cell and be accounted for. So I was able to complete my concert but then everybody had to leave to get back to their cells.

JL: What kind of music did you pick to take them out?

MJ: It was a real joyful piece called *Wildflower*. They were connecting with the joy of the music I was playing as well as with the sadness. I think that when you draw people into one dimension, it brings the others to life, as well. The one polarity of joyfulness naturally brings up the other polarity of sadness.

JL: Tell me about the AIDS hospice.

MJ: It had some of the same feeling as the penitentiary, in terms of what came up for me being in a setting like that. The staff and volunteers needed this music as much as the patients. They are so over-extended and they're working with people who are terminally ill. It takes a tremendous toll on the volunteers; they are working with their own mortality while working with somebody else's. They are dealing with patients, who become friends, who are passing away.

It is the same thing, I find, that in settings where I feel into the energy–in settings where people are marginalized like that—it can't do anything but stretch my music. If I am willing to be open to that energy, let it guide where the music is moving and not just play pre-set pieces.

JL: So you go in and play whatever comes through? No previous compositions?

MJ: I may have a piece that I start with, that I am familiar with, but I really can feel how it starts to open up more quickly from just feeling something in the room that needs to be addressed in some way, in terms of how I am working with the sound. I want to be open to that as well. So that tends to move me into a music that I probably would not play in another setting. I hear it in a particular way in a setting like the hospice or prison.

JL: Can you make a distinction between the concert hall, prison and hospice in terms of what it brings up for you?

MJ: They are very different places. In both the prison and hospice, the dreams have died. Yet there is a paradox here. I found more life there than you would find out on the street. It seems that in the giving up of one thing, they touch more deeply into another dimension of life.

Generally in a concert hall, even though I know that people know and love my work and are there for it, I have to pull the energy from the inside. Though it is wonderful to play to, it's very different. In these other settings we've been talking about, most people don't know my music, so it is not my audience, in that sense. There are people who are in pain in many different ways. Is there some way that I can be there, to be present, to offer something that can not cover over the pain but can help them hold it in whatever place they are?

This is where I feel myself to be of service with the music. I'm not there to be a performer. I'm there to let something through the music be present with that group. That is the common link. There certainly was a tenderness in the AIDS Center that I felt more immediately. There were attendants with people in wheelchairs, men who were in advanced stages of various diseases connected with AIDS. I could certainly feel my vulnerability because it was new for me; not being acclimatized, not having been in a center like that. I just walked in and saw all of this.

I was getting a little shaky. So that was another thing that I could let be in the music. Part of the challenge for me was to not close up because there was something in that environment that was difficult for me to handle. This is probably where part of the opening is–that I could feel the woundedness that was there, and feel my own, and let that be some of what I could play from.

JL: What quality did that give to your music?

MJ: I could feel the grief in the hospice. I could feel the people who were going before their time. All the life that was not being lived, the friends who had been lost. I could feel the presence of all of that. And the paradox again wasn't necessarily that I had to go into deeply sad, minor, heavy music. I think that opened up the other side again -

another place where more joyful music could be played. Its like the clown is sometimes the saddest person on the block. But what it draws out is it's opposite. That's what can be lent is the opposite. It hasn't been that the music I played has been very minor. It had its own joy but it was grounded in it's opposite. That's what I experienced being there; how to come out of the opposite. This way, all of it is there. Joyful music can be played out of feeling the grief that lies beneath it.

Music that Opens the Healing Heart

JL: Michael, we are meeting here at a colloquium investigating the healing aspects of music. How do you see the use of your music in this context, in a balancing context? So much of this concept, as exemplified this weekend, is pretty nebulous.

MJ: Yes, it is nebulous to one part of our mind. Our intellect has difficulty with these concepts. It doesn't quite fall within those parameters. That's why it is somewhat difficult for me to answer the question. At some level, I don't really know. I haven't really known aside from having an instinct or impulse to follow my music in a particular way. There has been no particular overdesign to what I have wanted to do. I haven't ever said, "I think that what I want to do is compose healing music." The truth is, I wouldn't have known how on earth to do that anyway. I couldn't even have said–even though I know people experience this, "I want to create music that opens the healing heart."

JL: Who says this?

MJ: People who respond to my music often say they find it very heart opening. That it creates a safety for them. They put it on right before they go to sleep because they feel safe with it. They put it on for their children, or people put it on because it warms their heart, it opens their heart quality.

JL: This is what you are told?

MJ: This is what people say back to me. I think that my salvation has been that I didn't know any of that. I didn't set out to accomplish any of that so I had no willful intention or design to have my music perform a certain function in the world.

I think probably what happened was that my early exposure to the place of music in life for me had been in nature. I used to play at a summer camp; I would be there in the midst of a thunderstorm with the waves and wind, and the sparkle of light on the water, and the whisper of the wind through the pines. Being a Romantic from my classical training, I was just so taken up with all of the moves and the feel of nature I wanted to create a language from which to communicate what I experienced there that words cannot do. So that was one very strong element of it.

I think that the other was that I had really good experience, in my early years in the church, where I had been an organist for some time. There was something about the sanctity of that sacred space that I wanted to in some way find a way to express musically. There also were experiences for me, when I was younger, where in moments, accidentally, I suddenly found that I wasn't playing the piano. It was playing me. It was flowing through me in ways that seemed very mysterious and mystical.

I loved the sense of the mystery that was there and I didn't want to do anything to change that. And yet, it could be gone as quickly as it appeared. It was like a fleeting glimpse; as soon as I put my attention on it, it was gone.

JL: That creative flow state is not something that can be bottled and jarred. And when it happens, it makes you a strong believer in a Higher Power, doesn't it?

MJ: It does. I am a strong believer that there are more than two hands on the piano during those times. I think that my dedication, through most of my life, has been to learn how to be in that place with the piano for longer and longer periods of time.

JL: How is that pursuit going?

MJ: I think I have about another fifty years to go. I feel that I am able to get more into it. But I know that there are more places to go with it. I loved hearing Vladimir Horowitz, at age 75, say that he felt like he was just a beginner at the piano. That is what is so wonderful about that instrument. There is absolutely no ceiling. No matter how much people rave about how fine you might be as a pianist, I realize that in so many ways, I am still a beginner. I found here at this colloquium, as I was doing energy work with somebody, that there is a whole other dimension of music that is opening up right now for me that I am just starting to feel into for the first time. I know that it is an ongoing thing. It is like a sacred trust that has been entrusted in me. I get that I am mandated to continue exploring. When I first experienced that sense of being played, it was something that I didn't openly share with people. I felt it was a sacred trust, something for me to explore, respect and work with intentionally and very carefully.

INTENTIONALITY

JL: There are two key words here–sacred and intention. Let's talk first about intention. You have a common response when people say, " Your music really opens my heart." Thank goodness you didn't feel that responsibility of, "I'm now going to write heart-opening music." That would be quite a burden to bear. But what do you think would happen if you did approach your piano with that intention?

MJ: I think there is a paradox here as well. I can have the intention, and want that to happen, but I really have to stay out of the way in how it's going to be executed. It could be in an infinite variety of ways. And, it may not happen the way I want it to happen! As soon as I sit down and say, "OK, I'm going to open up these people's hearts by playing *this* kind of music," I'm in difficulty.

I can feel this difficulty because now I have got some kind of attention and concentration placed on how I'm going to work with the piano. I suspect this interferes with the very process I would like to bring about. So it needs to be something that I need to hold very lightly. In some respects, I don't know if it makes a difference whether I hold that or not. People who heard my music twenty years ago said it was opening their hearts. At that time, I didn't consciously know anything about hearts, awareness, energy, etc.

JL: Have you been doing conscious work with your heart and feelings?

MJ: I've done a lot of different forms of work over the years. Part of my motivation has been because I was curious. I'm a learner. My graduate work was in adult education. I've been a teacher for many years. But I think the way that I taught has been through learning.

JL: How do you teach through learning?

MJ: One of the ways is through asking questions rather than from giving information. I love to learn from other people. I'm inquisitive and I love to listen to people talk. As a teacher, I did a lot more facilitation when groups really began to find their own meaning of things and then we would experience things collectively.[4]

JL: So do you think your music reflects the work you're doing on yourself? We are talking about a very subtle use of music now. What is the energy inside of the note? The intervals become almost subservient. What is it that creates the sweetness, the golden quality that soothes people's nervous systems?

It is a subtle quality that's very elusive; you can't quite put your hands on it. But I believe that it ultimately does come down to intention.

It is not that you say, "Now, I intend to go to that piano and write something that is going to have this effect." Maybe the actual paradigm is not planning the effect, but rather having the intention to become as whole a person as you possibly can be. Therefore, whatever comes out of your fingers and thoughts will reflect that personal resolve. Maybe intention is understanding that everything we produce reflects our own individual process.

MJ: Yes, this sounds like a very honest intention to have. I have the intention of being in a place of openness to let the emotion of my audience translate through me. I could come into the AIDS hospice, not with the intention to heal these people, cure them, or even open their hearts, but instead with the purpose to simply be available, to do whatever needs to be done in that setting. Letting the music do whatever it needs to do, for whomever needs to receive it, in whatever way. It wouldn't necessarily be to take away someone's pain, but in some cases it might facilitate going even more deeply into it. It is beyond my capacity to second guess what it is that people need in that respect. So it's not an honest intention, I don't think, to decide what people will get. Perhaps it is more about integrity. I can, with integrity, say, "I'm here and available to do what needs to be done." I have, in my own work, tended to trust and rely upon grace.

JL: We love ol' Grace don't we?

MJ: I think this is another way that the forces work with us. I love some lines that came out of Norman Maclean's book, *The River Runs Through It.* He opens his narrative by saying, "God comes to us by grace, grace comes by art, and art does not come easy." I thought those were wonderful lines because in one sense, it does come by grace. And grace, when you are in the midst of it, seems perfectly ordinary. But when you are not in it, it feels like the most impossible thing in the world to recapture.

I have probably taken the last forty years of my life and committed it to being in a place where grace could be there. So I love that line, "Art does not come easy." You work and you work with a lot of intentionality or whatever ways you do it. And yet, ultimately, when the grace is there, that is when the presence of greatness comes through.

JL: I am most interested in exploring this concept of intention with you, Michael. I know that all sound is a consequence of frequency. Anything that moves creates frequency, and frequency creates sound. Since *everything* is made up of atoms, and the atomic structure is based on movement, then everything in our world is buzzing with frequency.

In the same way as a fiber optic cable can carry the frequency of my voice across town-or the world, for that matter-and re-transmit it, is it not probable that frequency serves as a carrier wave for our own intentions. Isn't it possible that a piano wire would reflect, or transmit, the vibratory rate of the person playing it? In this discussion, we keep coming back to the idea that intention is really a very personal directive of thought energy. Does this make sense to you?

MJ: Yes, it is something that I have been playing around with also. Sometimes, I've felt that if I had a strong intention towards something, it might be the intention for the wrong thing. In terms of, "Where is this coming from?" So much of our vision potentially comes from the ego. And the ego has it's own particular agenda in terms of where it wants to be in the world, which may not be consistent with where our deeper purpose is. Unless those are really aligned, and that is not always the case. So I have been a bit mistrustful of my intentions because they can be a somewhat self-serving and they are not really serving the music.

I've had an intention with a composition I thought I wanted to do a certain thing. And I've discovered something else that the composition has done on it's own, that wasn't part of my intention, but far more magical and deeply touching for me than my own particular conscious design. So, it is not as if only I am playing because there certainly is a partnership I feel I go into. It is a co-creation. There is a lot of thought that goes into the feeling, the mood, and the shifts within a composition that unfolds; enough breathing space for things to open up in the performance of it.

I know there is help coming along the way because things simply appear that weren't there three minutes before. And then it gets recorded in a way that is quite different from how I have been playing it for two years. So there is a lot of stuff that is going on that is certainly outside of my control. I have to just be patient with all of that. There is a lot of stuff that goes on that is outside my realm of intention–at least my conscious intention.

I think, perhaps, there is a deeper intention at work, that has to do with a deeper sense of longing for what it is that I want to give the world.This level of intentionality is not as conscious or as explicit that I can articulate, but it is certainly very much alive throughout the work I do. It is quite possible there is a very deep desire I've had to touch the world in some way. Maybe the music that I create is my expression of this. It has nothing to do with album sales. It is the sense of wanting to open the heart of the world. This comes from such a deep level. It moves my actions in a way that I am not conscious of day by day. It is not something that I give thought to, day by day. It is a deeper current that moves me.

JL: I wonder about consciously bringing our deeper motivations to the surface, translating them through the keyboard.

MJ: It has the potential of being very powerful. I certainly do trust that there is a very deep intention that we carry, that is rooted in the longing I was speaking about earlier. It is the longing of our heart. It is the heart's choice to do that in the world. It is not coming from the intellect or our strategic mind. It has a whole different quality to it.

The Sufi poet, Rumi, says that "...it is the intensity of the longing that does the work." The intention that comes from that has a real different quality to it. His book talks about "... crying for a vision." He speaks about the nature of vision and the nature of seeing. There is something that comes through the tears that really touches into the depth of vision that is possible for us. But we don't see it until we have the tears. That is how I am taking his meaning. My interpretation of that is that so much of our visioning comes from the willfulness of the ego and it doesn't really touch into that deeper dimension of life. And yet the tears take us into a place of vulnerability where we connect with the deeper longing of our heart. That kind of vision and intentionality really touches closer to the essence of what we are here to do, what our work is here in the world. When we are connected with that, I think we have something we can trust. When we are not, I think that we can easily find ourselves way off track, with a belief that we have all of the language, but we are not really connecting with the truth of what we are here to do.

I think that the ego throws up a lot of tricks. And that is where it is a tricky business in our work with intention. Unless we can really connect with the source of who we are, and move with the intention that flows from that, that is behind our identity, is behind our attachments, behind the kind of language that we use to fool ourselves, then I think that we easily get drawn off into a number of very subtle traps and believe we're really doing something, which in fact is more self-serving and is not really serving a deeper and larger purpose. Knowing that, if you don't trust where the intention is coming from, you trust that grace will move you towards where the deeper longing is. That is the value of moving with the deeper movement of things and feeling where that movement is. The paradox, as the old wisdom tells us, is that if you know where your path is then you are not on your path. If you can see the road map then you are on somebody else's trip, you are not on your own. So it does mean that you are entering into the space of the unknown and trusting that what is there for you, your treasure, lies in the unknown and in the shadows. It is not always where the light is. ✧

ENDNOTES

1 The music of Michael Jones is available on Narada Records.

2 Michael is the author of an award-winning book/CD collection of stories and reflections that celebrate his life at the piano entitled *Creating an Imaginative Life* (Conari Press).

3 These colloquiums have continued annually. For information regarding upcoming events, contact Lumina Productions. (See Appendix C).

4 The music for Michael's most recent release, *Touch* (Narada, 1997) was composed and performed in dialogue sessions designed to help individuals re-imagine their organizations, their work, and their lives.

7

BIO-TUNING

A conversation with
Jeffrey Thompson, D.C.

Investigations into the field of *whole brain synchronization* brought me from the venerable Monroe Institute in Virginia to North Carolina's therapy-based Acoustic Brain Research. From there I travelled to Washington's Theta Technologies, and then down to San Diego and Brain/Mind Research.

My primary exploration in this corner of soundwork revolves around modulating sound waves known as *binaural beat frequencies.*[1] These frequencies, when applied through headphones, have the effect of entraining brainwaves up or down, from Beta to Delta. Binaural beat frequencies can produce altered states in the brain, are used with sound and/or music, and can be used for psycho-therapeutic, meditative, health, educational, or mental enhancement functions. In a word, they are an astounding sonic tool.

This is an expanding and exciting field of great depth and proportion. Some companies market singular sound frequencies, simply masked by environmental sounds, for relaxation or insomnia. Others utilize whole brain synchronization to generate intensive physical and emotional change, sub-conscious access, or intentional out-of-body experiences. In San Diego, Dr. Jeffrey Thompson uses frequencies to cause the brain/mind to merge with what Carl Jung calls the *collective unconscious.*

Jeffrey Thompson weaves multi-layered sound frequencies into the fabric of each musical note and sound to invoke the sub-conscious.

"Primordial Subconscious Processing™," developed by Thompson, awakens deeper levels of the subconscious with the use of sound recordings from the body, from nature, and from specially processed NASA space recordings not recognizable to the ordinary mind of our 'waking' consciousness. He makes an end run around all conscious brain filters, as he heads for the deep regions he calls the "Organic/Biological Intelligence." Thompson believes it is this intelligence that knows how to grow a body from two cells.

Touchdown… on Jeffrey Thompson, December 1992.

THE "WHO I THINK I AM" SYNDROME

JT: I've been a musician since I was a kid, playing all kinds of different things. I always wanted to produce an album. I started fooling with electronic sounds when I was twelve. I'd take my parents tape recorder apart and do weird things with it, make it make weird noises.

Another thing that I liked was slowing down sound. The first thing I ever did was a pencil sharpener. I'd take a pencil in a pencil sharpener and record it at fast speed. I'd then play it back at its slowest speed while recording it on another tape recorder at its fastest speed. Play that back at slow speed and record that at fast speed. By keeping on slowing it down that way, probably a dozen times, each time I was dropping the speed in half, by an octave. So let's say I dropped it by a dozen octaves, now what I heard was a series of long, drawn-out explosions, lasting about 40 seconds. Each explosion was the sound of the blade slicing its way through the pencil wood. It was like a sonic magnifying glass.

Fast forward to present time, and here I am in my studio at 44 years old. I have created these pulse frequencies, this entrainment business, built into a sound track to do something to your brain waves so they follow these pulses and put you into this altered state of consciousness. Hopefully, at this point, your sub-conscious mind is more exposed, and the rational thinking part, that doesn't usually allow things in, is out of the way. Now that you have the sub-conscious mind exposed, you are in a perfect position to be centered, to be in touch with something that is more real than yourself. You are in a better position for a therapeutic interaction with a psycho-therapist, bodyworker, hypnotherapist, or somebody doing visualizations or affirmations. You are closer to being the programmer of your own computer because all of the peripheral stuff is out of the way.

The way I look at it is that my thinking, rational consciousness, *Who I Think I Am* doesn't have anything to do with who I really am. In reality, *Who I Think I Am* is just a social growth.

When I am born, I am this raw, essential aliveness with consciousness that goes about the business of interacting with my universe. Touching it, eating it, smelling, interacting with it, having a great time. I want it all, information, interaction. And then, as time goes on, those interactions are blocked. Its as if I'm bringing it to my mouth and its held back. "You can't have that!, you can't eat the sharpened pencil, you can't play with that piece of paper, you can't pull my books off the shelf, you can't, you can't, you can't!"

Each *you can't* makes me cry. I have a fit because I'm being blocked from interacting with myself, with my externalized universe. I can't bring it in to me, I can't explore it. Somebody is holding it back from me. So, as I get older, I am exposed to successive layers of "no"! And the uninhibited spirit has no way of dealing with that whatsoever. So it creates a buffer to deal with "no". And its also all wrapped up in "Oh, you're supposed to be this way with other people, you're supposed to wear clothes, be polite, not vomit on your neighbor." You're not *supposed* to do all these different things!

The part of us that learns to behave and not do all these things is this social growth that starts to emerge–as a specialized tool that the essence grows to buffer out and deal with those rules–so the essence can still be untouched. The essence doesn't know "no". It doesn't know "yes" either. Its just into interaction, there to feed on itself, on the universe. So this new social growth becomes our identity because as we grow up, more and more of our time is spent with other people, other situations and things that we're supposed to do, rules and regulations that we're supposed to behave by.

And before we know it, the social growth part becomes so exercised, like a strengthened muscle, that one day it takes over. One day it completely closes our essence off. This takes place at about seven-years–old.

In pediatrics, around this age, when all the teeth are in, the final personality cements. A seven-year–old is just about at the point where they finally solidify their personal identity; its around that point that they have their first experience of personal awareness. This is when a kid looks in the mirror and goes, "Oh! That's me!" So at that moment, who it is who says, "That's me!" is this social growth, the *Who I Think I Am*. *Who I Think I Am* takes over *Who I really am*, which is the essential biological organic intelligence that knows how to grow a body out of two cells. That part gets merged; different people have different ages when that closes off.

What is also interesting is that the Pineal gland goes through a crystallization at age seven. The Pineal gland is synonymous with the seventh chakra and is actually located in the middle of the upper head. It is the seventh endocrine gland. When I was going through school, studying anatomy and physiology, I did a special project searching out all of the endocrine glands. Specifically because of all the esoteric stuff I had been involved with in the past and because the endocrine glands are the counterparts of the chakra system. I wanted to see what modern medicine knows about the physiology of this system.

I intuitively understood that this body is like a textbook of universal law. Its all right here in my glands. So if I studied the Nth degree of anatomy and physiology, and really got it down, on a cellular level of detail, that as I went through that voyage of discovery, I would see all the stuff that I know from my esoteric studies reflected here in this body.

What I want to do with brain entrainment is to get this part of *Who I Think I Am* out of the way and expose the biological organic intelligence. I want to get to that part because that's the identity of me that is creating my own reality. That's me with a capitol I. That's my real identity. That identity happens without words, without thoughts, and without time. It is the immediate, now, living Tao. *Who I Think I Am* happens in time.

This idea of our essence being covered over by the *Who I Think I Am,* and all the different types of modern techniques that you see now, of hypnosis, for example, all are attempting to get this *Who I Think I Am* out of the way.

JL: What else besides hypnosis explores this level?

JT: Monroe entrainment, meditation, and in particular, looking at how human beings have, for centuries, used sound to alter consciousness and to enhance meditation states. I made some interesting discoveries about that after I had solved the problem, for me, of this entrainment business.

Once I went through school, graduated, had a chiropractic clinic, and was a doctor, it was an interesting experience. You graduate from one kind of strata of person to another strata. When you become a doctor, a whole different thing starts to happen. Its a real trip trying to get used to that, trying to step into that bodysuit, so to speak.

SOUND AND CHIROPRACTIC

JL: How old were you at that time?

JT: Thirty-three. I become successful, made money, and realized that I was going to be able to afford to buy some musical equipment. So I put some gear together to create this album of electronic music that I had always wanted to do.

JL: So you still had the musician in you even though you were becoming a successful chiropractor?

JT: Yes. I always wanted to do this.

JL: Why did you go into chiropractic as opposed to being a professional musician?

JT: I was a professional musician in high school. But the reason that I became a chiropractor was to become a holistic health practitioner. The only way that you can become a physician in this country, and not be a medical doctor, is to become a chiropractor. If you want to do acupuncture, homeopathy, and all the other weird stuff, and get paid by third-party payers, you become a chiropractor. Then you are recognized by insurance companies.

My first attempt with therapeutic sound was making chiropractic adjustments with sound frequencies. It was based on a very simple idea: sympathetic resonance. If you hit the right note, the wine glass begins to vibrate because of atomic resonance of the glass molecules. So that is the same thing with every substance; if you can get the right frequency vibration wave for a piece of oak in a certain size and shape and dimension, it will resonate.

JL: And if you increase the amplitude, or volume, than it will over-amp?

JT: Yes. So like everything else, dosage is everything. Its a homeopathic idea. Correct dosage; therapeutic. Overdosage; poison. We all need water, but too much water, you drown. We all need salt, but too much salt, you die. We all need oxygen, but too much oxygen and you get a stroke.

Since then, I have discovered that there is a whole science of acoustic resonance in building. So for instance, if you go to the nearest airport and you want to build some cement high rises, you have to consult an acoustic specialist from a certain corporation, who comes with expensive equipment to test out the type of concrete they are using, and will advise you on the acoustic properties of concrete that are anti-harmonics to the tuning of the jet engines. Because if the concrete is in the same harmonic as the jet engine, it is going to crack. And it won't take long for it to crack. So for every type of building material, there is equipment for testing it out, to expose it to different frequencies, looking at oscilloscopes and seeing what its fundamental resonance is.

So the same thing with the body. Each bone, each vertebra is a different shape, density, mass, and size. So you should be able to resonate it with its own fundamental frequency. In the beginning, I had this one headphone connected directly to the wire, and placed it directly over the bone that was out. It would take about 30 seconds to resonate the bone back into position, never touching it with my hands.

JL: You mean that if I had a subluxation, you would apply this headphone to that area, and it would vibrate the vertebra back into alignment?

JT: Exactly.

JL: Why is that bone out in the first place?

JT: Either it is external force that is caused from an injury, like being hit by a car, or it is an internal, non-coordinator of your internal events.

And that is the central nervous system, your brain. Your brain is the ultimate coordination of everything that goes on in your system. Your brain is telling the bones what position to be in. What's holding those bones in position are five different layers of very complicated muscles that go up and down the spine. The brain can contract these muscles and move the bone into any position that it wants. So the brain is telling everybody where to be. The brain is telling all the organs how to coordinate with each other. The brain is doing the chemical reactions, the neurological reactions. And it is all happening at once. We know, through testing, that the rational brain can process 500 words per minute, max! The sub-conscious brain can process information at a rate that we can't even measure. Possibly, in my opinion, at the speed of light.

It was exceptionally easy to adjust spinal vertebrae using sound frequencies. What I realized though, was that it took 30 seconds to do it with sound, and it only takes one second to do it by hand. In my practice, I was seeing 30-40 patients a day. Even though I had stumbled across the ultimate low-force technique, I couldn't use it practically in the kind of practice that I had. What I did notice though, was that the corresponding organ to that spinal bone was also responding and normalizing. So I began to explore resonating organs with frequency tones because each organ is a different shape, mass, and density.

This was new ground. I began cataloguing frequency vibration rate patterns for different organs. I had this holistic health center at the time, and one of the things that I did there was something called a Chemical Blood Screen. This is a blood test to determine what your nutritional needs are. When you do this test, you can see exactly where your metabolic weak points are, and you know exactly what nutritional things to give. So when I would see a patient who had liver enzymes that were out of range, I could do a sound treatment on the liver, exposing the liver to it's own fundamental frequencies. I'd see the blood values change. Then I knew objectively that this work was real.

JL: How did you establish the notes for each organ?

JT: Because I saw the liver responding when I was doing, for example, work on the eighth thoracic, (a person with a gall bladder problem is going to have a 4th thoracic vertebra problem every single time.) It is a typical thing for a chiropractor to see a patient come in and say, "I've got this pain between my shoulder blades and nobody can do anything about it, and it's just killing me." You go back, sure enough its out, so you adjust it, and by the time the person walks out, its out again.

JL: Because it is really about an organ that is out of balance?

JT: Yes. The organ is out of balance and the bone is popping out like a circuit breaker. Unless you fix the organ, the circuit breaker is going to continue to overload. As soon as I give this person nutritional support for the liver, the pain between the shoulder blade disappears.

I was doing a lot of Magnetic Therapy at the time, where I would put a certain strength of magnetic field over the liver and watch the bone go back by itself. So it is the same thing with the sound. You put the correct frequency over the liver, and within a few seconds, the bone goes back into place without even touching it.

JL: Are most spinal problems organ related?

JT: No, but a good percentage of what goes on back there is. I was just pinch-hitting with a sonic frequency what I used to do with a magnet, acupuncture points, reflex points, or with a hands-on therapy. Instead of putting a certain magnetic field over the liver to see if that would put the subluxation back in place, I was putting a certain sound frequency to see if that did it. And it did.

The critical point for me was when I realized that the brain was also an organ. The brain's function as an organ is the coordination of all the other systems. So if I could find the fundamental resonant frequency of the brain, and expose it to this frequency, and that organ normalized, what would I expect to see as a result of that? I'd expect to see a global realignment of all the organs with each other, of all the spinal elements, of all the acupuncture systems. I should see some kind of grandiose rebalancing of all the body systems.

When I set that up and started experimenting with it, that is exactly what I found. It was an awesome experience. It was like breaking into King Tut's tomb. It was as if I was simply vacationing in Egypt and finding something that nobody else had ever found, and then understanding that I had discovered this titanic thing and realizing that, "Oh my God, I think I better go to archeological school and become an archaeologist!" You can't walk away from a titanic discovery and go back to teaching school or something.

So that was when I sold my practice and my house and moved from Virginia to California. Virginia, forget it! I was having a hard enough time explaining to people why cracking their backs had anything to do with health, never mind resonating their brains with sound frequencies to bring about total healing.

BRAINWAVES RESEARCH

JT: I moved to San Diego County in 1989 and opened up a place called Brainwaves Research. It was a combination research lab with a sound table, recording studio, and the rest of it was a brain spa. I had all kinds of different brain entrainment equipment, the light and sound devices. The public could come in and try any of these interesting and new tools for mind expansion. Or they could come into me for a one on one session where all of these tools would be tuned to their individual system.

JL: Did you have a lot of people coming in?

JT: Oh yes.

JL: What was their motivation?

JT: Everything. From miracle cures of whatever was ailing them, to doing it for fun because it was psychedelic. People came in for stress reduction. I had a lot of meditators come in to break through to a deeper level.

Previously to this time, there were two branches of my work with sound. One branch was this idea of resonating the physical body as a bio-mass with sound, either separate organs, or the brain, whatever. The spin-off from that was resonating brainwave function for changing states of consciousness. I found that resonating the brain itself would cause profound changes in brainwave function and altered states of consciousness. But I approached it from the entrainment idea of exposing the brain to pulse rate frequencies that slow down over time.

Since I was in Virginia, just a stone's throw to Washington, D.C., I had access to the National Medical Library in Bethesda. This place has a copy of every research paper written by anybody in the world on file. I went in there to see who was doing research into consciousness and brainwaves and found that most of it was in the field of sleep research. When I started doing one-on-one sound therapy sessions with patients, what I was searching for was this fundamental sound frequency pattern for your total bio-mass, or your brain's central nervous system- to cause a coordination of all the parts. I was doing that by testing a number of different body systems, structural, muscular, acupuncture, and organ balance. Finding the imbalances-but not fixing them as I went along-like I usually do. Using these imbalances as something to observe, because now I'm hoping to eliminate all of the imbalances, at the same time, in a number of different body systems, with a single frequency. My first approach was, if I'm exposing the brain to its own fundamental frequency as an organ, and that organ normalizes, I should see a related response.

JL: Is that true?

JT: That has been true. And there is an emotional response. It depends on where your imbalances are. On the other hand, the work that I was doing with entrainment resulted in a series of tapes. The world sees that part of what I am doing. What they are not seeing is the private session work with resonating the body.

JL: What was it that you were looking to accomplish with the tapes?

JT: The most effective way that I could come up with the entrainment of the brain.

JL: Slowing it down?

JT: Yes.

JL: And then what would take place when you slowed it down besides relaxation or having somebody peacefully fall asleep?

JT: The research that has been done with meditators, or with expansion of consciousness response, or increased awareness response, all has a certain brain picture that shows up on the EEG. That brain picture is usually lower brainwave frequencies, generally in theta someplace. Hypnogogic states, easy visualization state. People like this state, as I was to learn after *Isle of Sky*[2] was out. This tape was very successful; within a month of its release, it was picked up by fifteen New Age distributors. It got good air time and was adopted by the National Hypnotherapy Association.

JL: Why do you think this album was so successful?

JT: At the time, I thought it was successful because of the subtlety of how I built the entrainment into the sounds. I was also trying to entertain, to capture the attention of that mind that needs to be entertained. Take it-grab it and move, and don't let it go-on a fantastic journey, a sound journey that would entertain it as much as watching *Star Wars*. The mind is now very sophisticated in what it wants to entertain it. All I wanted people to do was close their eyes, put headphones on in a dark room, and go on a sound journey with me. And when they did that, what would happen is they would go into an altered state. What would come out of that altered state was change.

By the time I came out with the second tape, *Egg of Time*.[3] I realized that there is never a time when the brain is just alpha or just theta, or just anything. There is this complex pattern of multiple levels of alpha, beta, theta and delta that form highly specific patterns. Those patterns are coincident in certain exact states of consciousness.

This work was done by Maxwell Cade, a British researcher who showed the patterns of relationship of alpha, beta, theta, and delta as fifteen different frequency patterns. He took a machine that measured brainwaves around the world on a two year tour, looking up the most profound meditators that he could find. He would go up into the mountains of Tibet, China, and India, find these lamaseries and get the head of the whole place to come out, hook him up, have him go into his highest state of meditation, and see what patterns showed up. Over the course of two years, there was this single pattern that showed up so many times, that he called it the Awakened Mind Pattern.[4]

As I was going through and working on *Egg of Time*, I began taking each instrument sound, each bird and nature sound, and building a different frequency amplitude brain pulse frequency into each one of those that would mimic these patterns.

JL: Did you then use his work as your model?

JT: Yes, and I started to discover things on my own. You can refine different states. You can combine different states. But from *Egg of Time* onwards, the format then became multiple levels of brain frequency patterns built into every sound that you hear. Each different sound is a different one of those frequencies in a global picture. And all of them, over time, are moving into another picture.

FUNDAMENTAL FREQUENCIES

JT: The entrainment part was one aspect. The other part of what I discovered was in my one-on-one session with people. I'd find a fundamental frequency and play it through a specially designed sound table into a person's body, using a basic synthesized tone. I realized that in order to get that tone as perfect as possible, out to a fifth decimal point, we already had a musical instrument built into our body. The vocal cords. God did it for us and did it better. Not only that, but it is a stringed instrument and a wood instrument at the same time. It is a blown and a plucked; you are plucking a string with wind. How beautiful. It is the best of both.

So, the idea was that if I am trying to find the fundamental frequency of your bio-mass, your vocal chords are part of your bio-mass. So in a microcosm, what I am really trying to do is find the fundamental frequency of your vocal cords. The fundamental frequency of your vocal cords is the easiest note to sing. Your body is an ecological system, just like the earth, so it is trying to get the most work out of the least amount of energy expended, a true ecological system with the least amount of waste.

At the point where the vocal cords hit their fundamental frequency, you get the most volume with the most relaxation. When the vocal cords are hitting their fundamental note, their fundamental resonance, this is the time when you are getting all of the harmonics and overtones you need to hear. That's when you can hear more than one note coming from a single person's mouth. Because now, the fundamental frequency of the vocal cords is also the fundamental frequency of the densities of your face, of your mouth, your tongue, palette, teeth. They are all going to start singing and resonating also. Each of those are going to resonate at a harmonic.

So what I did was have a person sing their most natural note, sample it, build brain frequencies into it, play it in different octaves. When you hear this recording of your vocal cords hitting a fundamental frequency, slowed down four octaves, your rational *Who you think you are* doesn't recognize it for what it is anymore. It is this beautiful, incredible cosmic choir, with all these harmonies singing in the background. This deep, primordial, biological intelligence that grew the vocal cords from two cells, sits right up and wakes up. It says, "I know that sound. Not only do I know that sound, but I know that pattern!" Its not just a sound. It is the fundamental frequency pattern of those vocal cords. You are hitting a pattern that was used to design it out of two cells. Its a deep response!

JL: So when you do that, what is the effect?

JT: It is very dramatic. Everybody responds differently. Some people have this grandiose response. Other people jump off the table and say, "Oh, that was real nice. I feel real balanced, thank you." And then over the course of the next six months, their entire life changes.

There was a friend of mine from the 60's, who was the youngest PhD in the country. He had this statement that has stuck with me: "I am not who I think I am. I am not who you think I am. I am who I think you think I am." In other words, you live your life, based on what you think I am expecting you to be. I become who I think you expect me to be. And you, being the whole world; my parents, my friends, my peer group. Its all the pressures that come to bear on me from the world all around me, who are all screaming for me to be this way and this way and this way and this way. And I accommodate and be that. And what I end up with is a multi-facetted accommodation with no substance of *me* at all. I am not there at all.

Who is really there–buried underneath that fantasy–is my biological organic intelligence; outside of time, without thought, without ego, going about the business of being meditation in action. The witness, the objective observer in my life. And I am separated from that. The whole idea behind this, is the same idea that has been done with sound for thousands of years-using sound to get this part out of the way and expose the deep part.

If you can expose yourself to the deep part, and get in touch with it, you've come in contact with all your own answers. You don't need a therapist, you don't need somebody to tell you what's wrong with you. You've got those answers in yourself. All you have to do is come and contact them in a non-time/space. When you do that, you arrive at your power spot. And every time that you do that, your exercising it like a muscle. Its been under exercised for years, its been atrophied because all your energy has been out here, being *Who I think you think I am.*

As soon as you cut through that, come back in touch with that, and do that again and again, come back in here and be on this table with your frequency, again and again and again, and I take that frequency and put it on an audio tape, and then you use it every single day, again and again, then you go into this space within yourself, again and again. You are exercising that part of you and as it exercises it gets stronger. And over time, as it gets stronger, one day it gets strong enough to challenge *Who I think I am* for *who is real.*

As that day approaches, your life is changing. You are, all of a sudden, starting to have a yardstick inside, to measure your external world by. The big mysteries of your life become painfully obvious after awhile. It becomes obvious why you are unhappy, why you have no love, why you have no money, why your job isn't working, your life is not working. Your life is not working because you are out of touch! At a core level, you are unhappy with yourself and this situation, because you are not fulfilling your dharma, your purpose on earth. You are not following your path. You are spinning your wheels with a job, paying a mortgage, trying to live up to other people's ideas of what a husband/wife and a father/mother is supposed to be. And you are not coming from your truth. As soon as we come from our truth, we cut through all that stuff with the people around us. All of a sudden, our relationships are utterly different. We can't change that core part of ourselves.

JL: So what you are essentially doing is helping people rediscover their own fundamental selves. You believe people can heal themselves by getting back to the fundamental, tone and all?

JT: Yes! And that is what I have been attempting to build into the tapes. One-on-one sessions with people is not enough. The purpose and potential of that, if it works, is bigger than just seeing a patient. If I could do that on a tape and sell the tape to 10,000 people, now I have 10,000 people on my table. Because when you come to that point in yourself, and you have that experience, you realize that you are really one cell in the bigger brain. And out of the joy that comes with touching yourself, is an immediate sadness because you are surrounded by people who aren't in touch, and immediately you are shouldered with this responsibility. You can't be happy when people around you are crying, particularly when you can see why.

JL: So your knowledge becomes your cross?

JT: You have to do it. You can't turn your back on it without stepping on your own truth. Because those people that are crying are you. They are not somebody else. So to be truly happy at your core, you have to make everybody happy around you. You have to share what you have seen[5]. ✧

Partial Discography

- *The Thinking Music Series* (2 album set). Designed to enhance concentration and focus. Applied Sound.[6]
- *Brainwave Suite* (4 album set). Introduction to the use of binaural beat frequencies. The Relaxation Company.
- *Brainwave Journey with Owen Morrison* (4 album set). Guided imagery with frequencies. The Relaxation Company.
- *Psycho-Sensory Integration Series* (6 albums). Designed for therapeutic applications. Brain/Mind Research.
- NASA Space Sound Series (11 albums). Brain/Mind Research.

ENDNOTES

1 For a brush-up on this sonic brainwave technology, See Chapter Two, *Demystifying Binaural Beat Frequencies.*

2 *Isle of Skye* is available through Brain/Mind Research. See Appendix C.

3 *Egg of Time* is available through Brain/Mind Research. See Appendix C.

4 Maxwell Cade's American protege is Anna Wise, one of the world's leading authorities on the use of MindMirror EEGs. Cade's work has been further developed by Ms. Wise and can be found in her book and audio series, *The High Performance Mind* (NY, Tartcher, 1995). Audio tapes by the same name are available from the mail-order catalog, Tools for Exploration, (888) 748-6657.

5 As of the date of this revised edition of *Sonic Alchemy* (6/99), Dr. Thompson is the founding director of the Center for NeuroAcoustic Research at the California Institute for Human Science in Encinitas, CA.

6 *Thinking Music* is available from Applied Music & Sound. See Appendix C

8

Psychoacoustics

A conversation with
Tom Kenyon

Whole brain synchronization (WBS), in simple terms, is the synchronization of the right and left hemispheres of the brain. *Bi-lateral hemispheric synchronization*, another term for WBS, is a natural brain state occurring momentarily throughout the day. At these times, our brain-power is at its height; we are highly focused, productive, and fully coherent. This idyllic state of mind is illusive to most of us-for it is not accessible upon command.

However, WBS, induced by specific audio frequencies and stereo head-phones is changing this accessibility. New sonic techniques now give us, at will, access to this prime state of awareness. Additionally, audio technologies modulate the tempo of our brainwaves, from high beta states to low delta and then back again. These powerful, non-invasive tools explore, develop and maximize our consciousness, our minds.

Robert Monroe's sonic discoveries in the 60's provided the groundwork for many organizations which have adapted his findings to their unique pathworks, adding, subtracting, mixing it up, painting it their own.[1] I believe these organizations want to make a difference; they realize the power of this technology and the potential benefits for us all.

Acoustic Brain Research (ABR) is the brainchild of Tom Kenyon. Established in 1983, ABR grew out of Mr. Kenyan's successful utilization of sound and music in his psychotherapy practice. A high-tech alchemist, Tom Kenyon combines guided imagery, subliminal messages, specific tonal and musical patterns, as well as sophisticated brainwave technologies to create a *tonal matrix.* These sonic potions of voice, sound and music have proven highly effective to manage stress, accelerate learning, increase intelligence and creativity, induce recovery, self-healing, and in meditation. ABR tapes are highly respected and used world-wide.

Wonderful and strange sounds, odd rhythms and shifting harmonies characterize Kenyon's imaginative and unique albums. After weeks with my Walkman headphones in place, I realize that the seeming random structure is deliberate. There is hardly an unplanned element to be found. In fact, I wager there is rhyme and reason behind every sound. An amazing aspect of these tapes is *what we don't hear*; specific sub-audio frequencies and sound patterns that only the brain registers–totally by-passing our conscious hearing process.

After listening to ABR's *Sound Meditations.* I feel as if I just awakened from a deliciously deep afternoon nap. My head feels funny, light, altered, great! My body is calm, fully relaxed, and I'm not really concerned about anything at this moment. I feel connected, whole, at one.

Reading the *New York Times* didn't make me feel this way. Meditation, using TM, didn't make me feel this way. I ate an absolutely perfect peach and didn't feel 5% of the sense of wholeness, peacefulness and perfection I now feel. How does Tom Kenyon do this? There is something really wonderful going on beneath the surface.

The following interview took place in August, 1992.

THE TONAL MATRIX

JL: Tom, tell me how you began.

TK: I was a professional musician, putting myself through undergraduate school playing in various pop music bands. Then I got my Masters in psychological counseling and started doing extensive work in Eriksonian Hypnosis and altered states. At that point, I realized that music could facilitate trance state through certain rhythm patterns and tonal keys.

Different scales and chord structures have specific effects. For example, if you do something in a minor key, you will have a different emotional tone to it than if you were in a major key. By building certain kinds of tension within the music, when a person is in a trance state, which is really internalized awareness, then the tension that is in the music will transfer into a kind of tension in their psyche. If they are going through imagery work, and the music starts to move into a kind of tension, like a crescendo or resolving of the tension, it seems that the person's internal process parallels the music.

JL: In other words, the music carries them along.

TK: That's right. So I did a lot of experimentation with this, and then I sought training in neurology. I studied with John-David back in the 70's. Putting all those pieces together, I started making tapes for my clients and realized they would facilitate and deepen their therapeutic process when working with my tapes between sessions.

I then invited independent researchers, including five major universities, to become involved. One of my goals was to scientifically document psychoacoustics, which is the effect of music and sound on the brain and the nervous system. They would document people using these tapes, and then come back and say, "I didn't think this was possible, but this is really happening." There was a lot of excitement on our end having scientific proof of what we believed to be so effective.

JL: In your catalogue, you mention the term *tonal matrices*. The sense that I have is of you putting down layer after layer of information on a multi-track recorder. The image that comes to mind is you saying, "O.K., we want to get to mid-theta, or high delta, so we're going to create specific combinations of these different technologies to get there." So each different frequency, sound, vocal instruction, etc., goes onto discreet tracks of tape, just in the same way as if you were multi-layering pop music; you would put the base drum on track one and the guitar on track two. But the difference is that now you are working with knowledge and technologies that allow you to pinpoint exactly where in the brain you want to bring somebody, and then to do something with them once you get them there.

TK: Yes this is true. But I would say that it is more the general area of the brain then a pin-point specific. Actually, some of the independent research that has been done has shown that if you give a 4Hz signal, which is a low theta signal, depending on the person, sometimes their brain wave will go down to 4Hz, some people, their brainwaves will lower, but not all the way down to the 4Hz level. They'll kind of float around it. Some people will go below the 4Hz level. But what you are doing is nudging them into the domain that you want them.

JL: So once you've determined that domain, then through the use of these different psychological, musical, and brainwave frequencies, you create an aural experience whereby the body goes into a specific relaxed state?

TK: Yes. It is the mind that is in a relaxed state whereby they are able to have a series of experiences that they would not normally have in a higher brain state. What happens with the tonal matrices, with the use of stereo headphones, is the creation of a world that is totally controlled, or elicited by the sound, and the person can enter that world and have transformational, healing experiences. Then there are other aspects of it where there are sound tone patterns that have nothing to do with creating the experiences, but they are creating physiologic effects on the brain. Another part of the tonal matrix is the music, which is crucial. It is not used as a pretty mask, it is a very important part of the process. This is based upon Manfred Clynes' work, from Australia, known as *Essentic Forms*.[2] His work was centered around findings he gathered while traveling the world with a computer device that was able to track the waveform characteristics which convey essential human emotions and qualities. Clynes found that the waveforms were similar in all languages. So there are universal emotions that have the same universal waveform characteristics; anger, love, etc. So if you have these waveforms in the music, or in any type of movement, even a dance movement, it will tend to elicit that particular emotion.

JL: How are different frequencies determined?

TK: If we want a person going into a deep state of rest, and have totally an internal experience, where there is no experience of the external world, and we want their brainwaves, respiration, and heartrate to slow down to the lowest possible state, so we can get a deep state of rest, then we are going to put them into delta, ranging from .5 to 4Hz. If we want to create a transformational dreamlike experience, in which, again, they are not attentive to the outside world, but they are aware of their bodies, and energy is moving through their body, then we are going to target theta, which is 4-8Hz. If we want them to have a relaxed awareness, whereby they are aware of both their internal imagery and the external world, then we are going for alpha, which is 8-12Hz.

In our *Acoustic Supported Learning* tapes,[3] used to accelerate learning, these are in the mid-alpha range, because we want the person to be relaxed but also aware of the external environment. In the *24 Minute Nap*, we don't want them to be aware of the external environment at all. We want them to go into a deep state of rest, so we would use low theta and low delta.

THE DANGER OF BRAINWAVE TECHNOLOGY

JL: With this understanding of brainwave states, and the ability to sonically entrain the brain into specific rates, you have the power to take somebody through the full range of awareness, voluntarily if they are aware, involuntarily if they don't know. Is there a danger in any of this?

TK: Yes, there are dangers in the technology, because anything that has such power can be misused. I was approached by a hotel chain in Asia. They wanted to pay me a large sum of money to develop a series of tapes that would be playing softly in the lobby, instructing people to go downstairs to the shops and buy things. I have been approached by movie companies, who want to use this technology to make the emotions of the films even more impactful, as in horror films, for example. We are talking about the ability to imprint the nervous system. And of course, I would not do it for them. I am very careful and attentive to the dangers of this. It all has to do with integrity.

JL: To your knowledge, has there been a misuse of these technologies?

TK: Well, I don't want to point any fingers... And yes, there has been.

JL: Within the major companies that are advancing this technology and putting product out on the marketplace, do you feel that the public is in good hands?

TK: Yes. I don't think that any of the major companies are doing anything ill-intentioned. Sometimes, their technological approach does not deliver what they say it does. Some of the claims that they make simply cannot be documented scientifically. When somebody says, "Listen to this tape and you will have a state of genius and perfect memory just by listening five minutes a day," you've got to know that this kind of claim is beyond the realm of documentation. Also, some aspects of the technology are actually being misused by certain agencies in different governments.

JL: I'd be surprised if the CIA's of the world weren't fully cognizant of this power. Its like a sacred trust falling into the wrong hands.

TK: That's exactly how I hold this knowledge, as sacred. In the ancient mystery schools, music and sound was used as one of the main healing modalities.

PERSONAL EFFECTS

JL: But aside from music and sound, the brainwave technology has allowed us to become acutely specific. We now have the ability to get into the nervous system of the human being. How long do our brains stay synchronized after listening to these tapes?

TK: It varies from person to person, anywhere from a few minutes to a few hours. For some people a few days. We are in a realm that is still a lot of theory. But the best guess that we can make, from a neurological and psychological standpoint, is that it has to do with the personality structure of the person, and how rigid they are in their perceptions. A person who is more fluid will tend to have stronger effects and will last longer. Whereas a person who is more rigid in their personality and has higher control needs, the brain snaps back to attention as soon as they are relaxed. Or they may be relaxed for twenty minutes, experiencing whatever they are experiencing internally, and then as soon as it is over, the brain, because it so habitually has to snap back to attention, be vigilant, and in control of the environment, then those people tend to have shorter effects than on the people who are more free-floating.

JL: Does whole brain synchronization take the place of meditation?

TK: No, it doesn't. This is where I disagree with a lot of people in this field. I feel that the highest use of human consciousness is self-mastery.

My goal is to assist people into states of experience that they can reproduce themselves. I see the tapes as a way of assisting people to levels of consciousness that they may never have had access to before. But once they have gone to them enough times, the goal would be for them to be able to go, by themselves, simply by recalling the state and going to it.

THE FUTURE OF SONIC BRAINWAVE TECHNOLOGY

JL: Where do you see this work going?

TK: Well there are several levels of it. There is a lot of research going on with high-beta frequencies. We know that there is a certain frequency that will stimulate the Kundalini energy. And there are certain frequencies that will cause a person to have an out-of-body experience. There is a lot of research going on with something called the *sensory motor reflex* frequency, a high-alpha frequency. What this does is increase muscle coordination, improve memory, improve certain learning disabilities, such as dyslexia, and in some mild cases, seems to reverse epilepsy, or put the symptoms at bay.

This is all very exciting stuff. This is looking at specific frequencies and what they can do in terms of physical and mental effects. I see that we are going to be much more precise in the use of frequencies. Also, we will be much more precise in the use of language and understanding. There is a whole new science of language: Dr. Chomsky's work with linguistics, Dr. Milton Erikson's work, as examples. We will be much more precise in how we can create resourceful internal states and motivate them. I think that we are going to create much more powerful transformational tools using sound.

I also believe that there will be a lot more medical application of sound and music in the next twenty years. There is already a growing recognition in the medical field of its use.

JL: What are you working on at this time?

TK: I'm working with one of the foremost cardiologists in this country, Dr. Bruno Cortis, out of Chicago. We are working on tapes that will be used to reduce anxiety and accelerate healing for cardiac patients. Heart attacks are the biggest killers in America, and anxiety is a very big problem with cardiac patients, which of course makes the cardiovascular problems worse. So this series of tapes are designed to facilitate both an emotional and physical healing while they are going through their other medical procedures.[4]

We are doing more work with accelerated learning and accessing genius states. We are completing one of the major projects, called *The Inspired Series*. Another project is with specific high-beta frequencies, looking at stimulating the Kundalini energy and creating out-of-body experiences.[5] ✧

ENDNOTES

1 Robert Monroe (1915-1995) was the founder and guiding force of The Monroe Institute. See Chapter Two for further detail on this extraordinary neuro-sonic researcher.

2 Dr. Manfred Clynes, *Sentics; The Touch of Emotions* (NY, Avery Publishing Group, 1989.)

3 ABR tapes are available through S.E.E. Publishing. See Appendix B for further information.

4 Entitled *Mind Your Health.* Available through S.E.E. Publishing.

5 In my introduction to the interviews, listed in Part II, I asserted that some soundworkers have expanded their reach to the point that current work bears little resemblance to the sentiments on these pages.

This statement certainly refers to the current work of Tom Kenyon. In the five years that have passed between the interview and this publication, Tom has become a channel; a reluctant intuitive, at that. Priding himself on a clinical, scientific approach to life, he was thoroughly surprised when information from the Hathors—a group of Egyptian sound priests dating B.C.E.—started to fall from his lips. Not an occasional experience, Tom has become an abundant conduit for extraordinary spiritual and practical information. He artfully combines this new/old information, including frequency work, with his therapeutic and musical background (including a 4 octave vocal range). The net result: In this writer's opiniuon, Tom Kenyon has become one of the most powerful sources of sacred sound available to the public.

He is a gentle teacher and tireless seminar leader. Currently, he travels extensively, instructing throughout the United States. If you have a chance to participate in one of his programs, I whole-heartedly recommend you take advantage of the opportunity.

9

Awakening the Amnesia of Wellness – Sound as Bodywork

A conversation with
Vickie Dodd

"I wish to speak to that cell that remembers; to speak to it in its own language, in its rhythm, that it may pulsate and vibrate to move and spread itself through more cells, more dimensions, and start a revolution, an evolution, a call to awaken.

WAKE UP, WAKE UP
Hello in there
Are you alone in there?
Are you home in there?

WAKE UP, WAKE UP
And listen to me
I need you to see
You make a difference to me.

I'm going to AH you
I'm going to CALL you
I'm going to do whatever it takes
to make you ALL me

I know that one upon a time
to be blind
was sublime
was the way to survive.

WAKE UP, WAKE UP
I'm not saying it's too late
        or that it's even your fate
I'm just wondering if you are tired
        of having to fake
        That you're not AWAKE?

I can hear you singing joyfully,
I can feel you hugging yourself
I can smell your sense as you exude
        sweet thoughts to you and yours.
I know you are in there, whole and well.

And, I know for so long, you've
        been afraid I'd tell
                that we are truly well
        that we do love ourselves
                that we are fine
                        and couldn't complain
                                about a thing.

But, how, what would all the others think?
        That we are for sure
                in blind denial?
                        delusion?
                                idealistic?
                for sure not facing reality.

The habit is great to be sick
        The support is there, if you please:
        I make my living on this disease.
        Why and how could I displease
                so many
                        by my release
                                of sleep.

My greatest fear is that you will
        know I am well
And will not need me anymore
will not feed me any more.

My greatest fear is that I am
well, and I can not
find anyone else to admit
that they are also.

The risk of being well
is the warrior of the future.
is the belly warrior
is the heart warrior,
is the will to see Well.

One little cell is all it takes
to change and re-arrange
one's entire fate,
one's entire notion
and quotion
within the vast ocean
Of Self."

- *Vickie Dodd, from "The Well Cell"*

In all my sound sleuthing, I have come across no one as delightfully mind-altering and controversial as Vickie Dodd. With less than 5 feet of height, this woman is a giant in terms of her impact. Often times, she does not speak, but omits a sounding that seems to contain 'languages' that seamlessly 'morph' from one emotion into another. It is spell-binding to witness. The first time I saw and heard this, I had to go out and take a long walk to figure out what I'd just experienced. Simply put, I'd just experienced Vickie Dodd matching frequencies. Matching frequencies? What does this mean?

Vickie is clairaudiant. She distinguishes the singular sounds of an individual's internal frequency field. With the mantle of this innate extra-sensory perception, Ms. Dodd has walked, at times, a personally perilous path. It is difficult to always hear the truth regardless of what someone might be 'saying.' There are few teachers to instruct in the constructive usage of this sensing. For the last thirty years, Vickie has combined her 'listening' with the field of bodywork.

The following interview–conducted in Boulder, Colorado, in 1994–may appear abstract at times. This fifth draft is as 'simple' as I could draw forth. Like the sounds she hears, Vickie's thoughts are both linear and expansive. It is well worth your time to follow these geometric lines of logic. Her thinking about sound is evolutionary.

HISTORY OF A CLAIRAUDIENT

JL: I am interested in your ability to sense frequency. Tell me about this.

VD: I was always able to perceive so I never knew that other people didn't.

JL: When was your first memory of this ability?

VD: In the womb.

JL: What do you remember?

VD: I grew up in a small town, Eldorado, Illinois. It is right by Kentucky and Missouri. Both grandmothers lived with my family. They were both very strong, powerful women.

When I was in the womb, they scared me because one of them seemed almost evil. It was as if she did not want me to be born. The other one kept on loving me and served like a guardian. So, I was confused about the grandmother that didn't want me to be. That was when I first started learning how to hide my mind and my light. It was from her. I didn't understand when I was in the womb what they were up to. I understood later as I got to know them.

Basically this grandmother was afraid for me. As I got older and started understanding her more, I realized that she wasn't evil. And it wasn't that she didn't want me to be born. She was concerned about my being born because she could see me and she didn't know how it was going to be for me. Also, I was being born into a culture where there was not much freedom for a girl child.

JL: What stands out in your memory from your childhood?

VD: By the time I was a little girl, I would have visions.

JL: Tell me about them.

VD: One that I still really love was when I was about four. I was asleep and these lights woke me up. They just filled me up and danced around, and they were just loving and stroking me. This happened to me often through my childhood, but this one particular time, I remember thinking it was Christ. So the next morning, I told my mother that Jesus had come to me last night, and she said, "Oh, that's nice honey..." and went on cooking. I love that part about my childhood, that none of this was considered special or strange.

JL: What else stands out?

VD: I knew Grandma Reister, Grandma Baggott, and Grandma Reeder-On-The-Hill. All these old women... Everyone went to them for various maladies; arthritis, heart problems, warts, growths of any sorts. That's just what you did. These weren't considered medicine women or special people; it was just what they did.

And, my Mother, she did their hair-in our kitchen. And I spent most of my time underneath the kitchen table. And they lived their dreams; they talked their dreams. Dreams were real and dreams had messages. So a lot of time was spent talking about dreams.

People birthed each others babies, they looked into each others eyes, they knew what was going on with each other. Years past, I studied many forms of diagnosing, and realized they were practicing some form of iridology. They were doing many forms that we now call Neural-Linguistic Programming.

When Grandma Baggott removed a wart from my inner lip, she touched my shoulder and said, "Honey, let me see that, you won't have that tomorrow". It was all so simple, then. I don't think these were exceptional beings. I think they were practicing common sense. I think I happened to have been born, at a time, in a pocket of this country, that still had not been televised. We didn't even have refrigeration in the 50's. I was raised with an ice box. And, I'm not in my eighties. But the lifestyle was as if I could well be.

JL: When were you born?

VD: It's not about the time I was born; it was that little cultural pocket, where somehow I was protected. I used to say when I first started realizing my frequency perceptiveness—that the biggest difference between me and others I had met with heightened sensitivities—was that I wasn't educated, medicated or 'religioned' out of my inherent knowingness. There is something to say for being left alone. What I have found with so many of my students and clients was that they all had a lot of perception. Some of them can actually remember. Some of them after working awhile can remember more of their perceptiveness. Their greatest pain is knowing that there was a time when they remembered more that they do now! And that is what I find most prevalent. The family structure that I came from had no educational overlay on top of their essential wisdom. And, for me this was a fortunate placement.

JL: As a child, you were sensing frequency?

VD: Yes, but I didn't know I was sensing frequency. Like most of us, I thought my reality was what everybody else's was.

JL: How did that look? How did it sound?

VD: Well, I talked to all the plants. I could hear them talking to me. It was wonderful. To be quite honest, it was like being friends with the plants and all of the little creatures. It's a language. It's a listening. That piece was wonderful. It didn't hurt me. I would lay on the ground and I could hear the sky and the clouds. That was my favorite thing-I could hear the sky.

JL: How did that sound?

VD: Well, my voice box can't make most of these sounds. But, remember the movie, *Close Encounters of the Third Kind?* It was the first time I heard anything that kind of matched. The tonal sequence with the space ship resembled what I heard. If you kept following that five note sequence, you would get most harmonics in many languages. It was the harmonics I was hearing.

JL: So in your normal soundscape, as you were going through your day, you were hearing the harmonics, or frequencies, of everything around you?

VD: Or the dissonance!

JL: Didn't it get a little loud?

VD: Oh yes, very loud. And, so I used to dance a lot to let the sound move and be experienced through my body. I think I came out of the womb dancing. I was teaching tap-dancing when I was five years old. I toured the mental hospitals in Kentucky, Illinois and Missouri, tap-dancing for the mental patients. I loved it and they loved me! Years later I realized that one of the things the tap dancing did was to allow the frequencies that were unable to be expressed in these people to be moved or touched in some way. And I knew how to do it because what I was doing was dancing the things that I could hear. Emotions are coded in rhythm. Each emotion has its own little tap-dance.

JL: Vickie, what was the quality of the sound that you would hear?

VD: Like orchestras.

JL: Like orchestras tuning?

VD: Yes, that was a part. Also it was always changing, it wasn't like a finished piece.

JL: So when you talk about what it is like being around someone who lied to you, would that manifest in a horrible sound around you?

VD: As a child I would hear the integrity or falseness in people and situations. Hearing is probably not a very good word because it's really the whole body. What I was hearing was their own internal dissonance with themselves, especially when what they said, was different than what their frequency was saying.

When I was twelve, my family moved to Chicago. I didn't have enough discernment for my nervous system to be able to maintain my open state. So I shut down. It was only when I got to be about 17-years–old, and started on my path of trying to heal myself–which was basically trying to heal my nervous system and learn discernment–that I started being able to unravel the effect that my sensitivity to sound had on my body.

JL: What was the effect, how did it feel?

VD: In the brain, it sounded like screeching train wheels on a track; they are braking and the metal is scraping against metal. It just felt tighter and tighter in my head. Very high frequencies. I think that this was crazy-making. It short-circuited my wiring.

JL: Can you remember ever having to literally run away from a circumstance that was creating sound that you couldn't bear?

VD: I didn't physically run away, but what I started doing was withdrawing deeper and deeper into myself.

JL: You became an introvert to survive?

VD: Yes. And that started me on an intellectual pursuit. I began reading all the time. Before that, I had nature and dancing. Once in Chicago, I started looking for a truth in books and politics. I started using my mind in different ways than before.

Sometime, when I was about seventeen, this very loud sonic-boom voice came to me. At different times in my life, it had saved me. This time, it said, "If you do not learn how the motions live in the physical body, you will be dead!" And that was it. I was so glad to be given an assignment. All of a sudden, I had a focus. I hadn't heard that voice for a long time and wasn't feeling connected to any other source. I have always felt a connection to Spirit, to Will, to God. And, I was feeling very disconnected in Chicago as a teenager. Trying to adapt. I think that was because I didn't know how to plug in as well as when my receptivity was wide open in the country. I didn't know how to listen in a new way. So that began it. And from there, I just soared and it hasn't stopped. And it has gotten steadily better; my understanding, that is, of how the emotions live in the body.

In the years that have passed, I have come to think that a lot of people are equipped to perceive as I have. But, I think that they knew how to shut down as soon as they came out of the birth canal. They got it immediately! For whatever reasons, I didn't know how to shut down. Now in some ways that is good; I am learning that we can actually survive with this increased perception. And, I can be assistance to those who want to re-open and re-plane that level of intelligence. This is why I feel so many people are drawn to this work-because the cellular memory is still there. And because the experience is embodied, it reduces the tendency to want to mystify this work or knowingness.

JL: Vickie, what I understood you to say is that in hindsight, you've realized that a process did not happen with you that takes place with other people. That for survival, most of us shut down a level of perception at birth. However, you were safe enough that you did not have to flip that switch, in whatever mechanism, so you were able to come in with this heightened perception. Your belief is that many have a sense memory of the perception, but, can't quite get back to it. Because of this shutdown, and the resultant experiences in life that basically tie us down, your work is a process of reminding people, through the depth of your frequency connection, that we can basically untie that which binds us-including the ability to sense frequency. Am I in the ballpark?

VD: Yes, you are. And, it is actually a reality of embodiment, and not just a theory. We have to come to a place where all of our learning and wisdom is not just something we have, but something that we are. If I use my body as a laboratory to learn what I know, then when I work with you, there is a trust that is established because I've embodied my experience. There is a believability factor.

JL: Otherwise it is superficial and technique-driven?

VD: Yes, and, basically that is true in many of our professional societies; we have trained technicians. This seems to even exist in the alternative training programs. I would like to see this interrupted. To reach the places most in need of healing, we as practitioners, must now embody our training and wisdom. This of course, is suggesting a major consciousness change. To suggest that the means and measures of how we get the results are equally important as the results.

JL: When did you first study sound or frequency with a teacher?

VD: When I met William David. He is a wonderful teacher who needs to be more recognized in the Sound world. He started the first American Sound School in Houston in the early 60's. One of his schools is still there. His research facility is now outside of Phoenix. William is in his 70's now. He was the first person who really affirmed for me that I was up to something. Up until then, I was working with sound, but I had not met anyone else who was.

JL: How did you meet?

VD: In the early 70's. I was still in Chicago studying color and light. A woman brought William in to work with our group. He and I had an immediate, beautiful rapport. We became very good friends.

JL: And you studied with him?

VD: Yes. Mainly what he suggested was that I start working with vowels, with color, and the emotional qualities associated with them. He had a system for this study. So, I started toning and my emotions moved in a way that I had never been able to do . He was such a beautiful teacher, he presented his material and said, "I want you to take this and create your own from it." And he embodied what he taught; his roots of information continue to grow deeper.

JL: And how did you take this process?

VD: I started putting the vowel and consonant work into more of a body context since I am a body worker. I have always been involved in movement. Some of the questions I always had were... How do you use your body to get there? How do I start matching the shape of the geometry of that sound in my body?

TEACHING THE GEOMETRY OF SOUND

JL: What does it mean to match the geometry?

VD: To start learning how to follow the geometry. It is almost like gathering all of the threads, or all of the tentacles, of the roots of that feeling. Since I've always been able to perceive sound frequencies in people's bodies, I listen to what is there. I can tell by listening where the emotion is inserted in the system. I use my voice to 'sound' the place that presents itself the most. I try to match it's rhythm, emotional content, pitch, and direction.

In some ways, my feeling is that I'm sounding what has been unexpressed, denied, forgotten. Hopefully, I'm engaging that unexpressed place in a sort o dialogue. And most times, I sense that this crystallization is so grateful for finally being acknowledged-having waited to be called, sung, re-connected... for so long.

Now I'm using concepts that I learned from Judith Aston, the originator of a body work called Aston-Patterning.[1] I've studied with Judith since 1976. The Aston work emphasizes listening to individual tissue, bone and joint preferences, rather than imposing one posture on everyone, so that the work can allow and facilitate the way a person needs to 'unfold' organically. It's based on the premise that each person's body has an inherent intelligence of it's own. Integrity calls for the practitioner to follow, 'listen' to that person's intelligence, so that the person has the choice to reveal that which their system has the ability to support. Emotionally as well as physically. I've translated these principles into my work with sound.

JL: Vickie, how do you teach people to "reclaim the truth" in their voice?

VD: I educate about how to reclaim the voice from a place of not tearing the tissue, but, rather following the tissue. The word tissue and the direction of tissue I am using symbolically; to give texture to the layer we are touching with sound. One of the things I learned from Judith Aston was If you meet resistance, go in another direction. That is how you can start finding the geometry that I have been talking about. That is the secret. It is so simple: If you meet resistance, go another direction. (Vickie tones a bit and then says...)

It's almost as if you go in there with your voice and you go this way, and that way, and around here, and over there, and around there... You see what I am saying? The places where the sound alters, where it turns, stops, illustrates the boundaries of the shape of the geometry. The body will show you the geometry; you do not have to know it. You just need to know how to listen and follow it.

I know that learning to sound our truer voice, comes from learning to listen. Since many of us do not know how to listen to our emotions without judgment, I demonstrate how to follow the judgment into a place of grace, or acceptance by initially using my voice, as I'm wanting to demonstrate the immense variety of possibilities and give them permission and choices for sounding their own. They start hearing how the most discordant sound will always move into a place of tone. This is because the body is so loaded with grace that it will always take one into a place of acceptance. This is how I teach people. I teach to follow discordance into a place of tone. As the harmonics live within the discord. It is a study of letting the body do the singing, instead of the mind.

Many times people will really want to move a strong emotional feeling in their bodies, and they will use their voice to try to blast through, the same way we might use force to move the physical tissue, to muscle through it. This is what I call using our mind to listen to our emotional or physical bodies. So we usually miss the geometry, the spatial design, the appropriate timing and rhythm of the body. So we may get temporary relief, as sound does break up crystallization, but many times it is not sustainable. And, again that takes us back to value of how we get the results and not the fact that we can create change.

Some places are so compressed, so restricted, that you have to be willing to not try and push them open, blast them, or tear them. No, it's through sounding the smallest opening that is there. This encourages trust and a resiliency in the tissue, a fluid, the tissue actually starts being hydrated. This is *Sound as a bodywork* that I'm talking about.

JL: So, hypothetically, a person comes to you with grief, knowing they have an emotional restriction. They can feel it manifesting in their body and psyche. From what I understand, you do not even need to use your hands. You can basically scan their sound field. Do you hear the places where the energy is not moving and what does it sound like?

VD: I do hear/sense it. And it is not like one sound. it is a unique geometry of sound, a formula so to say of that particular placement.

JL: So it's like the extraordinary sounds you make?

VD: In some ways, but my voicebox cannot even get close. Maybe with several other voices working together. That is part of my vision; that sound practitioners could actually cooperate to such a degree, and love one another that much, to assist people in coming to their greatness. The limitation is great with only one voice. I may not be able to match the total accuracy of what I hear. But I can match the emotional component, the particular rhythm, the inflection, or the in-between-notes.

JL: When you reflect back, matching with sound, what are you hearing?

VD: By matching the emotion, feeling, blockage, or wound, you are acknowledging its presence, its qualities, itßs identity. You are touching this place in a way which is like reaching through a doorway and inviting it to move through. A familiar example of this dynamic is matching the components of frequency of a crystal glass and it shatters. The crystallization of memories in our nervous system can be restructured similarly.

This can not be accomplished through set formulas, it must be done through listening, feeling, matching the components of the individualized placement.

JL: So in teaching people your system, how to do your work–I gather that it is not about set techniques, but about how to listen.

VD: Yes. We seem to think that formulas are a much more intelligent system than the system we are listening to.

JL: Talk to me about listening.

VD: To listen means that you are not going to know. To listen means that you do not know where that body is to move to. It is not listening when a practitioner assumes they know where a client's body is going to go. And they immediately impose a stroke, a posture, or a sound into the body. We then get impressed because we create a change, forgetting that change is probably the easiest thing to create. The body is a malleable system, a water and fluid system. So getting change is not very difficult. But does it sustain? And does the person look more like themselves or do they look more like a system? Are we liberating their more essential wisdom or are we imposing a formula? Does the person lose one part of themselves to reclaim another? That is what I am the most interested in.

If we are working toward an evolutionary form, the person will look more like themselves. You wouldn't be able to identify that they had done this or they had done that kind of work, or they were of that culture. What you would notice is that they seem more confident and comfortable. They seem to have more grace about themselves.

JL: How do you accomplish this?

VD: This is quite a process. And it varies with each individual. Generally speaking, I focus on teaching others how to move their own emotions without hurting themselves or someone else. Initially, we start with expressing or moving that which is not ours-just stuff. It might take the form of a daily ritual of sounding the superficial layers that our environments (physical, emotional, psychological) create and shape. This is the beginning of learning discernment.

I challenge my students to become more and more passionate about this process of getting acquainted with themselves, learning to follow and track their various 'fragments,' judgments, and opinions about who they are, how they've been, etc. It's the challenge of being intimate with oneself. And the main focus is listening to oneself not another. The practice of listening is so multi-faceted. Listening is having compassion. It is not trying to impose healing or a belief system. In the context of the body, listening is being willing to not know where the direction of the movement to receive sound is. Being willing to not know so that one is available to change frequency, direction, or rhythm when needed. It takes dedication. But, the results are so rewarding. One starts being more honest with themselves and truly begins to embody more of Self. Eventually the results of this gathering of the various fragments of self can be felt physically, as more sustenance, more security, and more Self present. And that means more choices, more freedom of expression-and finally, the possibility of cooperating with others, the ability to start listening to another.

If I know what's mine–what actually gives me my uniqueness. I don't have to worry about having more or less than others, or about something being taken away from me. I can then accept what makes me different from others. This is the awakening of the part of the memory that knows cooperation is the most efficient use of our relationships.

JL: So it is very much a teaching of the honoring of our individual process.

VD: Yes, and I believe we're now on a threshold of needing to let go of that which was in order to go into a place of not-knowing. This is an evolutionary step. It is a definite shift from a mindset that considered one form, one mantra, one chant, to be appropriate for everyone in the group-to accepting an individual, intuitive knowing of what is right for oneself.

THE WELL CELL

JL: I notice you pick your words very carefully.

VD: I treat my words very carefully when I am talking to someone because I think that the power of sound is great. I never say to someone that they have a blockage or that "you are off here." I basically say, "I think there could be more movement there, more ease, more room." I truly do not know what anyone's healing looks like. It looks all ways. And after nearly 30 years of tracking what I have thought healing or wellness was, I am presently at not-knowing. And, actually it really isn't even my interest these days to know.

I try to talk to a person's well cell. You can track and chase what is not right forever. There is no end to what's not right. I'm an expert at it and most of us are. We give people degrees for their ability to critique. We call this intelligence. I call this indulgence. In all genuineness, I would like to see what would happen if we tracked what I call 'the well cell,' the place before the original cause memory said, "God doesn't like me. I'm not good enough for God."

Years ago, I got to listen to a Norman Cousins lecture. He touched me deeply. He was one of the first people that said the diagnosis was what speeded up the dis-ease or actually even a wrong diagnosis had the power to kill. The power of the diagnosis is enormous. And people coming to us, listen to us. It is a huge responsibility.

JL: In listening to your album, *The Well Cell.*[2] I hear a major concept of yours is waking up the amnesia of wellness. So in talking about a person who comes to see you, they have had life weigh so heavily on them that....

VD: ...They can't remember that they're up to anything, that their life is meaningful. That they have a purpose. It can happen to any of us. None of us are immune to it. That is what we need to remember when we are with someone who has forgotten. When we are living honestly with our own stories, then someone else's story is not so unmanageable, or uncomfortable for us. So when someone drags themselves in, on some level, I just say, "I hear you, you've got some amnesia!"

JL: Right! No blockages, just a little amnesia!

VD: There is an amnesia epidemic out there.

JL: The foundation of your thought is that we forget how well we really are?

VD: Yes. And, I think that it is really supported. I think it needs a lot of reminding. It is a daily affair to try to stay awake. That's why I try to remember to track my *Well Cell* along with those that I am working with.

USING SOUND IN TREATING ABUSE

JL: Let's talk about the use of sound in relation to abuse.

VD: Through the years, I've had many clients that I initially could not touch them with my hands, but I could touch them with sound. Many times they were coming to me as their therapists knew they needed assistance in remembering. Many times they were coming because they already knew their story, but knowing the story intellectually might not move the paralysis in the feeling/emotional body. Or free up the body of memories they kept at the chronological age of the abuse.

My work is to give the body the freedom of expression that has been achieved on other levels. What I have learned and have been able to assist many folks with is the possibility to mature memories. Bring the memory to present time. And Sound is a wonderful tool of teaching people how to use their voice to keep the movement in their bodies. Especially if they should go through a crisis, or are in environments that cause them much fear. Sound is a remarkable tool for empowering people. People actually get to reclaim their voices. And, it doesn't have to be through many of the dramatic, sensational ways, we were using in the late 60's and early 70's, what was called Primal Scream. It worked for many and for many it was shattering and not an honoring of the timing, rhythm, geometry or the support for such expression. Sound can not only work on a tissue level of stored memories, but has the ability to work at the cellular level.

JL: How do you do that?

VD: In the exact same way I would work with any other person or concern. The basic principle is in listening. And the many ways of listening are longer than this interview. Many times, the words of describing listening start sounding so complex, even though the practice of listening is a complex math. We're always looking at timing, rhythm, the angle, the dimension, what is above and below, how is the body being supported, is the environment creating a holding pattern, how am I in my body? Am I diagnosing my own holding, my own judgments, and on and on...

Mainly listening comes from a place of being in acceptance with whatever the body is revealing. And, not trying to impose some idea of healing.

JL: When I think of geometry, I think of grids and patterns; being turned at different angles, as if on a computer imaging screens. Do you think that all emotion basically has an end point and a beginning point? That if you can tap into what that emotion is, then through sound, you take it back out through all of the different patterns until finally it is completely out of the system?

VD: Or into the system or wherever it goes. I primarily think that what happens is that the memory gets accepted. Acceptance seems to create trust, trust seems to engage rest, rest helps create movement, movement assists transformation. I think that a layer of emotion has a beginning and an end, but in the body, it's not going to look so linear or symmetrical as the memory guides us closer to the root of inception. A lot of what we name as emotions, may not be emotions; they may just need to be sounded to create the atmosphere of movement. The actual sound shapes of different emotions create a geometry or vortex , openings into places we need to enter. This is a major piece in my more advanced trainings-transforming the limited belief structures of how many emotions we have and the various opinions and judgments we may have about them. However, initially we must know our own stories, and be honest about them, to be willing and able to let them go and take the risk of not knowing what comes after our stories.

JL: So instead of making these negative, or hurtful feelings and thought forms into an adversary, you make them into an ally?

VD: You neutralize them. You move from a place of them making your life unmanageable, to a place of neutral. You move to a place of some choice. Instead of having to follow the mind or the emotions down any track they may want to go, you become more the director of yourself. This is not through denial, not through imposing another thought form, but from expressing what is there Through practice this becomes quite easy and very quick... seconds. And for many of us this is a daily affair to become available for neutrality. To keep experiencing that harmony lives in discord is a huge lesson in itself.

USING SOUND IN TREATING GRIEF

JL: I'd like to know more about the use of sound in dealing with grief.

VD: I made a tape expressing grief, entitled *Transforming the Blues into Gold.*[3] I did this out of my own experience of losing some of my dearest closest friends and family members between 1985 and 1992. I felt the loss of about 40 people from cancer, AIDS, accidents, a variety of ways.

I learned a great deal about grief needless to say. I learned that it looks all ways, just like any healing, and that the way a person dies is as unpredictable as the way the are birthed. I had been a mid-wife, prior to being with people dying. I sounded a lot of memorials, a lot of ashes. I made the tape because what I experienced was that most of us have very little permission to grieve, even from ourselves, and seem to know very little about it. *Transforming the Blues into Gold* is about how to unravel the process of grief, permission to express, and assistance in doing so. There is a lot of anger and a lot of not knowing, sadness, craziness and despair. And it keeps moving and moving and it is like a spiral. It spirals into a lullaby. It is a variety of the Blues.

JL: So when someone comes and you sense that they are bound by grief, what is your process in helping them move this emotion?

VD: When someone comes to me and they are dealing with their own grief–on whatever level it may be–betrayal, rejection, incest, loss through death, their own dying, surgery... It's always basically the same process, just different formulas, to fit the uniqueness of the person and their situation.

Many times, people need more support from themselves before they can go any farther with their process. They may have lost parts of themselves through their situation. So, that would be the priority, finding ways for them to feel more present. It is probably not possible to heal or feel if we not embodied in the body, literally. Grieving our loved ones, grieving our own dying, is so very challenging as we keep trying to find answers, to make this somehow perfect. And maybe intellectually it all comes out clear, but possibly emotionally, it doesn't matter to us, if it was their time, or God's way. Grieving has such a spectrum of feelings; it looks and feels all ways. And it literally takes it's own time and shape. Grieving becomes a major teacher in not-knowing.

JL: So your grieving client comes in, wants to move through the blockages. Your ability to match the sound that you are hearing, and to be able to essentially let that energy know that is not alone, that it is okay, that it doesn't have to be changed, that it can be acknowledged, that it can be sung with, touched, that you can find harmony with it…

VD: …That God hasn't forsaken us. That we will or can live through this.

JL: So where most of us feel like we become discordant, dissonant... to the point that it starts affecting our systems, our organs, our functionality, you work to help make peace, find the harmony within, through the use of sound?

VD: Yes, through the use of expression of sound. Voicing the discord and following the discord. What I learned as a child-which I didn't know until I got older-was that the discordancy that I would hear in most humanity, if I listened to the discordance and followed it, would travel into harmony or harmonics. Always.

JL: If you followed it?

VD: Yes the same concepts of listening, accepting, not pushing, not working hard, letting the body dictate the song. This is learned. I do not mean to suggest that is simple. Although it is once we are introduced bodily to this understanding. Following is truly not having an agenda, a recipe. It is like the path many of us are on, there are no maps. We have to rely on the inherent blueprint of the intelligence of these systems. It is truly an example of walking our talk. If I had one thing that I could assist or teach it is somehow to reduce the fear of taking the risk, the risk to not know.

THE MOMENTUM OF THERAPEUTIC SOUND

JL: Vickie, why do you think that therapeutic sound is gathering such momentum at this time?

VD: Mainly, as it is in incredible tool. One of the more powerful possibilities around. And, we actually know very little about it.

However, it is clear that one can use sound and create very dynamic change rapidly. And we, as a people, love that immediacy. But, a fix-it system of sound will not necessarily engage cooperation and acceptance. Sound has the possibility of giving us a more powerful tool to date, control, manipulate, and re-arrange form. Sound has forever been used for healing as well as for the use of control.

And, without an internal integrity system to cue us, to give us feedback; that this is not mine, or I choose not to have that imposed upon me, or I choose to allow this frequency to come in, or that is not my business… a discernment system needs to be in place. So then I find I have great concern on the many possibilities in the future that sound could possibly be used or abused. There is a responsibility, we as practitioners have, to truly do our own inner work on a daily basis and to always promote this for our students and clients.

I am very excited about sound as a *fix-it* tool. I would like to see us being able to match frequency as an example, with the accurate dosage of insulin and inject the frequency of insulin. This is just an example. I question bombarding the body with frequency instruments. As I do not know any instrument [machine] that has the discerning ability to know how to differentiate the emotional/feeling body. And, to be able to measure the appropriateness of dosage given the full history of the client, not just the symptoms.

I feel we have so much to learn in the use of sound as medicine, as therapy. I caution us not to try to move so quickly from the place of our excitement. Rather, to gather ourselves individually and then as a group. To take the risk to cooperate and not-know together for a moment and pause and see what is revealed.

And, pause so as not to repeat history. Not to be too impressed by the fact that sound can create change, produce shape. But to sit with that knowledge, or information, and see what actually happens to us over some time and see its sustainment and cause and effect. In our own personal laboratories, we must not market formulas. This is a liquid system. Very ready and available for change. Change is about the easiest piece to come by.

JL: What is so important about sound as self-embodiment?

VD: The key factors of knowing one's own rhythms, frequencies, varieties, is that cooperation seems to start being a possibility. That if I know what's mine, which actually gives me my uniqueness, then I do not have to fear that you have 'more or less' what I have or that you can take for me and so forth.

Actually, I believe the more we embody ourselves, the more willing we are to want to cooperate with others. Again, this is part of the memory that feels lost, the memory of an inherent intelligence that knows cooperation is the most efficient use of our relationships. One major key is in the acceptance of our differences. And this is an inside job. The outer is a possibility, if we do the inner.

The evolutionary form begins with the willingness to take the risk-of-not-knowing, to support harmony within discord as it evolves into cooperation. This requires patience and trust. This harmony within discord exists from the tiniest molecular level through our physical and emotional bodies. It lives in our relationships to self, environment and others. Take a risk; continue moving. ✧

ENDNOTES

1 Aston Patterning information is available from Vickie Dodd or P.O. Box 3568, Incline Village, NV 84450. (702) 831-8228.

2 *The Well Cell* can be purchased from Vickie Dodd. See Appendix B.

3 *Transforming the Blues into Gold* can be purchased from Vickie Dodd.

10

The Power of the Drum

A conversation with
Arthur Hull

Arthur Hull is the author of *Guide to Endrummingment,* a small book and video.[1] He is a master percussionist and instructor at the University of California at Santa Cruz. Having traveled the world studying rhythm and percussion, Mr. Hull has become a leading facilitator of *Village Drum Circles.* These workshops use rhythm as a pathway to community building. In 1994, he conducted over 150 workshops at Fortune 500 corporations throughout America. Arthur is a warm and humorous fellow. He perceives rhythm as fun, sexy, communicative, transformative, cohesive, and a link back to the beginning of time.

This interview took place in Berkeley, California, September 1995.

Entraining — Or is that Train Wrecking?

JL: Let's talk about entrainment.

AH: Entrainment is a very powerful element inside a community drum circle. I bring that up in my programs. I say to my groups that one end of the spectrum is entrainment and the other end of the spectrum is a train wreck. The difference is very minor. One way, everyone is playing their thing, but they are not playing it together with an agreement about pace or pulse or a point of reference. The other way, everyone is still doing the same thing, just about, but the small adjustment is that they are all focusing towards, and giving up a little bit of what they do, in order to be a part of a pace.

JL: How do you define entrainment?

AH: The art of giving up the small self to be a part of the big self.

JL: As someone who has been using, playing and teaching rhythm all your life, what would you say are the effects of rhythm on the nervous system?

AH: The nervous system is something doctors want to come up with quantification of effect. This is what the organization, Rhythm for Life,[2] is doing with music therapists. They are trying to quantify the effects of rhythms on certain aspects of health. They are studying the effect of rhythm on Alzheimer patients, the elderly, etc.

Yet, here I am, on their advisory board, and I don't have a scientific clue as to the effect of rhythm on the nervous system.

THE POWER OF THE GUN, GO, AND PA

JL: What was going on in that drum circle today?

AH: It was different for every single person. I have to stay generic and let each individual take the effects of drumming with a group of 25 strangers into their own deeper experience.

In a drum circle the other night, there was a woman and she was crying. My first reaction was that I hadn't even done my *heart meditation* yet. Basically, she got in touch with something on an emotional side and it was time to release it. So she sat there and she just quietly cried. Tears were running down her face. She was in total ecstasy in the drum circle, in touch with her pain. The rhythms had opened up something, someplace, somehow. She was crying, didn't want to stop. She wasn't embarrassed, she was so deep inside the release. It wasn't the pain, but the release that was the ecstasy. She was releasing pain, and this means that the pain was leaving her body. It is like Rolfing; you get in there and squeeze that place where something has been held for many years. And rhythm has the ability to do that.

JL: How is that?

AH: It isn't the rhythm, but the tool that sends the rhythm. There are three basic sounds on these drums: there is your base note, your tone, and your slap. We are talking about any drum that has a body, even a frame drum has a tone and slap, but the bass is weak. It is essentially a finger drum. I am talking about body drums like a *djimbe, dumbek, conga*... there are thousands of drums with bodies that are longer than the head is wide. Within these hand drums, there are these three basic sounds that you will find on any body drum on the planet. These sounds are from the African master drummer, Babatunde Olatunje. Any other African would give you another name for the exact same sound according to what drum they are using. The bass sound is *gun* (pronounced gune). A *go* is a tone and a *pa* is a slap.

When everybody hits a *gun* at once, that is the head of the drum vibrating air out through the body of the drum, out the smaller hole. It is a compression note. It is the body of the drum vibrating, not the head. The *gun* pushes the air out and creates a sub-sonic wave that can rattle windows, break glasses, and can travel for miles. It goes to certain chakra points. A sub-sonic wave is a wave that is not heard, but can be felt. It is so big that the bottom of it would start at one end of a large room, arc up to the ceiling half-way through the room, and reach the bottom end of the arc of that sound wave at the other end of the room. This means it has the powerful potential to travel through walls and long distances without deteriorating.

JL: So what happens when that wave hits your body?

AH: It makes you want to move and dance because it is vibrating the movement point in your body. This is the area of the second chakra, also known as the *hara*, the *don chen*, the *kath* point. Give it a culture and the culture will give it a name.

This brings up an interesting thought. Do the dancer's make the drummer's drum, or do the drummer's make the dancer's dance? The answer, of course, is yes.

So that *gun* sound goes to that part of the body, right below the navel, and that is what makes those elderly folks call the police when we hold drum circles in Santa Cruz. It's not the noise, it is the sub-sonics massaging an area that they never gave anyone permission to massage. They don't know this. It is an unconscious thing.

JL: So when you speak to a drum circle and say that the people in the circle have just been very intimate with each other, that they ought to at least get to know each other's name, this sub-sonic sound is what you are referring to?

AH: If they've just been drumming together for the last two hours, they have been making love with each other.

JL: You are saying that the rhythms have the effect of essentially creating a sensual massage effect?

AH: You bet. Here I am in the middle of 400 men at a gathering. One large reason why drums are a part of the men's movement is not just because of the search for the primal self, but the fact that you can sit in a circle and massage all these men, and get a massage in a very intimate way from all these people, without necessarily touching. Then when they are done, they give each other a hug and don't even know each other's name.

So this is level one, with *gun*, the sub-sonic bass note of the drum. Level two is the *go*. This is the tone and it goes right to the heart chakra, the place of the emotional context. These tones are the melody of the drum and are the perfect balance between the body note (*gun*) and the head note (*pa*). The tone is the drum head itself, singing as it vibrates the drum. The *gun* is the drum vibrating from the head pushing the sound out. The *go* tone is on the edge of the drum between the center and the edge of the drum. This is the tone that vibrates the emotions.

The third tone is the *pa*, the slap on the drumhead that affects the thoughts in the head. It is this sound from the drum that actually stops time. It is really a lot of it mixed up together that stops time. But the slaps have a tendency to get the words out of your head. It makes space in your head; you stop to listen to the space between the thoughts. This is the goal of *Vipassana* meditation. To get to the place where you can create the absence of sound, through the drum, then you have created a perfect meditation effect of clearing the mind. It is then that you can hear the silence that allows for the inner wisdom to come forth. The slap knocks your thoughts away. The slaps are vibrating both the head of the drum and the head of the drummer. When you hit the tone, you are hitting the balance point between the head and the body and you are vibrating the emotions.

JL: Have you experimented with these different tones?

AH: I do over 140 drum circles a year. When I work in the corporate zone, I don't dwell so much on the effects of these different sounds. But when I work in the personal growth seminars, I really do concentrate on these different elements. People come looking to do this part of work.

For example, I will say that we are going to do a *go* song. We play mostly in the region of this sound for 1/2 hour. When we finish, people will often relate a sense of pain from long-held, unreleased experiences.The tones are the melody lines and the melody lines sing the songs. And the songs soothe the emotional states and what came out was lots of emotions about relationships and pain or loss.

When we did nothing but slaps *(pa)* for a half hour, hardly anyone could talk after that session. In the heart, everyone was crying. In the body, everyone was into a darker and deeper physical stuff. You have to remember, this was not about rhythms, but about the tones.

We are back to entrainment. We entrained together with our own personal rhythms. This whole alchemy works together in an on-going, never ending process. Rhythm mixes all these things up and goes right to whoever needs it, at whatever level. When we just worked in *gun,* we entrained into that experience. When we entrained in the tones, in *go's*, then we spoke from the feelings, the heart. In the areas of the *pa's,* there is mostly silence. The head space is the epitome of calming and quelling the mind. After playing here for awhile, hardly anyone could speak because the mind had been massaged and it stops time.

JL: What about the effects of the *gun* sounds? The ones that go to the sexual regions?

AH: Well this is what I was telling you about the elderly people that get so angry at us when we play near their homes. Even though they do not consciously know it, when they walk up to a drum circle, enraged, it is because they feel they have been violated sexually because they are getting their sexual chakras stimulated just by being in earshot of the sound.

JL: So it has nothing to do with the rhythm, it is merely the sound that has this effect?

AH: It is the sound of the drum that is being carried by the rhythm. But as a player, you have to be careful. If you play from just the place of *gun, go,* or *pa,* you can get stuck in that place. If you play from a place of imbalance, where you are just playing to the groin or the head, then you are not really martial-arting with your playing, you are attacking the drum. This makes your hands hurt, you get stuck and you are not letting it flow through you. If you are playing just from the heart, then you are inside your emotions and you might want to go and play by yourself. Your stuff is going to come up and interfere with your drumming. Having all those tones surround your heart chakra will cause you to release a lot of pain. These frequencies of the drum tones are a potent device and ought to be used with awareness. Like water, these vibrations go to the places where they are needed most. Water seeks its own level. In the same way, these vibrations go to the place in the body that is crying for attention.

JL: You are saying that the body, in its own innate wisdom, knows how to pull the nutrients from the sounds that are being carried by the rhythms.

AH: That's correct. I'm working with gang kids from San Jose. I work at the Foundation school where juveniles who have been thrown out of their regular schools can go for nine months before they are re-admitted. Many attend here because they are trying to stay alive. Otherwise, they are just out on the streets or stuck at home which is not as safe as school. The other day, this guy came to one of my drum classes. I saw him wailing on the drum. Afterwards, he came up to me and said, "I just came to school today, and I knew that I was going to hit somebody. It didn't matter whom, I just started looking for someone to pick a fight with. It didn't matter why, I just needed to punch someone. But I hit the drum instead and I feel really good because I don't have to hit anybody now."

This is one of the major powers of a drum circle because the rhythms create that massage. And each person uses it as they need it. Now a shaman, writing on their one-beat drone, can actually go into states of consciousness that actually transcend the limits of what we perceive to be our physical realities. These are states of consciousness that aren't just illusionary, but to the point where you can watch some guy lean on a spear, see it go right through his body and watch him stand back up again and say, "hi," and pull it out and no blood comes out. These kinds of states are totally amazing.

The drumming is the horse, on some level, of this kind of interdimensional work. It helps you ride through these places if you have the training or inclinations. There are many stories of the shamanistic use of the drum. The Shamanistic approach is heavily documented. What we are doing is addressing the healing aspects of rhythm.

Following the Heartbeat to the Beginning of Time

JL: Tell me about the rhythm of the heart beat and how you use it in your work.

AH: This is a universal pattern. Different rhythms in different cultures have purpose. Most cultures play rhythms for a purpose, not just a musical expression for rock 'n roll. They accompany rituals that connect them with the earth, or with each other, or connect them to the spirit. These three things are universal: the use of rhythm to connect to the earth, each other, and to the spirit. Part of the ritual is the drums themselves.

With these rhythms, for instance the *clave*, is a universal pattern. In fact, it is the representation of question/answer, push/pull, question/resolve, squeeze/unsqueeze. It is yin/yang. It is the exact same process that makes your heart beat. It is an ever-ending flow. But it also, in rhythm, represents the universal laws of rhythm in balanced motion. This *clave* beat represents that. The word *clave* is like a keystone that supports the two sides of an arch that would fall in on each other without the two-sided stone to balance it out and support the two sides. It holds them together and makes them strong. It is a universal pattern that I found in Bangkok, in France, in South Africa, in Beliz, in Mexico, even in Australia, inside the digeridoos.

JL: Are there other universal rhythms?

AH: Yes there are! When you look at the rhythms, each have purposes inside the cultures where they are played. But the purposes are different. But when you go to the rhythm of the heartbeat, the purpose is parallel. There are many universal patterns, but they have different purposes. The universal pattern of the heartbeat has a universal purpose which is bringing the community together.

When I use this rhythm in a drumming circle, I use this exercise to have people get in touch with their heart. I literally have people put their fingers on the pulse in their wrists or on their neck. They close their eyes and I have them listen to this rhythm. I guide them into the rhythm of their own heartbeat very slowly and deeply. Then I let them know that they are hearing the sound of unconditional love. This heartbeat doesn't care who you are or what color your skin is, what your religion is, or what culture you are from. It doesn't even care if you are a good person or a bad person. It just keeps on beating; it will not stop until it's time to stop or something dramatic stops it. It just keeps on beating. And once they get in touch with it and listen to it for a long time, I ask them to listen to it in a new way. I tell them it is not even their heartbeat, but it is their mother's. That she gave it to you, that she taught it to you when you were in her womb. It is the sound of unconditional love. And as we listen deeper, in complete silence without any drumming, then we are actually getting in touch with the mother's heartbeat. Recognizing that this was actually a transference; that it came from her, that she taught it to them, basically gave them this heartbeat. Listening even deeper, this is not the mother's heartbeat, it is your grandmother's. She taught it to your mother. All of a sudden, through listening to the sound of their own rhythm, they are kinesthetically in touch with their own ancestors that are living and pounding inside them. They begin to understand the deeper meaning of the genetic will to preserve the species. This is not even the sound of the grandmother's heartbeat, but your mother's mother's mother's, and it goes all the way back. By this time, we are following the heartbeat back to the source, to the great mother, to the beginning of time. Depending on the context of the community I am speaking to, I hand them the water and they drink it. By this time, we are all gone... It is a very deep experience. And as they come back out to the circle, they have a realization that everyone around them is actually hearing the same pulse, and that we really are all related, that we really are all brothers and sisters. It's a very enlightening thing and a powerful moment and prayer. When the rhythm starts to come out of this experience, it leads to an amazing drumming and personal experience. This exercise is my signature closing of most of the groups that I lead. I rarely do it in the corporate setting. However, the only time I felt comfortable doing this was at Apple Computer.

PERCUSSION*itis* — *I GOTTA DRUM...*

JL: Why do people drum?

AH: The drum calls them. Maybe 10% of the population are already drummers. They have *percussionitis;* they were born with it. I was one of those. I couldn't help not drumming. They express themselves rhythmically. They may not even have discovered the drum yet, but they are drumming in their sleep with their toes, grinding their teeth rhythmically, or tapping on the dashboard while driving down the road, or acknowledging the cracks under the car as they drive, and maybe even getting into trouble as they accelerate just to hear the change in the rhythm of the tires on the road. But they don't even know they are doing this.

Why do people drum? Like a little kid that discovers a stick... It extends his reach and he discovers the power in that. The drum extends your aura and your spirit. If you take the head off and turn the drum the other way, it is a cone, like a megaphone. The drum is nothing but a megaphone for the spirit. You put your hand on the drum, you touch and dance on the head. You are really playing with your front feet. With the drum, you dance the kinesthetic dance of your personal rhythmical experience. You have placement on the drum where the dance is. You add tonality and technique and a whole vocabulary emerges from which the unconscious speaks your spirit. It's kinesthetic, its the heart, and its the brain. And it massages everything and it expresses everything and it releases everything.

JL: Is there a negative use of the drum? Can rhythm be abused?

AH: Anything can be abused. Rhythm is just the vehicle to carry consciousness and the drum is the tool. Rhythm is the vehicle to carry the power to make things happen. In our world we think that power comes from machines or muscles. There are many cultures that have up to ten definitions of what power is. There is a kind of power that is generated in a world of time, through rhythm that generates the power to make things happen. You generate energy in a drum circle. You generate energy when you are by yourself, but when you drum with others, the power of your selves gets into the bigger self.

So what are you going to do? You can take it home and have sex. You can take it to a sacred place and transcend yourself through it. You can use it to heal. You can use it or you can say a prayer and send it out.

JL: Use it like a vehicle, like a musical note, for your own intention?

AH: Right. When we all get together and play together, with a joined intention, we are sending out a very powerful energy force field into the universe. Using rhythm with intention is a very powerful thing.

JL: Therefore just in the same way as different cultures can have different contexts for the same rhythm, I see that some people are tuned to toning, another use of sound, but different than rhythm. They are using tone as the vehicle for their intentionality. Other people are hard-wired to the use of rhythm and they use that vehicle to carry their images and intentions.

AH: Go beyond the belief to the experience. There are people who believe in the power of prayer. The power of prayer is the power to make things happen. Drumming and rhythm, at the core, is actually prayer in motion. ✧

ENDNOTES

1 Arthur Hull, *Guide to Endrumingment*. Available directly from Arthur Hull. See Appendix B.

2 Rhythm for Life, as of 1996, is no longer in existence.

11

ENTRAINMENT – THE EFFECT OF RHYTHM ON THE NERVOUS SYSTEM

A conversation with
Janalea Hoffman

Janalea Hoffman is a composer, author, music therapist, and self-titled "Entrainment Queen." This caught my attention. There are plenty of composers, music therapists and authors around. But in my travels in the world of sound, I've only come across one self-proclaimed *entrainment* enthusiast. And when you put music, words, and therapy together with the knowledge of this simple physics principle, there is a powerhouse to be recognized. Before talking with Janalea Hoffman, Kansas City author of *Rhythmic Medicine*[1] and thirteen therapeutic music albums,[2] let's look into entrainment.

The concept of entrainment is one of the theoretical pillars of the house of music and sound. On the most superficial level, entrainment is the reason rhythm is so infectious; it causes us to tap our feet and bob our heads. But internally is where the real action is taking place. External rhythms actually change our brain waves, heartbeat and breath rate. Simply put, *entrainment is a physiological process whereby major pulses of the body speed up or slow down to match a stronger external pulse.* Entrainment is a mysterious principle that few know about, yet it has been around forever.

Curiously enough, while accessing abundant research data-bases, I found little on the effects of resonance and perception of musical meter. The exploration of this field appears to be non-existent. We know that rhythm effects us; moving us, propelling, exciting or fatiguing us. But why does it effect us this way? Can we harness the power of rhythm to fuel us or cool us? How can we use this physiological phenomenon with awareness? These are but the initial questions that come to mind.

Understanding the concepts of resonance and entrainment is of great importance for anyone who wants to knowledgeably participate in the growing field of therapeutically-based music and sound. For it is through these related processes that external sounds and rhythms can either heal or create havoc. This pertains to dense cement walls and glass windows as well as the most delicate brain waves and organic cells.

Janalea Hoffman, an outstanding authority in the field of music and healing, is determined to introduce individuals to the power of music. Speaking at conferences and conducting seminars throughout America, Ms. Hoffman teaches the natural healing techniques she has researched and developed since forming her own company, *Rhythmic Medicine*, in 1978. Her work has been praised and supported by the medical community, as well as countless satisfied clients from her private music therapy practice.

The following interview was conducted in September, 1995.

JL: Let's talk about the history of your company, *Rhythmic Medicine*. Why rhythm?

JH: When I went through music therapy school, I learned about all the techniques and using music with children. When I got out of school, I did my internship in England with autistic children. It was fascinating to me the rhythmic movements that they made. Rhythm is important to everybody since we all have rhythm going on in the body all of the time. These autistic children, who weren't relating on very many human levels, had this association with rhythm that was really powerful to them.

Then when I came back to the States, I got a job at a psychiatric hospital and I tried out all the techniques I learned in school and found that a lot of these techniques were geared to emotional things and self expression through music. I began a search for techniques that I felt comfortable with. I ended up taking a course from Helen Bonny, who started the Guided Imagery through Music program (GIM).[3] I was very impressed with that and had some very powerful inner experiences with that myself. Some of the experience I had I would put on the cosmic level; they were very spiritual and internal. There was no questioning that the relaxation techniques combined with the music and imagery had really affected my life.

So I went back and started experimenting using the guided imagery and music with clients. I found that some of the clients really responded the way I had. Not everybody but a percentage did. So I left the state hospital and started a private practice because I wanted to explore the guided imagery with music more. I was told that this would never work in Kansas City because it is much too conservative. People said I would have to go to California to do this! But I stayed in Kansas City and the way I promoted it was with a lot of lectures and workshops, free lectures to drum up business. I found that every lecture I gave, I always got a few new clients. People seemed to be fascinated.

And then I worked in a private practice with a very innovative psychiatrist. This was in 1980. He was very interested in holistic health. He had a person in the office doing bio-feedback and me doing the music and relaxation work. This was a great opportunity to work with really mainstream clients.

At that time, most music therapists worked in institutions, like psychiatric hospitals or school systems. But mainstream America, with your average stress problems like ulcers and headaches, there were no music therapists working with them. So that was what I did I with this psychiatrist; work with people who had hyper-tension, migraines, mild depression. As I used the guided imagery technique, I found it was very effective with a lot of people. A little esoteric for many, but it worked.

Then I found the work of Dr. Lozanov[4] and his work with baroque music at sixty beats per minute. It was really impressive to me. I was working on my Masters thesis at the time. I decided to base it on helping people lower their blood pressure by using the 60 beats a minute baroque music.

I set up the study with 35 people. I had doctors referring patients for this study. It worked very well. I kept getting more patients with hyper-tension who wanted to use this process. And so that is how I really got started with the rhythm. It was after my Master's thesis using the 60 beats a minute music. It worked so well in getting people to relax. As I explained it to people, I found that they could relate to it, even the most conservative people could relate to the rhythm idea.

I found that about 30% of the people that I used this process with complained about the baroque music. Somehow, they had negative associations with classical music. So I started writing my own. With the exception of the baroque music, I couldn't find any other music that was really rhythmic to do the kind of therapy that I wanted. I began experimenting with writing in this tempo pattern and found people liked it. Ever since then, it has been a passion of mine–the whole idea that the body responds to rhythm so dramatically.

I love teaching people about it. The blood pressure study was so successful, that's what got me started. I also am into the esoteric aspect of all of this. But I think part of my mission is to be a bridge to the real conservative types that just can't relate to the guided imagery sessions at all. However, they can relate to slowing their heartbeats down to 60 beats a minute though. It keeps them alive!

In 1988, I made a tape called *Deep Daydreams.* One side was music at exactly 50 beats per minute. It was a very steady rhythm. I started using this tape to teach people to slow their body rhythms down. I call this method *Musical Biofeedback.* People relate to it so much that I've been doing that process since.

JL: Why do you think that the body responds to rhythm?

JH: Rhythm is the basis of what keeps us alive. The heart beating all day and night is all about rhythm. To me, real regular rhythms are a metaphor for life. The medical literature shows that your heart is the most regular rhythm when you are born. One of the big signs of aging is when you start getting irregular heart beat patterns. There is research showing that irregularity of the heart beat is a major sign of decay in the body. It is a sign of chronological age or if you are prematurely aging. They can tell just by measuring the heart beat.

MUSICAL BIOFEEDBACK

JL: How do you use music to deal with someone who has an irregular heartbeat?

JH: I teach them what I call musical biofeedback. I have them listen to music with a very steady beat that they can relate to, that they can hear—that is easily hearable and simple. I have them match their heart beat to the beat of the music and practice doing it.

JL: How does somebody match their heart beat to the music?
Can you control your heart?

JH: First of all, if you have music at 50-60 beats per minute, their hearts will try to entrain to that naturally. As you tell them to try and match their heart beat to that music, it is already slowing down by itself anyway. As they practice it, they feel their beats falling into synch with those rhythms and it feels good. They like it. It makes them feel in control.

One of the things taking place is that you are helping someone become aware of a conscious process. And by being conscious, they are combining a meditation technique known as focusing. You can achieve this safe effect by having somebody meditate by staring at a spot on the ceiling. But that is harder for people. This is one of my arguments for using the music.

If you tell someone who is stressed to go home and meditate, it is very hard for people because they can't shut off their thoughts. But when I tell them to go home and work with the musical bio-feedback, they have something to focus on and an excuse to go within and listen to their own hearts beating. It all works together and people are motivated to do this. I have found, with this technique, that people feel something happening that is dramatic enough that they are motivated to do it again. This is what happens with a lot of people who meditate. But a lot of people who took Transcendental Meditation stopped because the results are pretty subtle. Whereas with this process of musical bio-feedback, you really are feeling something happening. You are feeling more in control and there is more motivation to keep practicing it.

JL: So the net result is that someone who has too much stress or hypertension can listen your tapes, which are recorded at specific tempos corresponding to relaxation. In doing that, their heartbeat is going to naturally match the tempo of the music through a process of entrainment. And if they are intentional with that process, then it will happen even faster or easier. They basically learn to slow down their own heart beat or relieve their tension naturally. Do I have it?

JH: Yes. And another way to look at it is if a person is stressed, if you look at their life, they are surrounded by fast rhythms, where things are not calm in their life. By listening to the music, it helps them learn about slowing down. It gives them a point of reference.

When people get stressed, it is usually a gradual build-up. It gets worse and worse and it just feels normal to them. Their frenetic lifestyle is just so normal to them that they may know intellectually that they are stressed, but at some level they are thinking, "Well, this is norm, and there is no changing it." So by using the music, it is almost like giving them an example, a point of reference of another rhythm that works for them. I've had people say to me that they practice listening to the tape. Then they will be at work and they don't have the tape, but they will remember that rhythm and they will start to entrain just from remembering it.

I had a Parkinson's patient that I worked with rhythmic tapes a lot. Not just slow ones but fast rhythms also. Parkinson's patients get this thing where they may be walking along just fine but then they try to step over a door jam or a line in the sidewalk, and they just freeze and their leg won't move. This patient told me that if he just thought of the rhythms of the music, his legs would start moving again. I have actually watched this with a number of Parkinson's patients. It is so rewarding, but you have to get people thinking this way.

JL: Do you use musical biofeedback in your practice?

JH: Yes, a lot. And I find it to be very successful. People love it. I'm teaching a lot of nurses and social workers how to use these tapes and they love it also. So many professionals are attracted to the use of sound –they know it has an extraordinary power–but they don't have any musical talent and they don't know how to use it in their practice. The Musical Biofeedback tapes gives them a tool. Many nurses and social workers run relaxation groups and anti-stress groups and they relate to what I am doing because it makes logical sense to them and they can feel something happening in their bodies. They take these techniques and use them with their clients.

ENTRAINMENT — HOLISM AT THE HIGHEST DEGREE

JL: Let's talk about entrainment. How would you define it?

JH: To me, entrainment means that all living things are constantly trying to harmonize with each other.

JL: I think about that all the time. Here we are, built to be a strong, independent system, yet we have this entrainment mechanism inside, where we actually keep 'reaching' out. It's as if our different pulses are saying, "Oh, can I just come over here and merge with you right now." How strange that we have this mechanism built into all of us that is so eager, trusting, and willing to match up and merge.

JH: I think that's what intrigues me so much about entrainment. It is such a spiritual thing, really. You can't be exposed to anything for too long without it effecting you. That's why when negative things are on the radio or TV, and people say that it doesn't really affect anybody, that it's everybody's right to say whatever they want and that it doesn't have any effect, or launch violent shows and say that it doesn't cause violence. It is just amazing to me. When you understand entrainment, you realize that it everything affects everything.

JL: How have you researched rhythmic entrainment?

JH: Mostly by working with people. I haven't done too many formal studies. I've done some, but I haven't written them up.

JL: I've found there is so little formal research out there about this. It is basically an unknown concept in our culture. When you talk to most people about entrainment, they think you are talking about taking a train ride or something. Yet I believe, like you, that it is such a strong concept and that it completely changes your context. Why do you think that entrainment is so unexplored?

JH: I think it is because people want to believe that they are in control of their lives. Look at something as mundane as public transportation.

It is really hard to get people to carpool and share. They have their family and their lives and they want to be independent and in control. And the whole idea of entrainment is so spiritual. I think that when you understand entrainment, you get that it is affecting you all of the time. I think that it is a scary thought for people. It means that everything is connected and that you have to pay attention. And people don't want to.

JL: You mean that you have to pay attention to the fact that everything is connected.

JH: Yes. Entrainment is connectedness; it is holism at the highest degree.

JL: So there actually is no way to divorce entrainment from the concept of unity, is there? When I think about entrainment, I think it is ultimately a deeply spiritual device that our bodies come equipped with. Just in the same way as I have a colon or a liver, designed to do their jobs, my body is equipped with a process known as entrainment, whereby my autonomic pulses will reach out to stronger external pulses. I am amazed that there is such small attention given to such a big concept.

JH: I am too. I think it is incredible. Yet, when I talk about it, nobody ever argues with me.

JL: I know there is internal as well as external entrainment. That our organs entrain to each other just as our pulses entrain to external rhythms. Do you know anything about the natural flow of internal entrainment between the different body systems?

JH: I haven't really looked into internal entrainment. I know that acupuncture and energy meridians work together. I assume this has to do with entrainment. It seems that if one meridian is out of balance and the others aren't, then given the right extra energy, they'll all try to help each other and balance out. But I don't really know much about that.

JL: Do you think there is a danger in using external processes of entrainment? Can it do harm?

JH: That's a question that I get asked a lot. Someone will say, "I already have low blood pressure and heart rate. Will this slow music make it go any lower?" I've observed that people with low rates and pressure, when using the slow music, there is a balancing effect. It slows down whatever the stressors are internally that you can't put your finger on. And there is this balancing that occurs and they feel more relaxed afterwards.

JL: Can the process of entrainment be overused or abused?

JH: I imagine it could, especially if you are using really fast rhythms. Some people do that anyway; they are addicted to chaotic sounds and they are using it abusively. But if they knew about entrainment, they wouldn't do that. I believe they are using it unconsciously. I believe that they abuse entrainment in aerobic classes, especially when music is played with a real heavy metal sound. This stuff will make you feel sick! Heavy metal fast rhythms have a very negative effect on me; it makes me feel terrible.

JL: What are the most viable tempos for increased concentration?

JH: I think the 60 beats and the 50 beats both work for increased concentration. I know that sounds funny to say but that is what I have found. With some people, they need the slower ones. It is something I would like to do more study on.

JL: The difference between 50 and 60 beats per minute?

JH: Yes. But basically, most people will respond to both. One thing I'll get sometimes, with people who don't meditate or with whom the idea of going within is really new... When you play the 50 for the first time, it will be really stressful for them. It is so much slower than they are used to. It makes them feel out of control sometimes. It's scary when they feel this entrainment. I had this happen just last night when I was doing a seminar.

It was a very conservative church group. They were wanting to know more about holistic health. I was surprised to find how many of them admitted that they were afraid while listening to the 50 beat music. I asked for feedback and heard people say that they felt more stressed after listening to the 50 beats per minute music that before. I can predict, every single time, that somebody says that it stresses them more, that "...this is too slow for me, I need that faster music," that they have never meditated or done anything like this. What happens is they entrain so quickly that they interpret it as a loss of control. And that is scary. So what happens then is the body speeds up, the heart rate speeds up. That's why it seems like the opposite effect that they are supposed to get.

JL: So one needs to present a sense of safety with the entrainment.

JH: So when that takes place, what I do is take them through again. I say, "Let's do this again and think about it as losing control and that is what you are feeling. But this time, you know you are safe in this room. I'm not going to let anything bad come of this. Only good can come of losing control with this."

JL: When you've done a lot of self-work, losing control is OK. You have the understanding of the Big me and the Little me, and knowing that you can hand it over and that you will be safe. But I imagine without this work, the idea of losing control is a terribly frightening experience.

JH: Oh yes. Sometimes, when I do sessions with mainstream, conservative people, they get terrorized. But once I explain to them what is going on, it is a whole different experience. The second time, they're just thrilled when they feel their heartbeats going down.

There are some people that are walking around resisting changing their lives. Something is guiding them to change and they are just resisting with everything they have. They are the ones who are scared to death of this because if they did entrain and they listened, some voice would say, "You better do this. Quit resisting."

Once I explain that this fear of losing control is normal, and that it is just their body entraining so quickly and it is something they are not used to... Most people haven't heard 50 beats per minute music. Once I explain it–if they have any fascination to it at all–they start to open up.

JL: Do you find the idea of mixing 50 and 60 and even up into 70 beats per minute, works with the fluctuations of the body's pulses, since they don't stay at one constant rate for long?

JH: Well, that is an interesting thing. Musical acupuncture is pretty steady. But it goes from 65 down to 50 beats per minute.

JL: Did you do this using the ISO principle?[5]

JH: Yes, it helps when working with somebody who is a little more stressed, taking them down gradually. But I find people–I haven't done a formal study, but I have taken thousands of people through this–will entrain whether you start out faster and gradually slow down or if you give them the slow one to start with... they'll entrain anyway. There are a few people that do better with the principle of starting quicker and then moving down. I think that if you studied it, you would find that there are certain personality types that would relate better to that then others.

But the idea of the real steady, verses the rhythms changing some-some people really prefer a really steady beat. It is truly soothing to them and they really relate to it. Others, it just seems to drive them nuts! From an entrainment point of view, they will all entrain to the steady rhythm. Everybody, even if it drives them crazy, they still will entrain to it.

ENTRAIN WHAT?

JL: Are you finding that there are more people becoming interested in the field of entrainment?

JH: They are interested in the idea of entrainment. There is no field. That makes it sound like it is comprehensive. For me, I have noticed that there are more people showing an interest in the last year than prior to that.

In terms of seriously wanting to do research studies... I've tried for years to get people to help me do research. It's really difficult. I've been the only one really passionate about this. I've talked to so many people about collaborating on doing research on entrainment, and couldn't get anybody.

JL: Are their any studies on entrainment that you can refer to?

JH: My book came out in April '95. And I think that I found everything that existed which wasn't much. I am writing up a study that I just did with people with AIDS. We worked with entrainment and lowering heart rate.

Most of my knowledge comes from working literally with thousands of people, big groups, small groups, and individuals. Now, I am working on doing more research. I'm about to work with a group in Kentucky on the use of entrainment with Alzheimer patients.

JL: Do you think that rhythmic entrainment can be as effective as binaural beat frequencies?

JH: In theory I really believe in the concept. But I haven't heard any music containing frequencies that I have been able to listen to. I can't handle the synthesized sounds.

JL: In talking about entrainment, we've been addressing the use of external rhythm and how it effects the heart rate. What occurs to me is that binaural beat frequencies work directly on brain waves while external rhythms work more on the breath and heart. Have you tracked the effects on brainwaves, verses heart rate and breath?

JH: No I haven't. Again, only because of lack of research money. It is something I would really like to do. I am moving into a time of formal research; this is what I need to be doing for the next few years. This will help bring further credibility to the concept. I am just writing a grant for research into the use of entrainment with AIDS patients and how it would effect the immune system.

JL: What do you think are the most effective applications of rhythmic entrainment?

JH: I think it is wonderful for pain problems, hyper tension, heart arrythmias, migraines, depression. But to really work best with depression, you need a skilled therapist to work with. What I've done with that is use entrainment to get people beyond the barriers and then they find out why they are really depressed.

Entrainment and Pain

JL: Tell me about entrainment and pain.

JH: Just going within yourself really helps a lot. The idea of entraining your heartbeat… The fact that you are going within yourself… When people have pain, they just want to resist it. They want to go outside their bodies. So what you are doing is helping them go inside the body. That always helps relieve pain. It is one of the techniques therapists use. Hospice nurses will say, without music, "Now go right into the center of your pain." If someone really trusts their therapist, they might do that. But it is really hard. Who wants to go right into the middle of terrible pain? Everybody wants to run away from it. But it is easier when you are entraining with the music to go into it.

JL: If you go *into* the pain, does it actually lessen the trauma?

JH: It is like going into the eye of the storm. You see, the resistance is what actually exacerbates the pain. When people actually achieve going right into the middle of their pain, there is a dissipation effect that occurs.

JL: What other elements of sound do you use to increase the efficiency of the rhythmic entrainment?

JH: In my album, *Musical Acupuncture*, I use a lot of strings. I think they are very helpful. The other aspects of it are more intuitive for me. I don't really think that anyone knows about what intervals do what. With rhythm, there have been studies that show the effects. But when you get into what harmonies or melodies do this or that, I don't know of any data on this. There are too many factors involved. My orchestration is totally intuitive.

ENTRAINMENT IN THE FUTURE

JL: How do you see entrainment used in the future?

JH: I see doctors giving their patients tapes. If someone came in with heart arrythmias, they would try entrainment tapes before drugs. The doctors could have the patients find out if this is a stress reaction and have them practice entraining to a tape and solve it that way. That is often what the problem is. People have learned to cope with their stress by hyper-tension and then they get a heart flutter that becomes a pattern. Just like people have a facial twitch or blink their eyes as a stress thing. I believe that entrainment can help to reverse many patterns that we have created.

I believe that in the future, doctors will use entrainment tapes as a means of helping people de-stress.

JL: Do you think that de-stressing is the major power of entrainment?

JH: Yes, right now that is what we know. I think that it also balances energies in the body, but I don't know how really.

MUSIC AND CO-DEPENDENCY

JL: How do you use entrainment in your life?

JH: I'm so aware of entrainment that I use the knowledge of it as a monitor of harmony or discord in my life. If things are out of synch, I look to see what are the factors and analyze their effects on me. In talking with people, I find that it helps them define something that is going on in their life. The concept of entrainment helps them define something in their life that they haven't been able to put their finger on before.

This may seem like a funny analogy. But if you are familiar with the concept of *co-dependency*, a lot of people have been co-dependent in their lives and they have never been able to put their finger on what that behavior was. Then they go to a co-dependency twelve step group and realize that this is what has been driving their behavior. They come to understand that they have a problem with setting up boundaries with other people and that's one of the reasons that things don't go smoothly in their lives. But they never had the word *boundaries* to define it before, or the word co-dependency. And that is how I see entrainment; it helps people define things that they just couldn't put their finger on before.

JL: Janalea, I think that this is very original thought process here. I have never heard anybody talk about music, let alone entrainment, in relationship to co-dependency before. And you have an entire chapter in your book on this subject. Both the concept of co-dependency and entrainment are such extraordinary bodies of knowledge. Interestingly enough, they are both so subliminal in the psyche of the American psyche.

JH: The knowledge of both of these fields gives people a reference point, an understanding, a definition that they didn't have before. You can call it pop psychology, but if it is helping people to define something in their lives and make better choices, than it is a good thing.

JL: Author and psychologist John Bradshaw speaks about how the study of family systems and co-dependency will come to be seen as some of the greatest breakthrough work of the 20th century.[6] I am a strong believer in this knowledge of co-dependency.

Let's talk about entrainment and co-dependency. They come from such different areas and yet look at how they converge. You mentioned earlier about how some people have trouble with entrainment because they don't want to give up control. When you look at people who are into serious control over every aspect of their lives, from a co-dependent standpoint, it is because things were so out of control when they were children. Strict control is the only way they feel safe.

JH: I have found that some people who don't have good boundaries and they start entraining with somebody, then they essentially merge with the other and then lose themselves in the process. If they understood entrainment and co-dependency, or one or the other, they might not merge to the point of being so destructive. They would be able to separate and say, "Hey, I'm this person, and that's this person, and I'm finding myself entraining with them and I don't really want to."

JL: Within the world of co-dependency, is entrainment a merging on a certain level?

JH: Yes, I think so.

JL: And if one holds the concept of merging as being a behavioral pattern that you don't want to have–since merging comes about because of a lack of boundaries–then where do we sit with that?

JH: Usually the person who doesn't want to give up control, on the one hand, may be out of control on another level. They may be very co-dependent and merging like crazy on some level. It becomes pretty complicated.

MUSICAL ACUPUNCTURE

JL: Let's talk about your musical albums. Your most recent release is called *Musical Acupuncture.* You describe this project as music that "... can conduct and move energy in your body very similar to an acupuncture treatment without needles." Tell me about this.

JH: On the album, I instruct people to visualize the tones coming into the acupuncture points. If they do that, I have found most people feel energy moving in their meridians. I did a study with a health association where we took 120 people through the 22 minutes of the *Musical Acupuncture* tape. Heartrate and blood pressure went down significantly with everybody. But another thing they reported was that people who had an acupuncture treatment previously felt more energy moving with the tones than they did with the needles. I thought this was really fascinating.

JL: Well I listened to this tape about six times. It was over a weekend when I was in bed sick and I fell asleep every time I put the tape on. The fifty beats per minute just put me right out. I tried to stay awake to listen to the spoken visualization but never made it. But I appreciated how it allowed me to sleep when I was having so much trouble resting because I was so ill.

JH: Some people do use it for sleep but it is more commonly used for pain problems. When they visualize these tones coming in, it helps them feel pain being relieved. They feel tremendous. People report tingling and very intense experiences of energy moving in the body. What impressed me about this study was that people felt more energy moving with the tape than they did with the needles.

I think that there is a certain amount of anxiety about needles. Needles are not fun. Even with acupuncture, where the needles are thin and barely in your skin, a lot of people are squeamish. Whereas it is not scary to have a tone come in.

JL: Do you know about people who work with tuning forks, placing them on acupuncture meridians?[7]

JH: I hear that they get wonderful results but I've never experienced it myself.

JL: I love the concept of it, it makes such sense to me.

JH: I do too. But something that makes me nervous about it is that the tuning forks are so intense. Just the thought of having one of those on my body scares me.

JL: But you put on a set of headphones and take that frequency infusion right into your brain. And yet the idea of taking a direct tone off your body concerns you?

JH: Yes, a little. I'd like to experiment with that; I think its a great idea. It's a personal thing. I'm a really sensitive person. I'm a little person size-wise and super sensitive to external sounds or tools used on my body.

JL: I've experienced tuning forks once. I found it to be a wonderful experience. I loved the feeling of the tones spreading through my bones. Because I feel safe with tone, it was not a problem for me at all.

JH: When you were asking me if one could 'abuse' the concept of entrainment... Tones can be wonderful but they can be abused. For example, do you know of the Tibetan bowls? I worked with a Japanese doctor who said to me, "In Japan, we use these bowls one time to start the meditation. It centers everybody; you never do it more than once at the beginning or ending of the sessions."

But I went to a conference where someone had a booth where they were constantly ringing them. I had such a terrible pain that night. And I could feel the tone going right into my abdomen. I do believe that you can over do tone. A little of something can be too much.

JL: Could it be the same thing with rhythm?

JH: Yes it could.

JL: So ultimately, like anything... How much spinach do I eat? How much ice cream? How much aspirin do I take, how much Vitamin C? How much do I use a tone, ginseng, liquor?

JH: That's right. And I don't think that anybody really has the answers to that yet. But the positive thing is that tone is such a gentle, non-threatening thing, that I don't think it is too scary.

JL: Rhythm is?

JH: Yes, even the tones. For me, I knew when I'd had too much of the Tibetan bowl tones but I couldn't leave because I was in the booth next door. It made me sick but it didn't send me to the hospital or anything. That's what is nice about music and tone, it can be damaging but it is not like drugs and that kind of thing.

RHYTHMIC MEDICINE

JL: Which are your most widely used tapes?

JH: *Musical Acupuncture, Musical Biofeedback* and a tape called *Musical Massage. Musical Massage* is around 60 beats per minute, doesn't have a real steady beat in it. It is probably my best-seller cause it is really pretty. All natural instruments. People like that. My children's meditation tape is very widely used. *Music for Mellow Minds* features piano and cello. It has a guided meditation for sleep. *Musical Hypnosis* is specially composed metered music designed to take someone from a stressed heart rate of 80 beats per minute down to a relaxed heart rate of 50 beats per minute. This tape can be used to simply slow down physiologically or can be used to facilitate a state of hypnosis.

JL: Tell me about your videos.

JH: I have an instructional video that explains how to use music as a teaching tool. I also have a nature relaxation video that is mostly used in hospitals. It is 45 minutes long and the music starts at 60 and goes down to 50. At certain points, people are asked to match their heart beats. It is the musical biofeedback technique used in a video format. It is most effective in hospitals because people are lying in bed. It's nice for them to look at the visuals and do it with their eyes open.

JL: Of all of your tapes, which is your favorite?

JH: *Musical Acupuncture.* But I also have made a tape for a smaller market called *Music, Imagery, and Parkinson's.* This is just for people for Parkinson's disease.

I was invited to some of their symposiums and they were devastatingly boring. These poor people with the disease and their care-givers at the conferences would just be falling asleep during the sessions. They were only pharmaceutical in nature; nothing was ever addressed about the emotional aspects of the disease. So I made this tape.

There is research that shows that if Parkinson's patients visualize the neurons connecting in the brain, that it helps them reduce symptoms. You see, they are constantly resisting their tremors. There is an exercise on my tape where I have them do an exercise where they let their tremors go and just enjoy the rhythm of it in their bodies. And they love it. They are real relaxed afterwards and their tremors are a lot better after they do that.

JL: So again, it's about giving in instead of fighting?

JH: Yes. This Parkinson's tape is so obscure. And it is such a shame that there is nothing out there for these people. People aren't addressing the emotional aspects of diseases like this. And I believe it would make such a difference. ✧

ENDNOTES

1 Janalea Hoffman, *Rhythmic Medicine; Music with a Purpose* (KS, Jamillan Press, 1995).

2 Janalea's products are available by direct-mail. Call (888) JANALEA for a catalog.

3 Guided Imagery through Music (GIM) is the brilliant work of Helen Bonny. This musical therapeutic program is detailed by Carol A. Bush in *Healing Imagery & Music; Pathways to the Inner Self* (OR, Rudra Press, 1995). For information about GIM therapists or trainings, write: Carol A. Bush, Mid-Atlantic Institute, Box 4655, Virginia Beach, VA 23454.

4 The work of Bulgarian psychiatrist, Dr. Georgi Losanov, is highly discussed in *Superlearning 2000,* by Sheila Ostrander and Lynn Schroeder (NY, Delacorte Press, 1994).

5 The ISO principle, used in the context of the therapeutic applications of music or sound, refers to the process of 'meeting' the listener at the emotional or physical state when they are first introduced to the music, and then slowly, through entrainment, ushering them into different states of being.

For an excellent discussion on the ISO principle, as well as an over-view on the use of music as a healing art, refer to Kay Gardner's fine book, *Sounding the Inner Landscape; Music as Medicine* (ME, Caduceus Publications, 1990).

6 John Bradshaw is widely known for ground-breaking work with co-dependency, the 'inner child' concept, and family systems. He is the author of many

books, including *Bradshaw On: The Family* and *Healing the Shame that Binds You* (FL, Health Communications, 1988).

7 The use of tuning forks on acupuncture meridians has been studied by many, including French sound researcher, Fabien Maman. Dr. John Beaulieu's *BioSonic Tuning Forks* are designed to retune and rebalance the body's energies. Information and products are available from *Tools For Exploration,* (888) 748-6657.

12

THE POWER OF HARMONICS

A conversation with
Jonathan Goldman

Transformational music and sound is as old as creation itself. In the timeless tradition of exploration, the finest pioneers strive to bridge the wisdom of the past with the challenges of the present.

Jonathan Goldman lives high in the Rocky Mountains, 45 minutes west of Boulder, Colorado. Like Vickie Dodd, Robert Gass, Don Campbell,[1] and musician Kitaro, Jonathan picked Boulder as his base camp. He has helped to define this area as a Mecca of music and sound in the healing arts.

An authority on sound healing and a pioneer in the field of harmonics, Jonathan is the author of *Healing Sounds; The Power of Harmonics.*[2] He is founder and director of the Sound Healers Association and owner of a music label, Spirit Music. Recent recordings include *Dolphin Dreams, Gateways: Men's Drumming and Chanting, Trance Tara,* and *Song of Saraswati.*[3]

Jonathan has been empowered by the Chant Master of the Drepung Loseling Monastery to teach sacred Tibetan overtone chanting.

This conversation took place in Boulder, Colorado, October 1992.

JL: My first question about your new book, *Healing Sounds,* concerns your acknowledgments. You dedicated this book to many people, the most respected in the field, but first and foremost, to "...the Masters of the Sound Current." Tell me about that.

JG: This is an incredibly powerful first question.

JL: Are people such as Drs. Alfred Tomatis, Peter Guy Manners, or Hans Jenny, "Masters of the Sound Current?"

JG: The people you just named and the others thanked in my book are musicians, teachers, healers and scientists whose work has made an important contribution to the field of sound and music for health and transformation. However, I also have inner contact with different beings who give me guidance and teachings about sound. They give me information about what I'm supposed to do and why I'm supposed to do it. These beings are the Masters of the Sound Current to whom I've really dedicated the book.

JL: How do you work with them internally?

JG: In stages of deep meditation, dreamtime and soundings. If I have specific questions about the effects of sounds, how certain sounds may be utilized to benefit people, I will often be able to get information. One of the great pieces of information that I have gotten was to do my left-brain homework and gain scientific information that verifies the intuitive.

JL: I notice there is a 4 page, single-spaced bibliography in *Healing Sounds*. Which of these books have had a predominant effect on you?

JG: Randall McClellan's *Healing Forces of Music* , John Beaulieu's *Music and Sound in the Healing Arts*, and Peter Michael Hamel's *Through Music to the Self* are very important books. I also really like *Sounding the Inner Landscape* by Kay Gardner, *Nada Brahma* by Joachim Ernst Berendt and *Music: Physician for Times to Come* by Don Campbell. At the beginning of my journey into sound many years ago, Steven Halpern's *Tuning the Human Instrument* was a great eye and ear opener.

JL: Tell me about your book, *Healing Sounds*?

JG: My book focuses upon sound healing and specifically *vocal harmonics*, the ability to consciously create two or more notes at the same time. In my mind, vocal harmonics are probably the most powerful sonic healing and transformative technique I've come upon on this planet. I feel I am a privileged pioneer in the field of vocal harmonics. With the exception of certain esoteric traditions such as Tibetan monks, Mongolian shamans, etc., who seem to utilize these harmonics for sacred, healing purposes, most Westerners who currently work with harmonics have been doing it as an artform. I am really more interested in using these as transformative modalities. Not just because they are beautiful to listen to, but because they may have an extraordinary effect on the mind, body, and brain. Vocal harmonics may actually alter vibrational fields.

JL: You state on the back cover of your book, "There is no sound as pure as that of harmonics..." What exactly are harmonics?

JG: Harmonics are aspects of the sound spectrum which display universal principles. Through them, we may unveil the mysteries of vibration. By learning to create vocal harmonics, it is almost as though we are removing dark glasses and seeing for the first time. Actually, it would be more like listening for the first time. To be able to consciously hear and create harmonics is somewhat like being able to perceive the aura of sound.

JL: Are they only a phenomena of sound?

JG: Harmonics, or overtones, are found throughout the physics of the universe. Much the same way as a prism breaks light into different bands of the color spectrum, you can take a sound, which is complete with all sorts of other sounds, and break it into a fundamental tone with all these harmonics above it.

The overtones geometrically correspond to the fundamental sound. The first overtone vibrates twice as fast as the fundamental, the next overtone vibrates three times as fast, and on and on. This phenomenon is displayed throughout physics, botany, and chemistry. From the movement of electrons in the atom, to the planets around the solar system, it seems the concept of harmonics is a picture of a larger, macrocosmic aspect of consciousness. Things are harmonically related, the ratios are similar. Overtones are also responsible for creating the timbre of our voices. And without overtones, all instruments would sound alike.

FREQUENCY SHIFTS

JL: Jonathan, what does *healing* mean to you?

JG: I'd rather use the word transform. Transform means to change. I think of transformation as altering vibrational frequencies; bringing them up, or down, to another level. Transformation means change, and most change is beneficial. To me, healing is such an abstract concept.

Last week, I answered a letter from a woman who was suffering from numerous problems, and she asked if I had ever heard of somebody completely healing, or curing themselves using sound and tone. I wrote back that I had. And yet, on the same point, I have known of other people who have had similar conditions, who have used similar sonic techniques, and nothing has happened.

I suggest that healing might be a very complex, multi-level process. At what level is the transformation needed? Is the healing or vibrational shift needed on the physical and/or emotional, mental or spiritual level? Has one chosen to take a particular imbalance on as karmic belief, or because there were problems stemming from childhood?

It goes on and on. We could talk for an hour, speculating, trying to hone in. And yet, sometimes, you don't even need to know. Harmonics are so multi-layered that sometimes, without even being able to pinpoint a specific imbalance, it will disappear. Harmonics can resonate the brain, body and the etheric fields at the same time. This is a miraculous thing. And yet, sometimes, nothing may happen at all.

JL: Can vocal harmonics shift our frequencies?

JG: Absolutely.

JL: What do you mean by a frequency shift?

JG: The ability to change the vibrational rate of our beingness. In terms of pure healing, on the physical level with the use of sound, there is a metaphor that I employ as have others before me. When you are in a state of harmony, then you will also be in a good state of health; that dis-ease is an out-of-tuneness of self. There is the belief that if a particular organ is vibrating at a frequency that is out of harmony with the rest of the system, then this is called disease. If you can project the correct sound down onto that particular organ, you could cause it to resonate back into harmony.

RESONANT FREQUENCIES

JL: Is this what is known as resonant frequencies?

JG: Yes, exactly.

JL: Therefore, if I'm over-stressed, causing my adrenal glands to blow out, then by using the concept of resonant frequencies, it would be possible to correct my adrenal deficiency? That by using a series of tones, directed at these glands, it would cause them to shift back to their healthy rate of vibration?

JG: Yes, and there are a number of ways of doing this. I am particularly interested in using our own voices to do this. And there are a number of vocal techniques for this. There is also instrumentation that can project a sound wave into your body and there are tapes that will project sounds into your ears in order to trigger the area of the brain that stimulates the adrenals. There are mantras, whereby you interrelate your chakras with different body systems and the sounds that you make directly stimulate that specific organ. You can tone the sound and actually feel the adrenals vibrating.

JL: How do harmonics relate to resonant frequencies?

JG: They can be one and the same. Through using our voice, for example, you may find that specific vowels relate to particular parts of the body.

JL: And vowels are related to harmonics?

JG: Yes! A key to harmonics are found in the vowel sounds because within each vowel are contained specific harmonics that may be amplified through techniques to create vocal harmonics. Vowel sounds are considered sacred in a number of different spiritual traditions.

Edgar Cayce talked about ancient Egyptian priests being able to resonate the different energy centers of their body with the seven sacred vowel sounds. This dates back at least 5,000 years, and is probably much older than that.

REDISCOVERING AN OLD SCIENCE

JL: So when we talk about this *new* science of using sound in transformation, we are really talking about a very old science that we're newly rediscovering.

JG: Yes. For example, the Vedic traditions from India have mantric forms, different types of sounds that are used to effect, charge, balance, and soothe different portions of the body. It is speculated that this process of sound in transformation of the body and spirit goes back 5,000 to 10,000 years.

JL: So in the same way that the AMA can discount acupuncture as an untested system, given that it is only been practiced for about 5,000 years, the use of sound in healing is not taken terribly seriously.

However, we know that ancient shamans, mystics, and temple priests were also musicians. They worked with sound and music, not necessarily for entertainment, but as a transformative device.

JG: Yes. And we have taken this unique, extraordinary power of sound, of which each of us have the ability to use our voices to be able to become one with the Source, and instead we've created Gods and Goddesses of sound. And who are they? The superstars. We pay homage to them by buying their records and goings to their concerts. We have empowered them to entertain us, while forgetting about our greater ability to entrain ourselves with our own sounds.

Entrainment is the process of locking in with a more powerful vibrational rate. Perhaps, we have lost focus of our own ability use sound to change our vibratory fields and to come into Oneness with all. The ancient priests and priestesses used to do this. Even not so along ago, we would sound together; be it in churches, temples, or communal toning sessions. But it seems that we've mostly forgotten this; we mainly allow the professional musicians to do it for us now.

JL: This reminds me of how, politically, we have done the same thing; given away our personal, individual power to our governments. We now expect them to take care of us. And what I hear you say is that we have also given away intuitive, individual power by putting music and sound in the hands of others. We've created icons, and now expect them to take care of the sound thing; therefore, we don't think about taking care of it ourselves.

JG: Even one step further... We compare our sounds to the professionals, and conclude that since we don't meet the standard they set, it can't be a very good sound. Consequently, we should not make any sounds; just leave it to them! So many people in this culture have blocked throat chakras. Wounded singers, wounded listeners. So much of this comes about from comparing ourselves to other people.

We have this thought that if the sound is beautiful, its healing. I'm not necessarily sure that this is true. Sometimes, for example, to break up thought forms or energy patterns, a discordant sound is really useful and therapeutic. It can help to break us out of a mode. I'm not saying that beautiful sounds aren't wonderful and don't have a purpose. And yet, for ourselves, making different sounds can sometimes seem quite unpleasant to other people, yet they can be making us feel wonderful.

Don't get me wrong. I love beautiful sounds and they are very harmonically related. What I want to make clear is how judgmental I have discovered we are about our own sounds.

INTENTIONALITY

JL: There is a basic distinction that needs to be made. You are not talking about sound for entertainment; you are working with sound for transformation.

JG: Yes, they are totally different purposes. A lot of this has to do with intentionality. I was just reading *The Book of the Hopi,* and they talk about *The Spider Woman* creating the first two beings on the planet through sound. And one of these being's purpose was to go throughout the planet creating and activating sound everywhere. Why? To give praise and homage to the Creator.

This is what a lot of our initial sounds were about. When people got together to drum and chant, it was for ceremonial reasons, to praise the Creator. Later, they figured out the drumming could also be heard distances away and could be an instrument of communication. Communication was the secondary purpose of sound in *The Book of the Hopi.* The first purpose was to become the embodiment of the Creator through sound.

JL: It's interesting that many light years and continents away, Dr. Alfred Tomatis, the Frenchman whom many call the 'Einstein of the Ear', has a similar concept of the usage of sound and the ear. He believes the primary function of the ear is to charge the cortex of the brain, secondarily, to keep us in vestibular balance, and finally for communication purposes.[4]

JG: Dr. Tomatis is a brilliant man. He is also very aware of the sacred sounds of the planet and the therapeutic attributes they contain.

JL: Jonathan, where do you go to find sacred sounds besides chanting?

JG: The birds, the trees, the sounds of nature.

JL: Do you think that's why there are so many tapes on the market with environmental sounds?

JG: Oh yes. The sound of nature is as sacred as it gets. But anything can be a sacred sound, depending upon the intention we put into the sound. This aspect of intention is extremely important. In my book, I have a formula, *Frequency + Intent = Healing.* This means that the energy behind the sound, the consciousness if you like, is as important as the actual sound. Together, they create the transformative experience. It is very necessary for us not to get judgmental about what is and what is not a sacred sound. I was very judgmental when I first became involved in the field of healing with sound and music in 1980. I came from a background of playing rock n' roll and for a few years, I refused to listen to or play rock at all. Then I became aware of the importance of intention behind the music and I again opened up to the full spectrum of sounds found on this planet.

JL: What was the intentionality behind The Jefferson Airplane, The Grateful Dead, The Beatles?

JG: Some of those people, including, believe it or not, Jimi Hendrix, were interested in affecting consciousness and transforming with sound. There was research that indicated some of Hendrix's acid rock music was harmful to plants. This may be true–it depends upon which music and the energy behind it. I also have questions about the studies of the effects of music on plants. But what I do know is that we are not plants. Each one of us is such a unique vibratory being, all at different stages of physical, emotional, mental, spiritual and evolutionary development. Somebody who is 16 years old has a very different hormonal output than someone who is 40!

JL: Let alone a Philodendron or Ficus tree! So, in your offices at Spirit Music, there's a big picture of the Dalai Lama on one wall and of Jimi Hendrix on another. We know the effect of the Tibetans on you. What about Hendrix?

JG: A Hendrix piece, "A Merman I Should Turn to Be", from *Electric Ladyland* was the first trans-dimensional music that I ever encountered. That particular piece is a sonic journey into the evolutionary transformation of the human species. I would listen to it and travel to other places not of this world. In the latter part of his life, Hendrix was interested in healing with sound, as was John Lennon. There were interviews done soon before they died and both spoke of the possibility of healing with sound.

JL: Isn't it sad and interesting that both were taken from us when on the precipice of that work? Do you know of other popular musicians, aside from the New Age musicians, who are consciously using healing concepts in their sound?

JG: I know that Bobby McFerrin and Mickey Hart are both very interested in the healing properties of sound. I speculate that Sting and Peter Gabriel are aware of the ability of sound to shift consciousness.

JL: In the New Age field, who is commercially available that impresses you with their use of healing principles?

JG: Steven Halpern, Kay Gardner, Kitaro, Don Campbell, and most of the other artists on the Spirit Music label, Iasos, and so many more. Mind you, healing is such an individual thing. For example, *Sky of Mind*, by Ray Lynch, is one of the great heart-opening recordings I have ever heard. But since we are all at such different levels of evolution, what works for me, may not have any effect on somebody else. I've heard things that I perceive of as absolutely gorgeous garbage. Other people have extraordinary, metaphysical, healing experiences from the same piece that I can't even bear to listen to! I can't say to them, "Well that's not *really* healing music!" It's also true that music that affects me one way might have a completely different effect on me at another time and place in my life.

NEURO-SYNAPTIC HARMONICS

JL: In *Healing Sounds*, you speak of the power of harmonics as a particular method of the use of self-created sound to help to create harmony within the body.

JG: That's one aspect of it. Singing harmonics is like singing harmony with yourself. Its fun. Something that I am particularly fascinated with is the use of harmonics to resonate the brain. Specifically to stimulate different portions of the brain. Not just to stimulate the neo-cortex that Tomatis talks about, but the ability to make neuro-synaptic connections in the brain. I hope that in the future this will be more thoroughly researched. This could be very important in the field of head and brain injuries, for treatment of strokes and other rehabilitation.

JL: Having the ability to repair our own bodies from the inside out, with sound, is something out of Star Trek. And yet, it makes perfect sense. What other methods compliment this concept?

JG: If you can do self-generated thought coupled with self-generated sound, I believe that you are hitting the bull's eye. I've another formula that I discuss in the book: *Visualization (thought) + Vocalization (sound) = Manifestation.* This is an ancient and powerful formula that is found in many of the sacred spiritual traditions of this planet. Being able to couple thought or visualization with sound makes a much more powerful transformational modality.

INTERDIMENSIONAL WINDOWS

JL: Can anyone learn how to create vocal harmonics?

JG: Yes. Almost anyone can learn how to do the Mongolian (Hoomi) style. In terms of the Tibetan overtone chanting, that's more difficult, but I also give workshops, teaching this sacred technique.

The Tibetan voice is a multi-dimensional sound. It's a sound that is also found in the didjeridu, an instrument played by the Australian Aboriginal people. I wonder how these two traditions, so totally different, created a sound so similar?

The didjeridu is a blown instrument, found by the Aborigines in Dreamtime. The legend of the *Wandjina,* the Dreamtime people, is that they gave the didjeridu to the Aboriginal people, after they had created everything through sound. This was done so that when the Aborigines blew the didjeridu, they could contact the *Wandjina,* who would then come down to them. This is the same thing that happens with the Tibetans. They do an extraordinary visualization while they do this deep bass, guttural harmonic chant, with the intention to bring down their particular Tibetan deities. It may be that, in terms of their thoughtform consciousness, the way they manifest interdimensional, extraterrestrial, or stellar consciousness is through the Tibetan Deity forms. Its a different form and shape and belief system than the Aboriginal people have, but both these sounds create interdimensional windows. I'm quite interested in exploring this.

THE CALL OF SOUND HEALING

JL: Is there an additional book that you could recommend on overtone chanting?

JG: Not yet. There is nothing out besides my book.

JL: Overtone chanting has been pretty much a closed society, so to speak?

JG: Yes, I believe so. But it is my purpose to bring it to the public. It is time that we take these tools and learn to utilize them. They will empower us to explore and experience this extraordinary power of sound; to effect and change our vibratory rates, resonate our body, brain, our etheric fields.

JL: Is your work as a sound healer a calling?

JG: Nothing less. Ultimately I am interested in assisting people in making vibratory shifts using self-created sounds, if possible, or by listening to sounds, to assist in the vibratory shifts that are occurring on this planet. There are so many different changes and accelerations we are going through. Often times, our bodies, minds, our emotional levels are coming into points of total chaos. I believe, that through sound we can reform the chaos into another level of consciousness and being. We can shift our physical vibratory levels and everything else that is harmonically related to this. At this point in our evolutionary shift, it is not only necessary to learn how to do this, it is mandatory. We must learn how to use our own sounds, begin to work with these vibrational shifts, change our energetic levels, change our brain waves, release emotional imbalances, release the baggage that holds us back. It is mandatory for us to do this if we want to continue on this planet.[5] ✧

ENDNOTES

1 Don Campbell is the author of *The Mozart Effect* (NY, Avon, 1998), *Music; Physician for Times to Come* (IL, Quest, 1991), and many other fine books on the therapeutic applications of music and sound.

2 Jonathan Goldman, *Healing Sounds; The Power of Harmonics* (MA, Element, 1992).

3 Contact information for the Sound Healers Association and Jonathan's recordings can be found in Appendix B.

4 See Chapter Three, *The Tomatis Method.*

5 The author would like to gratefully acknowledge the fine research done by Jonathan Goldman, specifically in the field of sonic neuro-technologies. His chapters in *MusicMedicine* , ed. by Ralph Spintge, M.D. (MO, MMB Music, 1992) and *Music; Physician for Times to Come*, ed. by Don Campbell(IL, Quest, 1991) are great examples of the scientific reporting necessary to support this emerging field. Hats off and thanks.

13

LIGHT/SOUND MACHINES

A conversation with
Michael Stevens

I am fascinated by the possibility of greater access to the brain. For our entire lives, we carry this pound of grey matter. Yet we barely understand how the brain works, let alone how to work it better!

I know that I covet creativity, efficiency, proficiency, deep inner silence, health and balance. The brain is key to all of these states. While I use ancient techniques that still make sense, I am compelled to take advantage of high technology.

Marrying the study of the brain with high technology has birthed the field of *neuro-technology.* While still in its infancy, one of the manifestations of computer chips and mind exploration has been the creation of Light/Sound Machines (L/S Machines). Now available in units the size of a TV remote control, L/S Machines come with headphones and blackened sunglasses replete with light diodes. Utilizing the theories of sympathetic vibration, frequency follow-through, binaural beat frequencies in both light and sound, and other miscellaneous techniques, these machines qualify as the 21st century Pied Piper. Want to go to *Thetaland*, the *Alpha Zone*, or deep into the *Delta?* All you do is lay back and push the raised white button. What do you do when you get there? Well, it seems itineraries, hotels, and tour-guides are still being worked out.

Is this kind of inner journey safe? To what extent has it been researched? Is it of value? Long term/short term effects? Fun and exciting? Deep and profound?

In upstate Washington, Fall City is best known for its beautiful waterfall. There I found Theta Technologies. Forget the waterfall, what I want to know is, what's inside the purple storefront in this most conservative of one horse towns? I asked. I found out.

Michael Stevens, co-owner of Theta Technologies, put headphones on my ears, special glasses on my eyes, and pushed the raised white button. Through my closed eyelids came a flashing lights from a program entitled *The 4th of July.* In my ears were sedate electronic tones. There was no pretense of musicality; these were random pitches and irregular tempos. As I slid deeper and deeper (actually slower and slower) into my curious mind until all was very quiet and blissfully still, I realized there was nothing random in this L/S Machine experience. The lights and sound were still there, but way, way back.

The following interview took place in June, 1993.

WHAT WAS THAT, ANYWAY?

JL: What just happened to me?

MS: I'd like you to tell me what just happened to you.

JL: OK, I'm feeling very peaceful, yet alert, focused. I also feel similar to when I get into the very deepest part of a Transcendental Meditation. After a while, when I say, "Enough, time to go", than a part of my mind says, "Oh, not enough. Now we are *really* ready to get deep."

I felt that something was taking place for me when the machine turned off. It was that familiar sense of crossroads; I had the opportunity to drift further into my consciousness, into no thought and no time, or to redirect my energy to conduct this interview with you.

MS: Almost everything that you just experienced was exactly what was supposed to happen. What we did was to create an environment where there was no outside stimulus. We effectively managed to get your brain to latch onto the frequencies of the lights and the sounds that were coming to you. About 40% of your brain is affected by visual stimuli, and about 20% of your brain is affected by aural stimuli. So between the two stimuli, we effect, more or less, about 60% of your total brain mass. What that particular session did was slow the frequency of your brain.

When you lay down there, you were basically in a beta range, somewhere about 25Hz and above (your brainwave frequencies at 25 cycles per second.) That session starts about 30Hz and then it begins to slow, and slow, and you slow with it.

What we do, for the most part, is eliminate all outside stimulus. The only two things that you have to deal with are the lights and the sound. Then your brain attaches to those frequencies and slows to them. All the visuals, colors, or patterns that you saw, those were all from you. They did not come out of the machine. All that comes out of those glasses are little red flickering lights. You do this with your eyes closed, so most of the red is filtered by the capillaries in your eyelids. The rest of the light passes through the eye, to the back of the optic nerve, and causes a splash of neuron excitement, due to the stimulus itself. Your brain then translates that stimulus any way it cares to. So you could take any two people, put them on the exact same session with the exact same things going on, and what they would physically see would be two completely different things. Often times, people go deep enough, quickly enough, that they are not even aware of the lights being there anymore. They go into an altered space, a meditative, hypnogogic state. Often times, people will start with a session, they see the lights going, and then the next thing they are aware of is the lights turning off.

In first time use, it may be difficult to totally relax, simply because of the fact that you are analyzing what is going on. But if you use this machine on a regular basis, you can start calling these states up on your own without plugging into the machine.

JL: As I played with the different settings of light and sound, I wondered what would happen if I turned the lights off completely.

MS: Had you not had the lights on, you would have probably gone only 1/10 as deep as you did. The sound alone is not near as effective.

JL: Would the converse hold true if I were to turn the sound all the way off and it was just the lights?

MS: About 80% of the total effect will come from the lights alone.

The lights will stand stronger by themselves than the sound will. Both eyes are connected to both sides of the brain. Your right eye is connected to the right and left lobes, just as your left eye is. Whereas your ears are connected to only one side of the brain. They switch over; the right ear connects to the left side of the brain and the left ear connects to the right.

JL: Yet when I have worked with only binaural beat frequencies on tape, they have taken me very deep.

MS: With practice and experience, I think that is true. But for the average truck driver who chews cigars and kicks his dog, you could put him on this apparatus with the sounds and the lights, and he will go very deep. If you just put him on with only the sound, he is likely to become distracted fairly quickly. Learning to turn off your mind is not an automatic thing for most people in our culture.

A L/S machine creates an environment. The unit commands you to only pay attention to two things: what you hear and what you see. It could almost be called stimulus deprivation more then an abundance of stimulus. It commands your attention away from everything else.

JL: So while I was *under,* I heard you unlock the front door and come in, answer the phone, etc.

MS: Those were actually distractions. If that did not happen, you would have gone even deeper because there would have been nothing to call you back.

JL: So the process is to distract me with the lights and sound. This pulls me inward while at the same time those same lights and sound are slowing, or speeding up my brainwaves, via the process of sonic and visual entrainment?

MS: Exactly.

JL: Is the frequency of the sound and the modulation of the light in sync?

MS: Basically. There are fifty preset sessions in the *Voyager XL.*[1] In some of the sessions, the sound will go directly to 4 Hz using the binaural beats. For example, with 200 Hz in one ear and 204 Hz in the other ear, the brain can't hear two different sounds and hears the difference between the two, which is 4 Hz. So the parts of the brain that respond to aural stimuli from the beginning of the session are being told to go to 4 Hz. The lights, which are controlling most of what is happening, will start at a frequency more similar to where your brain is when you get onto the device. If the target level is 4 Hz for that particular session, it will slowly ramp its way to 4 Hz visually and then hold there for a period of time. And then ramp back out at the end.[2]

Now on some of the other sessions, the binaural beats will follow in synchronization with the lights. Each session is designed differently. Again, the lights are the more powerful part of what is going on.

JL: And the reason why the visual stimulation is so much stronger is the dual connection in the brain?

MS: Right. It is exponential. Partially what you have experienced on the *Voyager XL* is simply from laying there for twenty minutes. If a person could just lay down and shut off everything for twenty minutes, they would be extremely relaxed. The difficulty, in Western culture, is that they don't know how to do that. They lay down, they start thinking of all the things they have to do, and up they go. They just don't get into the deeper states. It is a real problem with the stressful lives we are living these days. People don't sleep the way they are supposed to. You can do a 1/2 hour session on the *Voyager* and get the same neuro-chemical response that you would achieve in 3-4 good hours of sleep. And you can do it in thirty minutes because it commands your attention. It takes you down quickly, it doesn't allow you to lay there and toss and turn.

JL: What brain state did my session bring me to?

MS: That particular session dips into everything. But you were spending most of your time in the alpha to theta ranges.

JL: And if I wanted to go deeper?

MS: Then we would put you on a deeper session.

JL: Deeper would be delta, which is normally considered deep sleep. So you would put me to sleep?

MS: We could put you to sleep or we could hang you on the edge of sleep. Right at the bottom edge of the theta range just before you go unconscious into delta.

MOTIVATION FOR L/S MACHINES

JL: What is the ultimate motivation for these machines?

MS: Stress relief. And getting people to take some time to think about what they are doing inwardly instead of what goes on just outwardly. We have all the answers. We know what is going on. It is just if we are paying attention to what is going on. So many people give their power away. They go to a therapist, to a hypnotist, a doctor, whatever, when God's intention was for us to be self-healing and to be complete beings on our own. Much of this we can do if we stop giving our power away.

The whole thought process of these L/S machines is to give you the power to decide how you want to feel and when you want to feel that way–instead of being at the mercy of your environment or at the mercy of where your brain wants to take you. You can literally be in a very stressed situation, had a bad day at work, got into a car accident, came home and found the dog had eaten part of the couch! You can then lay down with one of these machines on your head and you decide how you want to feel about all that. You don't have to be angered about it, you don't have to have high blood pressure.

When you take a human being and calm their mind, you calm their body, their neuro-chemistry changes, their releases along the lines of serotonins, beta-endorphins, norepinephrins, all these things that rejuvenate the system. And if a person doesn't get into these relaxed states, they don't get these neuro-chemical releases. If they stay in beta for too long, all they get is beta neuro-chemistry, the chemistry released in the beta frequencies.

If you catch people who have interrupted sleep cycles, they never get totally relaxed in their sleep cycle. If you watch their health, they will slowly degenerate. If you have a bad day, and you do thirty minutes on a light and sound device, you just don't care. You know that you had a bad day, but it just gets put into perspective. "So what, I got into a little car wreck in a traffic jam! So what that the dog ate the couch!" What is important? And you change the way that you feel. By the way, how do you feel?

JL: Quite wonderful right now. I feel very calm. I'm just loving sitting here, surrounded by this hanging ivy plant that is climbing around my neck. I feel pretty alert, not too fuzzy. And yet, at the same time, I am so relaxed I could lay down.

MS: Probably in the next 10-15 minutes, you will feel energized. What you are feeling right now is from laying there for twenty minutes and having your brainwave frequencies slowed. When you first got up, you looked like you had just awakened. Your eyes were a little puffy, a little red in the corneas. But now, your body's accepting all of the wonderful neuro-chemistry that was released in those lower frequencies. So as your body starts to use these chemicals, an initial sort of dopey feeling will begin to go away. And then as a little time goes by, your body will use that chemistry and you start to feel real good.

You asked what was the main thrust of this apparatus. There are several main thrusts. Stress relief is probably the biggest one. But secondarily, L/S machines have shown themselves to be wonderful for insomnia. Additionally, there have been studies done all over the country for migraine headache sufferers. People who have been on medications for thirty years who don't take them anymore. They start to feel a headache coming, they use a session, it goes away, it never comes. It is really extraordinary what the mind and the brain and the body can do if they are just allowed to relax. People are walking such tight wires these days.

People shooting at each other on the freeway. What for? If they all had Voyagers, they could put their rifles away.

The other applications that people are using this apparatus for is Attention Deficit Disorders, Alzheimers, all types of learning disabilities, let alone consciousness expansion. The list goes on and on.

JL: How many companies are there putting out machines like this right now?

MS: In the United States, four. In Europe, three. I don't know of any in Japan. I know that there are light and sound products being sold over there. But the Japanese are interesting, along the lines of what they will or will not jump into. Until the awareness of a product is so high that they know they can make millions, they won't really mess with it. They are into mass, mass production. The world is just waking up to this technology.

JL: When was the first utilization of this work?

MS: The first effective, marketable product was the *David.* That has been on the market for about nine years now. There are two Davids, a Junior and a Senior. The Senior version is really what is worthwhile. You need to have a technician there while you are using it to change settings and things of that nature. It's about an $1,200 machine. More recently, with the breakthroughs in computer chips and technology, it has become more affordable and more portable. Our *Voyager XL* sells for $330.

L/S AND THE MEDICAL ESTABLISHMENT

JL: Is there a danger in using these machines?

MS: The only contra-indication applies to people who have a condition that is known as photo-sensitive epilepsy, where flashing lights will literally trigger them into a seizure. These are people who shouldn't go near strobe lights or mirror balls. A train going by at night, with headlights shining from the other side can be enough to trigger seizures in them.

JL: Anybody who has this condition already knows about it?

MS: Not necessarily.

JL: So somebody could have this condition and not know they have it until they find themselves…

MS: They may have never been in a circumstance where light was at the right frequency, and when their brain chemistry was at the right place for it all to happen. Everything has to be just right for a seizure to be triggered.

JL: Well, what do you do with that, in relationship to your light devices?

MS: We estimate that there have been something like 180,000 people on our products. Of those 180,000 people, we are sure that there have been about ten seizures out there. The statistics say that one in 5,000 epileptics have photo-sensitive epilepsy.

JL: How is this technology regarded by the scientific community?

MS: Light and sound technology is still very much considered experimental. Interestingly enough, we have a lot of doctors out there who are aware of us, who use our apparatus, who suggest to their patients that they call us and get the apparatus, but who won't make any statements in writing. The first thing that happens to a doctor when they step forward with something is their peer group will immediately ask where the controlled test group is, which five thousand people were on the unit and which five thousand weren't?

JL: Is this one of the situations where holistic motivation, tied in with technology, runs into Western medicine?

MS: Exactly! The medical world is just a funny place, a very strange place, in Western society in particular. Its ridiculous–just insanity! This is an alternative to all that. So we don't particularly care what the Western medical people think about what we are doing because generally we don't care for what they are doing!

The habit of, "Doctor, I have a headache," "OK, go home and take some Valium for the next six weeks," has been out of control for a long time. When they do this, they are actually setting the entire person's bio- and neuro-chemistry completely out of whack. They are not taking care of the problem. All they are really doing is taking care of the symptoms. What we are doing here is going straight to the root of the problem. Most headaches are tension related. Many doctors will even tell you that if they have a patient who has a particular affliction or disease, if that person is highly stressed, their symptoms will be worse. If they can relieve some stress from that individual, they will be a less sick patient. Doctors are coming to the point where they are even willing to admit that all disease and all physical ailments are either directly, or indirectly, related to stress.

CREATING AN ENVIRONMENT TO GET AWAY

JL: If you have a machine that can help rollback stress, thereby increasing the strength of the immune system, then chances are their patient load will decline?

MS: It is very important to restate what you just said. The machine itself does nothing. The machine does not relieve stress. The machine simply creates an environment in which a person can actively get away from the stress. Where they can find a center for themselves, a meditative, hypnogogic state where those things fall by the wayside. The machine itself is not like a drug that you take that gets rid of a headache. It is just creating an environment that will allow you to de-stress. There is a session on the machine that is twelve minutes long that literally changes your whole thought process on the course of the day. You can just be up against the wall and wired tighter than a piano string, and just alleviate that stress using these machines. Simply through your own neurochemistry!

JL: Talk about changing thought processes, I'm feeling very laid back right now!

MS: Yes, you probably will be for another twenty minutes.

JL: As I'm sitting here talking to you, I'm noticing my body position. I'm so relaxed that instead of sitting here, I'd prefer to be laying down.

MS: Its the beta-endorphins that are still zipping through your system. These are natural opiates. You're loaded with them right now.

JL: How much of that light was designed to distract me, as opposed to being in a specific pattern?

MS: It is all designed to be in a pattern. That is so concise that even the distance between the flashes is timed.

JL: Binaural beat frequencies have been of great interest to me. As a student of the use of music and sound in the healing arts, this technology has grabbed my attention and not let go. What I find especially interesting is the varied ways different people use it.

Robert Monroe got into it because he was flying out of his body. He wanted to understand why, and then be able to recreate the experience for other people. Tom Kenyon, of ABR, is a therapist and uses it to facilitate psychological work. Brother Charles uses it to move people down their spiritual paths.[3]

HISTORY AND USE OF L/S

MS: It is so simple. It makes so much sense, why didn't somebody think of it before? But actually, people did think of it thousands of years ago.

JL: That was the function of Ting Shas, the Tibetan bells and bowls....[4]

MS: Yes, and even before that, the drums at the fire. That is light and sound in it's purest form! You got one guy over here playing, *dong, dong, dong,* and another guy over there, playing *ding, ding, ding.* And you are sitting between them with the light of the fire flickering at 7 Hz. Between 7-8 Hz is where a fire flickers. Your brain is used to being in a beta state at about 24 Hz. But if you stare at that fire for awhile, your brain is a creature of habit and is constantly looking for something to do. If you and I walked out on the sidewalk right now, the first 8-10 steps that we took, we would probably be out of tune. But after that, we would be walking side by side, stride for stride, even though we have different heights. Its just the way it works.

JL: You are referring to sympathetic vibration, where the weaker pulse gravitates to match the stronger pulse?

MS: Exactly. It's in everything we do. So when you limit your brain to only seeing and hearing specific frequencies, it locks onto them and goes there. That's what it wants to do; to grab onto something. Because your brain is bored.

Another thing that happens with light and sound technology is that you are actually stimulating parts of your brain that you don't normally use on a regular basis. We fall into what is referred to as *thought loops.* When any of us is hit with a particular stimuli, you can hit that person with the same stimuli over and over, and it will trigger a thought in the front of their brain that will travel down a specific path to the brain stem. And it will continue doing exactly that, as long as that person has the same thought process each time that stimuli hits them. Well, by using the Voyager, you begin to burn new pathways because you are creating stimulus in parts of your brain you haven't used. Something has to happen with that stimulus. Once it engages a particular synaptic connection, that signal has to travel somewhere else. If you have just alerted a neuron site that hasn't been stimulated for a period of time, that signal has to travel somewhere. It can't travel to where it would have before, it has to travel a new path to the brain stem. So you are actually opening new neuron pathways for thought processes.

JL: Dendrites?

MS: The dendrites are in the synapse which are in the neuron. They found, in the brains of rats, that by putting rats in enriched environments, they can actually densify the dendrites by creating more synaptic connections.

JL: And the net result of that is?

MS: More thought. More choice. We become such creatures of habit that we limit our own choices regularly.

JL: Is there a limitation to where you think this technology can go?

MS: Is there a limitation to the human brain? The more we learn and understand about the human brain, the further we can go. We are just scratching the surface with this technology. Consider the thought processes of a person like Einstein or Newton, knowing that they were only using 10% or less of their brains! And I compare myself to someone who thought like that, and I know that I can't be using but a 1/2% of mine because I should be capable of what they were able to do. And I'm not even close!

JL: That's frustrating, isn't it?

MS: Well, it would be frustrating if I was trying to be a nuclear physicist! We are just starting to understand what is going on. We are just starting to understand what stress is.

JL: Who buys this kind of device?

MS: Mostly people who are in a healing capacity of one form or another. Caregivers and people who are into meditation and the exploration of the mind. Our automatic clientele started in the metaphysical world and from there it moved into places like chiropractic, etc. We now have units placed at the University of Washington Hospital. They are using them in the cancer ward for people going through chemotherapy. Chemotherapy is a very ugly thing. It is a very anxious situation, no matter how many times you go for treatments, you still don't want to be there, you don't want to take the therapy because it makes you sick. So just to take the edge off, cancer patients are using the *Voyager XL* to help them go through the treatments with a little bit more flow, a little more evenly. They actually put these units on people while they administer the chemo.

At the Wenatchee Hospital, L/S machines are used in the maternity ward for women in labor. The U.S. Judo Olympic Team uses them for mental focus. Many college kids use them to help focus for study time.

You see, we know how the brain reacts in different frequencies. We know that the brain will follow what is given into those frequencies. So we can actually pinpoint different sessions, with different frequencies for different usages.

There are sessions for everything! From helping you to sleep at night to help revitalize you in the middle of the day, to focus for study, just fun, exploration. Allowing people to burn new neuron pathways through their brains allows them more choices. They become more open-minded. Their thought process is not as fixed. Their tunnel-vision diminishes. You start opening doors inside the brain.

JL: Tell me what are the effects of prolonged usage of this technology. You came across this only two years ago yourself. And you have told me that when you first got your hands on one of these machines, you used it every day.

MS: Every day for a year.

JL: Did you go to a twelve step group to get off your machine? Seriously, did you find that you were developing a dependence on it?

MS: No, not really. What actually happens is that there is a cumulative value to using it. Had you known me two years ago, you would see the difference. As we speak today, I am sitting here very still. Two years ago, I would have been sitting here fidgeting, always some kind of nervous motion. I was very high energy, and I still am, except now, I am more even. My general demeanor is much different. I was a grumpy guy. I had a tough beginning and it gave a definite slant to my thought process.

Then I went into the hard-core business world which prolonged that thought process.

Just simply by using a L/S machine and starting to open my mind, I have come to a totally different thought process within two years. I am now a mellow guy and I wasn't before. I am a happy person and I wasn't before. I did it by allowing myself more choices. By allowing my thought process to expand, by stimulating parts of my brain that I wasn't using, the sheer exploration of my own mind made me realize that the way I perceived things was stupid. I realized I really don't know what I am seeing, that I need to step to the side a little bit and try to view life from a different point of view. All these things combined is what has happened to almost everyone that I have spoken with who uses this machine on a regular basis.

It's a total exploration of your own mind. You grow quickly and change quickly. These apparatus' will bring change to you so fast it is unreal. You can't hide anymore. If you start entering these meditative states on a regular basis, the truth is suddenly known to you. And all of the rationalizations and all of the defense mechanisms that you have been using in the past, which prolong your particular behaviors, have to fall by the wayside. You can not justify the behavior anymore because you know the truth deep down inside. And rather than keeping the truth deep down inside, by using this apparatus, you start to become conscious in the alpha/theta ranges. And when the truth be known, when your defense mechanisms have dropped, that is when you wake up. And you start waking up slowly, bit by bit, until a year or two down the road, you are a completely evolved person from where you had been. And hopefully, continuing to evolve. That's what goes on.

JL: You used to employ it daily, but you found at a given point that you just didn't desire it in the same way?

MS: That is a question of addiction. This is the kind of thing that you use when you need it. Its like having a hammer. I have one in my garage and I don't use it all of the time. I only use it when I need to pound a nail in. Its the same with this L/S machine. After the end of the first year, I began to notice that my stress level was changing and that things were rolling off of me more readily and I wasn't absorbing so much.

I was more capable in dealing with things before they really got to me, or not dealing with them at all. If they didn't belong to me, I could let them go.

JL: This was all done through your own inner directed work?

MS: Just through using the machine. No psychoanalyst, no therapist, nothing.

JL: Were you a meditator before?

MS: No. But I can call up a theta state now in a snap.

JL: In other words, because you have learned how to 'voyage' to certain spaces in your head, that now, without the stimulus, you know the pathway and can get there on your own?

MS: Exactly. I can just call it up. My brain has learned the way there. Using the machine for a period of time, you remember the way to where you are going and you can just do it on your own.

JL: The whole purpose of meditation is to quiet the mind enough to reach a point of stillness whereby you can hear the deeper truth. Praying is considered the way to talk to God; meditating is considered the way to hear God. The techniques used in meditation have come down through thousands of years. What you are telling me is through the use of brain synchronization—achieved by binaural audio beats and visual patterns, that are choreographed to the frequency level of the beats—you are able to slow the brain down through the four or five different brainwave states. And that by learning how to hang out in these different areas, that would ordinarily take many years of meditation to be familiar with, you can now consciously bring yourself there, without any apparatus?

MS: Right. And most people, in a four month period of time, can learn how to do this. It is not as complex as people make it out to be. Meditation is not as hard as everybody says. But if you have never been there, then you don't know what you are looking for.

People have no patience. Two years ago, if you had said, "Michael, lay down and meditate," one of two things would have happened. I would have either laid there for five minutes and then got up, saying, "I don't know how to meditate," or I would have fallen asleep. Because those are the two things that I knew how to do. But by simply accessing these spaces, and knowing where they were, looking on the charts, knowing what the Hz level was of the sound and the light, and experiencing alpha for periods of time, over and over, and knowing what alpha feels like, and experiencing theta over and over, and knowing what it feels like, your brain remembers how to do that. But you have to learn how to do it first. You have to experience it before you can know it. By doing it over and over, now you can call it up and it is not so difficult.

THE FUTURE OF L/S

JL: Where do you see Theta Technologies in the next five years.

MS: I think L/S machines are going to be the Walkmans[5] of the future. But the reason that I am in this business is because about a month after I got involved with this business, (I was the first distributor), one of my friends came to a demo evening. She had migraine headaches for thirty years. Her face was the color gray of that desk over there. She walked into the room. I saw her and said, "You look terrible. What's going on?" She told me that she had a migraine for the last two weeks. She had come to try the L/S machine and she laid down, did a session, got up and her headache was gone. That was in November of '91.

Our local ABC affiliate in Seattle just had this woman on the news. They were doing a special on headaches and what people will do to try and get rid of them. She told the whole world, on national TV, that she has not had a headache since 1991, and all she has done differently in her life is use the L/S machine. She no longer takes the medication she was ineffectively on for thirty years! And that's why I am in this business. When this woman came to me and told me that she was off her medicine and was pain free, I suddenly felt like I had done more for mankind in that one instance then I had done in my whole life! ✧

GRACE NOTES

I walked out of Theta Technologies with a new *Voyager XL* under my arm. I went and saw the renowned Falls and they were quite impressive. But with my new L/S machine, I had mysteries of my own to unravel.

I'm impressed by the potential of this light and sound mixture. Theta Technologies has taken the impact of conscious brain travel a notch deeper by bringing on board seventeen program designers (therapists, scientists, doctors, teachers, etc.) to create supplementary audio tapes for their *Voyager XL.* Guided meditations, visualizations, Ericksonian hypnotherapy, et al, used in conjunction with the L/S machine, begins to address the concern of many of the ethics of brain/mind travel. Just because you can go to *Thetaland,* by artificial manipulation of the brainwaves, what happens when you get there? The deepest recesses of our minds are not public parks or recreational playgrounds. There is serious stuff hanging in the subconscious/ unconscious zones of our minds.

Given the current experimental nature of this technology, questions are of great value. Suitable answers establish credible basis for public acceptance. Clearly, the field of neuro-technology holds the promise of unlimited steps forward in the arena of human potential and consciousness expansion.

Dr. Frank Young, a Canadian psychologist with impressive credentials, has written an informative, intelligent paper entitled *Mind State Management: The Software of the Mind.* Located in the *Voyager XL's* user guide, Dr. Young's article strongly endorses L/S machines. In great detail, he describes the positive effects he has experienced, personally and professionally, with the use of this technology. This article and further information are available from Theta.

One of the things I appreciate about this technology is that it does not attempt quick fixes. I'm told the effects are cumulative. Hmmm... Why, I may be becoming a genius right now, and not yet know it. Maybe I'm becoming a millionaire right now, and I don't know it. Actually, I've always wanted to be a little taller...[6]

THE LONG ARM OF THE FDA

In June '94–one year after this interview took place–the Federal Food and Drug Administration closed down the major manufacturer of L/S machines in America, thereby stopping the flow of devices to smaller companies like Theta Technologies. Shortly thereafter, Theta was issued a cease and desist order for any further sales of L/S machines.

Over the last decade, multi-hundred thousand units have been sold, with results running the gamut from migraine headache reduction to deep relaxation and sub-conscious access.

The FDA has the mandate to approve all medical devices. The official definition of a medical device is, "...anything that changes or alters the function or structure of man." Clearly, with such a broad definition, anything from a toothbrush to a relaxation audio tape falls under this category.

The FDA has determined that L/S machines are medical devices and have issued numerous cease and desist orders to wholesalers. There has even been confiscation of inventory warehouses. When re-labeling of the product was requested by industry lawyers, the FDA's response was, "...that the public awareness is such that people will use L/S technology for medical purposes..." regardless of the label.

The price tag for appealing an FDA ruling is estimated at a million dollars and three years. The net effect of this action is the stifling of innovative and/or holistic approaches by small independent companies who cannot risk or afford entanglement with the FDA.

When asked why they were going after L/S machines, the FDA's Bothel, Washington office responded that there was a danger of photic epilepsy. This is epileptic condition can be activated by flashing lights, often to people who have no prior history of epilepsy. One of the L/S companies closed down–with sales of over 50,000 devices–knew of only one instance, in their entire history, of photic epilepsy resulting from their machines. On the other hand, according to a spokesperson for this company, there were 38 instances of photic epilepsy reported among children from the use of computer games in the last year alone.

With a third of the American population now using some form of holistic medicine, and $13+ billion spent annually for alternative care, one wonders about the financial/political motivations of this kind of move. The pharmaceutical/medical/insurance lobby is one of the most powerful in the country, strong enough to defeat governmental attempts at reform. As with the recent threat to over-the-counter vitamins and herbs, the 90's may shape up as a return to 60's style populist activism. This recent action by the FDA poses serious considerations, possibly effecting many avenues of the holistic community.[7] ✧

ENDNOTES

1 The *Voyager XL* is one of many L/S machines developed and sold by Theta Technologies. Resource information can be found in Appendix B.

2 See Chapter Two, *Demystifying Binaural Beat Frequencies.*

3 Information on the sonic/spiritual work of Brother Charles can be found by calling The Synchronicity Foundation. (800) 873-6114.

4 Ting Shas are Tibetan prayer cymbols. They are slightly detuned–thereby creating a binaural beat effect-and were created to help meditating monks remain in deep trance states. Ting Shas, along with Peruvian Whistling Vessels are among the first indications of intentional binaural beat frequency usage dating back B.C.E.

5 Walkman™ is a registered trademark of The SONY Corp.

6 The author ruefully admits that after five years of intensive usage with a L/S machine, he is not any taller.

7 As of this revised edition (1999), both Theta and their manufacturing partners are back in business. Part of the settlement with the FDA was the agreement to take the word *entrainment* out of all inclusive and promotional literature. The FDA deemed entrainment to be a medical term.

14

Resonance Therapy

A conversation with

Molly Scott, Ed.D.

The stark opposites of New York City and the backwoods of Massachusetts… A television performer evolving into a sound-working pioneer. There is a through line, a bridging, a constant seeking.

Like so many sound practitioners, Molly Scott was not content to be an entertainer, songmaster, or poet. In the course of twenty years, a media star grows into a Doctor of Philosophy in the most obscure field–Sound as a therapeutic modality.

Molly Scott has been called *Queen Molly, Ma'am…* and for good reason. She is dignified, vivacious, warm, and generous.

This in-depth foray into the sound mind of Molly Scott was conducted many times, on various coasts, between 1994-1996.

Birth of a New Therapy

JL: How did Resonance Therapy come into being?

MS: The birth of the model I call Resonance Sound Therapy (RST) occurred across a spectrum of early clients: Kelly, who could not coordinate her voice and her body; Alice, for whom sounds in the lower range opened up memories of past abuse; and Elena, whose voice held a key to her childhood trauma in war torn Europe. Working with these people and others moved me into a new profession and the development of an integrated therapy using the voice to modulate therapeutic change.

JL: What was your background?

MS: I had been a singer, performer, and workshop leader for many years when circumstances led me to start teaching voice lessons in my home. From the beginning, it was clear, that in opening the door to work with people individually, I was opening to something much deeper than the kind of "voice lessons" I had experienced in my own musical training.

As I encountered the problems these people had with their voices, I began to sense the systemic root system that blocked their expression, a disharmony that went deeper than vocal training techniques. The voice reflected the life like a hologram. As I worked with these people, question after question arose in me. Wanting to help, I followed my curiosity inward and found myself in a territory that was both very familiar and not at all what I had expected.

Somewhere along the way my students had become clients and their teacher, a counselor/therapist. At the point when this shift became clear, I entered graduate training in counseling and began the multi-disciplinary training and research which grounds the practice of Resonance Therapy in the world of psychotherapy, bodywork, and the natural sciences.

KELLY

MS: That autumn afternoon, twelve years ago, when Kelly stepped through my doorway, neither of us realized that we were both stepping through new doorways in practice and perception of what therapy means. She had many years of therapy, but never worked with the voice. For her, the door led to massive changes in life style, profession, location, and view of the world. For me, the door led to the creation of a synthesis of practices–Resonance Therapy.

Kelly brought her depression through the door with her that day in the sound of her voice. Flat and colorless, lacking in resonance or harmonic intonation, she carried that print of her emotional condition with her like a flag, there for all to read. The voice reflected other psycho/physical cues. Everything about her was heavy and down, her mouth, her weight, the dull colors she was wearing. She had come to me because she knew that I was combining voice work with counseling, and had the idea that her voice was an important part of her sense of herself. Indeed. Up to that point I had considered myself a voice teacher with a broad interest in other dynamics of my student's lives. After that day, I allowed my work to carry me into what has become the main stream of my interest and my practice: working with the body/mind as an elegant communication instrument for which the voice is a doorway, not only to the outer world of relationships and community, but to the inner world in the communities of intercellular and even sub-atomic communication.

That day I asked Kelly to do a simple exercise for me: to let her voice move up and down in a siren of sound, like a sigh, and as she did this, to trace the path of the sound with her finger on her forearm, moving up as the sound went up and down as the pitch of the voice went down. She couldn't do it. Although she understood the simple directions, she could not follow them. Her voice and body were in different worlds. In at least one sense, she didn't know up from down.

I had no idea what this information meant in neuro/physical terms, but I knew that this person was literally out of touch with herself, and I suspected that her voice might be a key to the integration of her fragmented life. I saw that a sense of pitch required a sense of herself in space which she lacked. I also perceived that pulse and tonal relationship could generate seed metaphors for the layers of the world in which this client moved. It seemed that when the movement in her body life was impaired–contracted and constricted–that her relationship to herself was as well, and that the metaphor of cell to cell communication played outward in widening circles from cell to self, and self to world.

The work that I have done with this client and others through the years has answered some of my own questions about the relationship of voice to psyche and soma and has opened many others. Along the way I have invented new ways and synthesized old ones, creating a flexible holding place for these ideas and techniques.

DEFINING RESONANCE THERAPY

JL: What exactly is Resonance Therapy?

MS: Resonance Therapy focuses on personal story and the healing capacity of the voice.

In practice, while it synthesizes and builds on expressive therapies, Psychosynthesis, family systems therapy, theater, and musical techniques, RST is distinguished from other psychotherapeutic approaches by the attention to the voice as a primary modulator of psycho/physical energy.

While it's common parlance in psychotherapy to talk about *voice*–as agency, as-voice-in-the-world. In RST we adjust the lens a little closer to observe the body's voice, the physical voice, positing it as a way to access the body's energy, the body's messages for the self.

A central tenet of RST work is understanding just how focused sound does affect the body/mind and how we can use the sound of the voice to jump-start healing in the system. RST draws its roots from the way that we intuitively modulate our physical, mental, and emotional states by the sounds our body makes: sighs, groans, grunts, hums, exclamations. The techniques and practices of RST build upon this natural facility, using specific and concrete interventions to effect the body/mind systems. We express these sounds out to the world and also give them back to ourselves through the feedback loop of our own hearing, through bone resonance, and the myriad metabolic and hormonal changes that occur in the act of creating sound.

In the RST model, we posit this adjustment process as frequency tuning. Tuning operates at every level of relationship: tuning between therapist and client, the client and world around her, tuning between client and the world within her, the inner voices or subpersonalities which motivate her thought and action, tuning between the various communities that comprise the organic life of her body, and the tuning that determines her relationship with her higher Self-her spiritual value system. Who she is (her resonance) is the composite of all these levels; health can be seen as the degree of interactive flow between them. In RST, the therapist needs to have a perspective and create an environment which can hold all these interactional levels in a container of practice.

I've developed RST as a compliment to other systems. People can use the concepts and techniques of Resonance work in whatever way works best for them; either in their personal lives, in their work, or in clinical practice. One person may use sounding the body as a form of health maintenance. A body therapist might work with clients using focused vocalization as a kind of inner massage to loosen and realign physical systems with their intentions and visions. Psychotherapists use the tools of Resonance Therapy to deepen their understanding and use of voice for relational tuning, accessing impacted memories, restructuring cognitive patterning. Human service and business people gain a deeper understanding of the role of voice as a modulator of communication dynamics, and as an important component in the energetic interplay of organizational structures.

JL: Do you use sound sources other than the voice in your work?

MS: I occasionally use acoustic instruments, drum, or piano. However, since I'm a singer, with a full life's experience of being an instrument for sound myself, the natural focus of my clinical practice and research is on the voice and its effect on the body/mind.

I know there is a whole armorarium of electronics therapeutic devices available in the field of sound and healing now. I am more interested in the human instrument and its connection to the life current through breath, voice, and body than I am in the instruments outside ourselves which have to be plugged into external sources of current-fascinating though they may be. In specific instances, I might use recorded music–but mostly not.

THE VOICE

JL: Let's talk about the voice

MS: Sound enters us as one kind of energy and leaves us as another. We receive it as breath, we give it as voice. A voice that is tuned with intention is a powerful agent in the world; it can create a resonant field that magnetizes other energies, it invites and engenders change. So in my practice I pay attention to Voice: my voice, the client's voice, the voice of the environment–wind, rain, light changes–and how we interact.

In Resonance work, we make our own sound, mostly with voice, both in and out of language. Sometimes, if we're in a time and place that permit it, we use the environment, walk in the woods, listening to a stream, and let what arises be inform us through image and metaphor. For example, when I took a spring walk with one of my clients, watching the rivulets of water flowing on the muddy road helped her to understand the ebb and flow of energy in her life and the importance of her intention. Questions arose from the living images: did she want to float along in the main stream, or was she moving off into a tributary? Was she stuck in the mud and not capable of flow at all? Audible sound wasn't involved here, but patterns of flow and relationship were.

Working with the voice, the first and most important thing is to set an environment where there are no wrong notes, where the constrictions of cultural standards of beauty and ugliness, good sound, bad sound, simply don't apply. The judge goes out the door. We work with the voice–or perhaps more to the point, play with it–as a conduit to the expression of what is true for us. Stretching the voice, making sounds that often people have never heard themselves make nor even known were possible, stretches their concept of the self, their range of emotion, the colors of their experience.

JL: You seem to be talking about something much more subtle than what we usually think of as sound.

MS: When I use the term *sound*, I'm using it as a metaphor for vibrational frequency in its multiple manifestations; heard, felt, sometimes seen. In RST we work with language and pre-language, the natural, pre-verbal sounds the body makes. We also work with *sound* past the audible impulse–with sound as touch, sound as movement.

JL: Can you speak more about the theoretical aspects of your work?

MS: The premise of Resonance work is that these coalesced forms are vibrating according to energetic principles that also govern the behavior of wave forms: sound waves, tides, rivulets, dunes, winds. And just as one focused vibration, like the sound of a bell, can excite another bell to ring, the rhythmically vibrating structure of our body can be called to response by focused tones resonating to similar patterns. We call this phenomenon *entrainment* or *sympathetic resonance.* It's also called phase-locking and is the basic premise upon which all sound therapy is based. Indeed, in my terms, entrainment is the basis for all therapy, period.

ANNIE

MS: Let me give you an example which incorporates both voice work and music therapy. Annie was an artist and writer who came to me with what she described as a communication problem. In fact, it was sometimes very difficult to follow her thought for she spoke very rapidly, interrupted herself often in mid-sentence, and jumping about in her narrative, leaving large parts of her story for me to guess.

As an illustration of entrainment, because I was attending to her so closely, I found my own breath getting short, and my own thought patterns feeling increasingly chaotic as I tried to follow her rapid delivery and cognitive leaps. I realized, as I entrained with her breath and speech patterns, that this chaotic method of vocalization both reflected and perpetuated her chaotic way of thinking. It seemed she literally couldn't get a handle on what was happening in her life because her mode of cognitive processing was so elusive that it slid away before it could come into coherent pattern. Interestingly enough, this cognitive disorganization was not so evident in her writing, which was lucid and thoughtful.

I had some simple behavioral suggestions for Annie which were helpful. Modeling through my own speaking pattern, I encouraged her to slow down her speech, to breathe more deeply, to finish her sentences and not start a new thought until she had finished the last one. I also highlighted some habits of expression ("makes me crazy", "drives me nuts," etc.) that reinforced a pattern of belief that she was acted upon by influences out of her control. I illustrated more coherent speech patterns and using my own entrained breath reactions as a litmus, stopped her when she began to wind up, go too fast and fall into chaotic verbal patterns. I also suggested that she center her breath lower in her body, and concentrate on feeling her voice in her body as she spoke.

This simple behavioral work gave her the opportunity to practice and amplify the new patterns so that the old ones could release into change. When she slowed down, not only did her speech get clearer, but her communication became much more coherent. Her attention to her body gave her flight-prone thought process a way to come to ground and, parenthetically, as her communication to me became clearer, her communication with herself did as well and she began to see her experience in a different way.

I've an interesting reflection here on the idea of coherence as it relates to understanding. Coherence is a concept in wave physics, implies a harmonic synchrony between one thing and another. And when we talk about something coherent, as capable of being understood, I think it's analogous to grounding a wave form–bringing it through the antenna of the self, into the ground. Grounding it is literally understanding it. This concept held true for Annie.

She was a highly intelligent, abstract thinker who had a serious injury to her spine. In energy terms, her spine is her central channel or antenna. When she began to swing off into litanies of abstraction, she experienced her energy as concentrated in her brain; she was energetically ungrounded. Slowing down, coming back to feeling the breath in her body, re-established her connection to the ground, her communication became less static. Entraining with her body, her thought patterns became coherent with the ground of her own being and with mine, and so, as she understood herself better, I understood her as well.

Another aspect of my work with Annie was drumming. When I first invited her to drum, her rhythms were very erratic, without a central organizing pulse; they reflected her interrupted breathing patterns and generally disjointed expression. I would encourage her to start drumming first while I would listen and wait, tuning in to her sounds. At some point, I would enter with a very simple repetitive pattern, slightly slower than Annie's, but close enough rhythmically to create a resonance of invitation. We wouldn't speak, and after a time, Annie's rhythms would begin to move into synchrony with mine. She didn't adopt my pulse–she kept her individual expression–but her pattern began to organize differently in relation to the rhythm that I was doing so that we were drumming together in complimentary patterns. At the same time, as the drum beat slowed and we came into sync with each other, the tension in Annie's face eased, her breath lengthened and so did mine. We continued drumming together with great pleasure.

In later sessions, we would follow similar patterns, playing at having first one person lead and then the other. This was all done non-verbally without cues other than the rhythm itself. It was part of Annie's taking control of her experience with me for her to take the lead as an equal partner in the sound. In music therapy terms, I considered the drumming to be an important part of the resonance work for Annie. Stabilizing her breathing slowed her heartbeat and steadied the flow of oxygen to her brain which contributed to her ability to think more clearly. Her cognitive disorganization went hand in hand with her interrupted speech pattern and choppy breathing. We were both gratified to discover that, not only could I understand her better and listen more attentively when I was not struggling to keep up, but most importantly, she understood and listened to herself. She developed a different relationship with her body as an instrument for breath and sound. She also adopted the process as a way of balancing her energy on her own and took great pleasure outside of sessions, using voice and drum to center herself when she felt "off".

In session, she gained a richer understanding of the resonance dynamics of our work. My discomfort, which she had attributed to fault and blame, she could now see as entrainment, and observe how the quality of our interactions changed as her breath/body relationship changed. I'm speaking about this rather simplistically to emphasize a point; as in any interaction between these complex bundles of association and memory that we are, our interactions had many dimensions, colored by her life and mine. But what I'm noting here is how modulating the way that her thoughts were expressed significantly affected us both. Through the time we worked together she was able to enlarge her sense of self–expand her container if you will–to hold both her past and present experience with a kind of equanimity.

ENTRAINMENT IN RST

JL: You've mentioned entrainment as a central concept for RST work. Can you explain the concept and process in more detail?

MS: Entrainment is defined in physics as the capacity of one vibrating body to call another into frequency alignment. The Harvard Dictionary of Music gives the definition of *resonance* or *sympathetic vibration* as the "...transmission of vibrations from a vibrating body to another body" and that this "... phenomenon takes place only when the two bodies are capable of vibrating at the same frequency (or harmonic thereof)."[1] For example, if two heart cells, beating in different rhythms, are brought close to each other, within seconds they will coordinate to the same rhythm. They have entrained, or phase-locked with each other.

Another example of entrainment is the simple acoustical demonstration that you might have seen in physics class: two tuning forks composed of the same tempered metal and calibrated to the same frequency or tone are set next to each other on a hollow box or resonating chamber. When one is struck and sounds in the other's presence, the unstuck fork will sound the same note, without being visibly touched.

RST is based upon the notion that we are tuning folks, that we're resonant instruments capable of tuning ourselves and each other by consciously aligning our frequencies to synchronize with another's. We do it all the time; it's natural to us. Think of the way we change our energy through our voices to soothe a crying baby, or comfort a grieving friend. The impulse that drives the molecular energy event, can be a thought, an emotion, a feeling. When the instrument is struck with intention, it generates a wave form that influences the molecular substance of the other instrument to vibrate in a similar manner.

Notice in this tuning fork example, the role of the sounding box. It's a hollow, resonating space. Without the sound box, the tuning forks wouldn't be heard. The entrained wave form would be present but not amplified enough for us to hear. We wouldn't be tuned by their sound. Note: if there's no container for the moving air, the sound won't get into the world.

We are the container for the voice of the body. As the strings of the cello need the hollow wooded chamber to transmit the vibration we call music, so we need clear, vibrant containers for our feelings, emotions, intentions, to have expression in the world. When our woundings are so great that our bodies are shut down, we are silenced in the world, just a like a bell that is damped and can't ring its song freely out into the air. The role of therapy is to free our capacity to sound in the world, to be resonant instruments for the truth of who we are.

JL: Earlier, you mentioned making sounds "both in and out of language." What do you mean by this?

MS: We use a sounding technique in Resonance Therapy that I call NLS (non-language sounding). Sometimes we call it *Free Speech.* I alluded to it when I talked about letting the body make the sounds it needs to make to come into alignment with its own template of healthy balance. By body sounds, though, I mean more than grunts, gasps and groans. There is efficacy in straight-ahead cathartic release, like Primal Scream, but RST has developed techniques to tune vocalization more subtly, more intentionally than raw catharsis, without cutting back on the power of the release.

In RST, we encourage a kind of spontaneous improvisatory sounding in which the vowels and consonants arise in free play, coming out of body rather than out of cognitive consciousness. That focused vowel sounds have effect on different energy centers of the body has been a tenet of spiritual practice–what we might call technologies of the sacred–for thousands of years. Prayer, chant, mantra. Think of Alleluia, Allah, Yahweh, Jesu–in terms of the musicality of vowel sounds and their feeling qualities in the body and you'll begin to get an idea of this.

Consider that every time we make a sound we are exciting and activating flows of energy in our body system and some sounds are more potent than others, depending upon whether they're spoken, sung, or chanted, and the intention with which they are expressed. We use this therapeutically by giving the body/mind the opportunity to express those sounds which it wants to make. What feels good in this instance is what is right. And although it seems like quite a leap to leave the seeming safety of known and structured language, once the leap has been taken people are astonished at the sounds which arise from them spontaneously and the effect that this flow of sonic energy has upon the way they feel. It seems to be a means of reaching material that is held deep in body–rather than in cognitive consciousness.

Recall the principle of sympathetic resonance. If the experience of a trauma was initially accompanied with a sound it will encode somatically in the centers which record sensory data but not necessarily be recoverable through structured language. A sound that resonates with the original sound can open up the held information and release it to language and conscious process. This is particularly true, of course, for experiences that occurred in the pre-language state of infancy but also applies to more recent experiences of trauma.

ELENA

MS: Many years ago, the first client I worked with in Europe gave a dramatic demonstration of this. Elena was Belgian, a therapist herself; she came to me because she felt blocked vocally and had a feeling that sound and her voice held some key for healing. When we started to work and I demonstrated a basic voice opening technique to her–a long sweep of the voice from very low to very high and back again–she hit the floor in terror, trembling in tears. The sound had awakened memories of the sirens in the city in the Second World War before the bombs hit. Her story was like so many others that I have heard again and again, but in some ways more poignant.

Like Anne Frank's family in Holland, Elena's life changed in one day when her family had to suddenly go into hiding during the war. They were Jewish and the Gestapo were arresting people to ship to death camps. She was 2 years old, just beginning to learn and enjoy speaking language. Within the space of a few hours her life changed from living in a comfortable Brussels neighborhood, to hiding in the basement of a city building with her parent and older siblings. During the day, the family had to huddle in the dark because the windows were covered over so that no one would suspect anyone of living there. Most devastating of all for an active two-year-old, was that she had to be absolutely quiet. Their lives literally depended on it! At night sometimes they would cautiously venture out on the street, but during the day they were silent in darkness. No peals of laughter, no childish screams of rage or frustration, no giggles of delight. No wonder that sound held such secrets for her.

Elena's family lived in that cellar for two years and they survived. But there was a child in Elena that she felt didn't survive, and her child/self's experience was encoded in sound. Ironically, for her, the coding was as much in the sounds she could not make, that experience of voicelessness, than in the sounds themselves. For Elena, the work of opening her voice was arduous but revelatory. Regaining a lost part of her resonance, she regained a part of her life.

JL: You're describing a situation where a child had no chance to play during an important time in her life. Is 'play' an important element in Resonance Therapy work?

MS: Yes, a very strong element. After all, since we're instruments for this energy, this music, we want to do what instruments do–tune in to the world around us and play!

RST is very playful and also very serious. Research in creativity tells us that we are at our best–most creative and productive–when we play. Resonance work encourages that kind of curiosity and playfulness, even when we are dealing with very serious things. It's that open-minded awareness I spoke about before. It cultivates flexibility, motility, the ability to hold many different states of being, like many colors are held within a painting, many sounds in a piece of music. It allows the new to arise.

TUNING WITH THE VOICE

MS: In theory we regard affect as vibrational frequency, and disease and illness as dysfunction in energy pattern. By using the voice as a tuner for modulating the energy inside and outside ourselves, we can invoke that tendency of our body/mind to come to a naturally harmonic state of resonance. In other words, we want to be healthy and whole, and when we allow ourselves to move from the deep impulses within us, we will come to balance. We have to know how to listen, how to attend to the vibratory frequencies which tune to our innately resonant selves.

This alignment means cleaning house; it entails encountering our shadow stuff, the heavy energies that clog our system and keep us bound in smallness. How we deal with this in resonance terms is the basic stuff of any good therapy: see what is there, acknowledge it, allow it to change. And the last part, the 'allowing' is the key.

We need to come face to face with who we are, and the role of the therapist is to assist in that process, to create an environment, like an alchemical alembic, in which change can occur. She helps by guiding and reflecting the process; her witness amplifies the resonance so that it can take on substance and manifest in the person's life.

THE HUMAN TECHNOLOGY OF SINGING

MS: The role of the voice is crucial here. When we resonate nose to nose with our shadow and can speak to and from that place of truthfulness, we seem to be meeting an organic criteria for change. An example that comes to mind is singing the blues. Singing is an act of consciousness change. When we can sing about something, no matter how bad it is, singing about it changes its color. The more we sing, the brighter we get. To do this is human technology, and we know how do it innately, although in our culture, we have blocked or mostly forgotten this capacity.

In traditional societies, people sing throughout the day, at work, at play. Singing makes the heart lift, makes the load lighter, the work go faster. Remember in Snow White and the Seven Dwarfs, "just whistle while you work?" A human use of human beings would be to encourage and allow each other to self-heal though our own instrumentation.

I find it very encouraging that story telling is rising in popularity again. It hearkens us back to the magic of the spoken world, the mystery of the fire circle, and the weavers work that the bard played in earlier societies. Sharing spoken stories is way of amplifying the richness of the experiences we share. A goal of RST is to help bring back these ancient and effective tools of community.

The similar process is active, of course, in what Freud called the "talking cure". The premise of free association opens the door to the stuck places and allows energy to move through and things to change. In Resonance Therapy we takes this further. By going directly to the body, and letting the body give sonic expression to the feeling, both in and out of language, the energy can move more quickly , more effectively. Sometimes a good cry–a time of weeping, moaning, wailing, or toning–is worth a thousand words!

A caveat here, however, (and this is a point that is sometimes missed in purely cathartic work including some bodywork and cathartic sounding): After a release of deep feeling, particularly of somatically held memory, we need to narrate what has happened, to make a story about it in language in order for it to have meaning for us. This doesn't have to be vocal, one can write about it in reflection, but neurologically, the experience apparently has to be rendered into language for the body to store it in a healthy way. I encourage people to try to put language about their experience as soon as possible because there is so much energetic richness in the act of speaking, sharing, and being witnessed.

VOCAL SOUNDING AND TRAUMA

JL: Can you speak more about the role of vocal sounding and memory?

MS: Meaning seems to evolves in ordered sequence through the circuitry in the mid-brain. If there is a blockage along these neural pathways-as in cases of severe trauma, post traumatic stress disorder-then we are literally stuck in the experience and relive the traumatic incident again and again, reverting in feeling and behavior to the age we were when the incident happened. That's what we call a flashback. It's a sensory reenactment without the necessary distance that language affords us to store the information in a useful, healthy way.

There is a growing body of research which indicates that in order to heal deeply traumatic experience, we have to re-experience it sequentially. Moving through the areas in the mid-brain, the Amygdala and Hippocampus, where the experience is stuck in sensory encoding–smell, touch, taste, sound–into visualizing and then putting it into language, allows us to tell the story of the trauma then move on from it. It's like a wiring diagram, an ordered sequence, and we can't miss a link or we get, literally, short-circuited.

By narrating our experience, we can step back from it enough to allow it to continue to process in us. Disengaging from the emotional locks–the fear and trauma–we move on through the neural pathways to the frontal cortex where 'sense' is made of the experience. It is appropriately filed and, although we may always experience some pain, the ability to narrate it unchains us from the experience of the memory. We can only go through this proccss whcn we are safe enough to do so. That's where good therapy comes in. Letting our sound go can be frightening for people in ordinary circumstances; when the sound is linked to traumatic memory, it's even more important to have issues of safety and boundaries in place and respectfully observed.

I'd like to see more research on the capacity of the voice to assist in traumatic memory work. We need to look at voicing as an analogic process apart from the digital nature of language itself. As such, vocalization is a doorway into a more ancient, primal communication system in our bodies, mediated by the old brain. We need to look also at the possibility that memories might be stored holographically as waves and interference patterns in every cell of the body, not just in the pathways of the central nervous system.

SOUND AWARENESS

JL: What do you observe going on with sound awareness in the American therapeutic community?

MS: There's an increasing interest in the sound/body connection. The concept that music can be healing, although it has spawned a lot of New Age elevator music, has had an educative influence on society generally. There has always been significant attention paid in therapy to the nuances of language, particularly in family therapy, the field in which I trained. I see an increase in framing therapeutic interchange as conversation, story and narrative. Some models, like Neuro Linguistic

Programming and Gestalt have paid attention to the quality of the voice as cues to body/mind states. It seems to me a logical evolution of inquiry for therapists to pay attention to language as sound, distinct from the content of speech. Sound plays with our neural pathways much as chemicals do. Sound is medicine for the brain/body, pouring through the physical ear, the ear of the heart, the ear of our senses. We know this in our gut and used to honor it as such.

JL: How does your therapeutic work with music and sound differ from that of a licensed music therapist?

MS: In Resonance Therapy, we are dealing primarily with the voice at a level of intensity and attention that most MTs are not trained to consider. Music therapists, as the name implies, use the organized structure of music, instrumental as well as vocal, to repattern and align their client's dysfunctional systems. I use techniques–as with the drumming I described earlier–which would be consonant with musical therapy methods. The over arching theory of energetic systems that animates RST isn't yet part of the philosophical base for most MT training, although one would hope that is changing. Certainly music therapists are a very important part of the changing culture around sound and healing. As a therapeutic discipline, MT has been positioned in the medical culture more as an adjunct to other treatment, as palliative care, rather than a primary medical modality on its own. More and more people are realizing that music is a primary change agent and there is a growing body of research to confirm that, much of it coming from the music therapy community. I have great respect for the field and the work that music therapists are doing in clinical and hospital settings. There is a growing body of research coming from the music therapy community that is advancing the field for all of us who use therapeutic sound.

JL: Did you find that formal training was helpful in your practice?

MS: Yes, but not for the reasons that I would have thought. It was not so much that I changed the fundamental focus of my practice when I received formal training, as that I greatly expanded my frame of reference. At the time I went to graduate school, I had already been practicing therapeutic sound therapy in group and private sessions for many years and had led workshops in this country and in Europe. Resonance work came out of my own eclectic experience, learning something that had yet to be formally taught. Like any teacher, I learned a great deal from teaching and from my students.

I went back to school to fill in some areas of my education, basic science, for example, that I had neglected in my artist years and was now very curious about. I hadn't intended to get caught in so much advanced degree work but once I opened that door I found that I was intellectually intrigued and hungry for the learning. Curiosity kept leading me on.

Exposure to the academic community gave me a variety of models of experience which have grounded my work in useful ways. I also entered new cultures, academia and the psychotherapeutic profession, with their own languages, mores, and socialization. All this added richness to the soup of the work.

Also, in order for this work to get out into a wider community of general practice, I think it has to be aligned with existing models and seen in the context of ongoing research and practice. If one is going to build a bridge, one needs to know what the footing is like on the other side before throwing the span. I've been doing that. Sometimes it feels more like a web than a four lane highway–but you know webs look delicate but are very strong.

RST — A COMPLEMENTARY THERAPY

JL: Where is sound most effective in a therapeutic context? Where have you found it be the least?

MS: I need to say, once again, in answering this question, that this is not a fix-it model. Resonance work is a compliment to therapy in many dimensions because it calls attention to the interplay between therapist and client in ways that expand conventional understanding. In this light, I could say that some of the techniques and practices are useful across the board. However, for some of the techniques-working outside of language, and voicing the body for example-require the client have sufficient will to change to take the first steps to leave the safety of their old patterns held in breath, held in language. For some people, this is too much of a leap without a great deal of preparatory work in more traditional modes of talk therapy. This is one of the reasons that I urge practitioners to have a grounding in basic psychology.

Sound/voice work has been effective for people suffering from identity issues, lack of self-esteem, and some forms of depression. It offers useful techniques for panic disorders, in association with behavioral work. It's also very helpful for people with histories of abuse. Women, in particular, find the voice work empowering at many levels.

The techniques of giving voice to subpersonalities, and voicing the body, need to be considered carefully when working with people who already have fragile or non-existent boundaries. The development of a strong central voice, the "I", is a primary goal in therapy, the resonance center of the wheel from which the rich complexities of the different aspects of the self can radiate.

People must be willing and able to take the first steps into the voice work. If they are not, other ways of tuning–talk therapy, behavioral work–are called for without, perhaps, reaching the depth that sonic work can reach. Everyone has their own timing, their own tuning. The therapist's job is to entrain to that place and resonate the possibilities that can emerge from it.

Resonance techniques work well with couple and family therapy. It's useful in relationship work to be able to get outside of the language locks that people get tangled in and still be able to keep communicating non-verbally. Sessions can be quite silly and then suddenly go deep. Major breakthroughs most often begin with silly ideas. It's that playful curiosity again.

RST offers a wide palette of possibilities for bodyworkers. Just the idea that sound is touch sheds new light on the interactions between client and therapist. Bodyworkers already have sensors highly tuned to subtle systems interaction. Adding the voice to that mix increases the possibilities exponentially. In my own practice, when I think it's indicated, I use the massage table and combine light *CranioSacral* body work with sounding, using my own voice. I encourage the client to look for the inner sonic image in their own bodies and sound as well.

The cranial work, a light manipulation of the flow of the cerebral spinal fluid, is about the resonance inside. It's effective for a wide range of somatic conditions and the sounding adds a focused vibrational component–like inner massage. I scan the body with sound, much as a person using therapeutic touch will scan the energy field with their hands, and then I focus in on the sounds that I sense are appropriate for different areas of the body.

JL: How do you know which sounds to make?

MS: How do we know what we know? This is a deeply intuitional process, and the best answer is entrainment. Somehow my hands and my voice feel the places where the energy is blocked and, because I have been listening to the body for so many years and have tuned my awareness this way, I hear a tone or tones in my inner ear and then sound them. I involve my client as much as possible in the process, asking for feedback, and inviting him to sound with me. This both amplifies the site energy and helps the client to understand what sounding his own body feels like. Whenever possible, I encourage people to be active in the sound rather than just passively receiving from me.

SONIC BOUNDARIES

JL: You mentioned training for boundaries. What are the boundary issues in this 'voice-on' work?

MS: The body/mind experiences sound as a kind of touch. We pay so little attention to the effect that sound has on us. We are surrounded with heavy sound pollution in our cities, our traffic, our electronics, and media music. It's little wonder that the subtleties of how our voices effect us and others tends to be lost in the din.

Yet, the voice creates a whole tapestry of effects both within us as we speak and around us, and in those who hear us. Sound as touch, as pressure, is transduced by the piezoelectric properties of the cells, and translates as electrical impulse in the body system. What this means is that we feel sound and sound, like touch, can be invasive.

And so–as we must with any other kind of touch–we need to be very respectful, very observant, of where each person's boundaries lie.

This is particularly important with people who have suffered deep trauma, physical or emotional, in childhood. The adaptive mechanisms that allow children to keep going in abusive situations are encoded in their body/mind continuum and can be triggered by sensory input including certain kinds of sound and certain levels of sound. For example, very loud voices, very soft voices, certain tones of voice, might be read as dangerous and trigger responses that are beyond conscious recall. At this point, training experience is critical for the practitioner. Not only must she be big enough to hold the client's reaction in her own field of compassionate and non-judgmental awareness, but she must have the resources to align with the frequencies of the traumatic response and help the client to bring it into a manageable form.

Better yet, as part of the groundwork process with this client, she might have first empowered the client to determine where the boundaries of presence, touch, and voice lay, so that these parameters were known and could be approached with conscious care. Everyone has different parameters of personal space. They vary from person to person, culture to culture. One of the things I notice when I travel, is how people align themselves somewhat differently country to country. Some cultural modes have much closer field contact than others. (Hungarians, for example, tend to stand very close when they talk to you; uncomfortably close if you're British or Scandinavian.) These things are so instinctive that we don't think about them, and yet they can be of critical importance in therapeutic work. So in Resonance training, we work with protocols for identifying appropriate sonic as well as physical boundaries.

ETHICAL STANDARDS

JL: Is there need for ethical standards in sound practice?

MS: Yes, I feel that there really is a need. We're getting more and more people interested in doing sound work and we need to have something in place that acknowledges the powerful effect that sound interventions can have on people's lives.

The question of ethics brings up important considerations. First of all it raises the old shibboleth that says you can't legislate ethical morality. Well, you can't effectively legislate it, but you can educate for it. We need to determine what those values are and educate people about them. It is true that no matter how many strictures and structures you put up to control people's behavior, if they do not have other people's welfare at heart as well as their own, there are bound to be abuses. But the shock waves of crisis in the therapeutic community over sexual abuse of clients, coupled with the confusions about the possibilities of therapist leading clients inappropriately in recovering repressed memories of sexual abuse, has resulted in a lot of thoughtful attention being paid to the basic dynamics of the client/therapist interaction.

Basically, whenever you have a one-up relationship–teacher/student, parent/child, pastor/penitent, therapist/client–you have an imbalance of power with the potential for abuse of that power.

What constitutes abuse? It's a heavy word and overused right now in the our society, but I would certainly use it in the context of sexual seduction of a client by a therapist. That's a blatant abuse of the trust which must be inherent in the therapy relationship. But there are numerous ways that a therapist can wittingly, or more often unwittingly, trespass upon the delicate balance of the relationship with a client–by playing guru, disregarding boundaries, breaking confidence, indulging in inappropriate dual relationships. And the mix is different with every situation.

The delicate blooming of interrelationship needs to unfold as freely as it can within limits and somewhat artificial confines of the therapeutic session. What constitutes dual relationship in one context may not be so in another. A small community where there are bound to be numerous overlaps of people known to both therapist and client, is very different from a practice in a big city. So a concern with the ethics of practice is not so much putting out rules–which would surely be broken anyway–as an affirmation of basic human values.

When people come to me as a therapist they are placing their confidence in me. This demands that I pay special attention to that power and how I deal with it. One of the things that I love about working with sound is that it tends to even out these imbalances. Not everyone sings, but everyone makes sounds.

When you leave the cognitive structures imbedded in language and free sound, the potentials for change are enormous. And, because you are in unboundaried space, so are the potentials for misuse, abuse of the client/therapist relationship. The therapist is like the nest that the fledging bird flies from, someone who holds the place, sounds the note, makes it safe to leave, and safe to come back. Sonic therapy may even require a deeper level of attention/intention than talk therapy precisely because it deals with territory beyond the structures of ordinary language.

The use of sound in healing is an ancient practice, as old as human beings are old. But the emergence of sound as a serious therapeutic modality is only now beginning to take hold in public awareness. It is my feeling that those of us in active practice, and those who are training people to use sound with other people, need to get the jump on this situation and set up some principles for practice which those just entering the field can learn from.

JL: What kind of standards do you think we should have in place?

MS: The basic principles are core human values–caring, respect, trustworthiness, responsibility, accountability, confidentiality. A health practitioner needs to hold the client's well-being foremost in their attention. Unconditional positive regard is the resonance that determines the parameters of behavior in practice.

I've been making a study of the ethics statements and principles of practice of professional psychology organizations to get a sense of what might be useful to transfer into the sound work. Perhaps the simplest and most direct is from John Beaulieu's *Polarity Wellness* group.[2] Basically it says: no drugs during sessions, no sex during sessions, all sessions are confidential so nothing can be revealed without client's permission, and caregivers should communicate with each other.

Accountability is one of the most important principles we need to attend to in this field where professional trainings are still so new. Other fields have internship and supervision requirements to assure accountability and I think that's a component of responsible practice that we need to consider. The apprenticeship model might work best for the sound field. Access to schools and institutions is not readily available and, as I've noted before, this is a special kind of learning. It is perhaps best transferred by the principles of resonance itself: by participation, entrainment, a kind of psycho-sensory osmosis.

LIGHT/SOUND NEURO-TECHNOLOGIES

JL: Molly, what is your thinking on the Light/Sound Machine technologies?

MS: I have a concern. My comments have all been directed to body/mind practice using the voice and natural sounding. I am concerned that people using the subtle and increasingly widely available sound/light technology have some psychotherapeutic training and be held to the same parameters of responsibility that I have been setting out for resonance practitioners. It seems to me that culturally we are numbed to the ramifications of our dependence upon exterior technology. There is too much that we don't see. We expect machines to do what we ourselves are innately capable of, leaning upon external devices, electronic pyrotechnics, to do things to us, to fix us up as though we were ourselves just machines to wind, oil, and set spinning.

Yet we are beings of such incredible subtlety that we cannot foresee a time when any mechanism we devise can even approach the wonder of our organic architecture. This is not to say that the technology isn't either fascinating or effective. Undoubtedly, it is both. And the field is exciting in its potential. But I have seen such things occur on the current of the voice/breath–the body that knows itself, that knows just what it needs. I would want to know that people who use the technology first have experience with their own energetic resonance through breath and voice, without the devices, before dealing with something as precious and precisely balanced as another person's body/mind.

TEACHING SOUNDWORK

JL: Do you think it is easier to teach therapists about sound than sound practitioners about therapy?

MS: What a provocative question! Depends on who they are, of course. Actually there are a surprising number of therapists who are scared silly to really open up their voices because they know that tight voices cork unexplored stuff in their lives. However, although they may not use this language, therapists have already developed keen sensors for subtle energy exchanges, and once they have dived into the resonance work, they will go deep in the process and know how to use it in their work and in their lives.

'Sound practitioners' now... who are they? If we're talking about people like music therapists who are already working with the psychological effects of sound, they are very open to this work, and rightly so. If we're talking about the sound practitioners with electronic instruments boys, then it's another story.

The number one anxiety in this country is public speaking. I think that opening and using the voice for therapeutic exploration holds unnamed terrors of self-discovery for people more accustomed to looking outside themselves for answers than within. And part of my concern, and the point of accountability and training, is precisely that the people who wield the powerful possibilities of sound technology have explored the possibilities of their own instruments first and know how to work with the effects of the technology on the living complexity of their client's body minds.

PRIMARY CONTRIBUTION OF RST

JL: What do you see as the primary contribution of RST to the health community?

MS: I think the primary contribution is in the synthesis of theory and methodology it offers from psychology, science, and the arts. It is of value too, to have an articulation of the principles of entrainment and energetic interaction relative to the field of mental health. RST also introduces rapid, efficient transformational techniques which can be learned by the client as preventative self-care. The self-care component is important with the trend in the mental health field towards short term psychotherapy and preventative health care. The body's ability to modulate its states through vocal sound is our own preventative system. Working with the voice should be a routine part of our personal health maintenance.

THE FUTURE OF SOUND THERAPY

JL: What do you see as the future of sound therapy in this country?

MS: Interest in sound and healing is growing at a rapid rate in this country. Sound is already being used in the high-tech. medical community with sonograms, ultrasound, lipotropsy. Actually many of the really phenomenal tools of medicine in use today, the PET and CAT scans and MRI, are really part of the an evolving energy medicine paradigm. It's a vibrational universe.

In the soft-science realm, I see sonic therapy as part of the same upsurge of cultural interest that puts Gregorian chant and world music on the best-selling music charts. Our ears are expanding. One can only hope that our understanding of each other and our world will not be too far behind.

On the practical front, I would like to see much more research done on the psycho/physiology of the voice, more empirical structures for the bridge between the paradigms that soundwork represents. But you know, whether that bridge becomes a four lane highway or stays a narrow span swaying in the winds of controversy, people will still cross over. We are creatures who use sound to bring ourselves to balance. We have always known this and always done this. And will continue to do so.

JL: Where would you like to have your work go in the future?

MS: I'll see training programs in Resonance Therapy and Creative Resonance work firmly established in this country as well as Europe. I'd like to see sounding work accepted in the medical pantheon as stress management is, and I think that will happen. I'd like to see therapeutic voice work be part of clinical psychotherapeutic training. For myself, I've got several books on sound to write. And a couple of books on other topics in the works. I want to have time to write music and there's always another album to make. ✧

ENDNOTES

1 *Harvard Dictionary of Music*, Pg. 276.

2 See Appendix C.

15

Chantmaster Extraordinaire

A conversation with

Robert Gass, Ed.D.

Robert Gass is a very impressive man, on paper and in person. He holds a doctorate from Harvard, has co-created Spring Hill, an educational center and community in Massachusetts, developed the *Opening the Heart* workshops through which over 100,000 have passed, has consulted with government agencies, corporations, and hospitals, set up hospice programs, and during the 70's, was a pop recording artist for Mercury Records. Now, where does this man find time to breathe?

If we believe that life deals us what we need, then Robert Gass had reason for introspection, perhaps some looking inside to do. In 1985, Robert suffered a malignant tumor in one eye. Ironic that someone so vigorously committed to care for cancer and AIDS patients now struggled for his own clear vision and survival.

This interview, however, is not about Robert's battle with cancer. Fortunately, he experiences fine health and full embodiment. I mention it with respect and admiration. Winning this battle is one of the highest accomplishments in his life's resume. To regain his healthful balance bespeaks a testament to his power as student, teacher, thinker, father, businessman, and musician.

Little wonder that Robert Gass nurtured Spring Hill Music into a thriving label and earned the distinction as the unrivalled chantmaster of New Age music. Since 1983, he has produced seventeen albums of transformational music with the 40 member Massachusetts choir, *On Wings of Song*. And with over 250,000 albums sold, Gass' *Chants of the World* series are distributed worldwide. He counts as his friends and collaborators such luminaries as Deepak Chopra, Dr. Elizabeth Kubler-Ross, Jean Houston, Steven Levine, and Dr. Bernie Siegel.[1]

Quite truthfully, I felt a bit intimidated approaching this interview. I feared that anyone with such an impressive history would be condescending, conceited, or simply annoyed at the bother of an interview. Fortunately, none of these projections bore fruit. When I called Spring Hill to make an appointment, I was told to bring walking shoes. Robert and I strolled around one of Colorado's perfect lakes. We talked enthusiastically, warmly, laughing often; it was a perfect day! I now understand why Robert Gass is adored wherever he goes. He is a gem, a sweetheart of a man.

This interview took place in Boulder, Colorado, August 1992.

WE'RE TALKIN' CHANTS HERE...

JL: Let's talk about chants. How many albums are you producing at this time?

RG: Two to three per year.

JL: Why chants?

RG: I have enjoyed chanting since I began my journey onto the spiritual path in the late 60's. I found that chanting with a group brought out a sense of community and commonalty amongst people. Aside from being a musician all my life, I have been a teacher and change agent.

In some of our early workshops, I used the chant *Om Namaha Shivaya*. I had a number of requests for a cassette of our group chants. I figured that all I had to do was take our recording down to a digital editing place, make a 90 minute duplicate, and maybe we'd sell a few at our workshops. What I was not prepared for was the floodgates of demand opening for this recording. We'd been trying to pedal our vocal music to New Age distributors for years. They kept saying, "Sorry, we like your music personally, but New Age vocal music doesn't sell." Then, all of a sudden, people from all over the world are writing and calling, wanting *Om Namaha Shivaya*, and distributors are coming to us, saying they are getting such a demand for this tape.

To show my innate business sense, I thought that it was a dumb idea from the start, and here we were, back-ordered, not able to keep up with the demand for this tape. Sometimes the universe sends it right in front of us and we just don't get it!

So, about seven years ago, I got into it. I thought, "Let me take this on as an artform." *Om Namaha Shivaya* was literally only about five minutes of music that we tape-looped. The next ones got a little more sophisticated. If you track over the years, you will notice a steady progression of greater musical complexity. At a certain point I realized that if I'm going to keep growing, I need to stop worrying about what people are going to like or listen to and give myself fully to it. So I have been definitely pushing the edges of this form in all sorts of directions. *Heart of Perfect Wisdom*, in which I was assisted by Jonathan Goldman and his overtone chanting, is an example of pushing the limits of the form. It is music that is extremely complex that sounds simple–until you really try and track it musically. Everything is in overlapping, interlocking tempos. No one ever knows where the beat is, but when it all comes together, it feels very organic.

JL: As a composer and arranger of this chanting format myself, I know what it is like to be locked into rigid structure. By it's very nature, a chant is supposed to be simple and repetitive; yet I too have strived to enlarge the form and make it creatively progressive.

RG: I've been making albums for 23 years, about 28 of them so far, which is different from doing one or two. So, in a sense, when you are looking at a lifetime as a musician, there is a balance that you have to hit. When you get known for a certain kind of music, your audience begins to expect that. The balance that you have to play is between giving your audience what is native to them and what they are comfortable with, and also educating your audience and trying to bring them along with you. I have noticed career musicians falling off on one side or the other. Either they give up on their own creative growth and just keep churning out what sells and what they are known for or they grow but lose their audience–and actually lose their capacity to keep making music.

JL: It is a difficult balance.

RG: I feel like I am doing pretty good with the balance that I have. Even when I am doing something that is incredibly simple, I bring my highest level of mastery and depth to it. I will sometimes sit there with one melodic line and work it for hours, changing one note one way or the other.

I think you will notice with *Medicine Wheel* how I am pushing it. On side one, it is a narrow dynamic range. If you wanted to put it on as background music, it could be done without being disruptive. On the other hand, if one wanted to put earphones on and really get into it, there is a lot going on, even though it is simple. People who have loved our music over the years will feel totally harmonious with that. Side Two will push people. The *Chief Seattle* song is a pretty intense dynamic range. It is quite complex musically, like what you would find in contemporary classical music. It is very challenging harmonically and melodically, relative to what our audience has heard before. Emotionally, it is disturbing. It is not love and light; it is the full range of the medicine wheel. You are talking violence to Native peoples and the rape of the land–along with a very positive message about our spirituality. But it is very demanding in that way emotionally as opposed to most New Age music which occupies a pretty narrow emotional band.

JL: How did you develop the concept of *Medicine Wheel*?

RG: What I do is pick a tradition, culture, or theme, and I immerse myself in it. In *Medicine Wheel*, I started devouring any Native American music that I could find. I went through catalogues and ordered chants and traditional healing tapes; I drank it in and got it into my cells. But in no way do I attempt to create music that is authentic to it's culture. Instead, using the indigenous harmonies, melodies, rhythms, and instruments, I create a mixture of their influence and my background.

JL: What is your musical heritage?

RG: Rock n' roll and Western classical music.

JL: How has *Medicine Wheel* been commercially received?

RG: It is our best-selling album to date! Some are drawn to it who are not attracted to our chanting music. For some of the people who have grown up on our chanting tapes, they get half way through it and stop because it gets too heavy for them.

JL: So what's next for you? I notice that you have adopted a catchy phrase, *Chants of the World,* which goes on the covers of all your new albums. Are you traversing the globe looking for new material?

RG: Yes!

THE EFFECT OF CHANT

JL: So after 10-15 albums of different chants, I think you qualify as a chantmaster. What is it that happens with chanting? Is it healing?

RG: Well, I am getting much lighter about things as I get older. I am not less passionate but I am less ideological about things. In a certain sense, is singing chants more healing than singing *You Are My Sunshine?*

My grandmother, who at age 80 was wearing mini-skirts and teaching dancing on the boardwalk at Coney Island, decided to study yoga. She would come over and stand on her head, in her mini-skirt, and she would be so excited. She confided to me once that she had been meditating for ten years. I asked her how she learned, and she said that she had taught herself. I said, "Well, how do you meditate?" And she said, "I say my mantra," pronouncing it man-tra. I asked her where she learned her mantra from. And she replied, "Well, I read in a book that you take an Indian word and you say it over and over and over again. So I picked my own word, and for ten years I've been repeating it every day." "So, what word did you pick?" I asked. And she answered, "Cheyenne, Cheyenne." She was confused. She thought that the mantra was supposed to be an American Indian word. But when she described the experiences that she had, she had the full range of experiences that one would expect to have having been given a devotional Sanskrit chant.

JL: As if she had paid $400 to the Transcendental Meditation Society?

RG: Exactly! Now I do believe, from my own studies, that certain syllables have intrinsic sonic qualities that may effect you in different ways than others. But in some sense, there is something that is intrinsically healing about making music, singing with other people. Both the making of music and the experiencing of music is healing. I used to have a strong ideology of what that was, but when I really open it up, there are many way that music is healing; the actual vibration of a sound, for instance. Now it also depends on what you mean by healing.

I wonder if healing is relative. Would one person's healing be another person's toxin? Clearly, by giving oneself a musical experience, either by participating in it or by simply receiving it, one's consciousness gets shifted. That happens with all different kinds of music. Various people create their own definitions of what kind of consciousness shift creates healing, and then will say that *that* is healing music. I think all music shifts consciousness. It is like a drug.

Chanting has many elements that create a shift in consciousness. These shifts are created by the actual quality of the vibration of the sounds being repeated over and over.

I remember that I used to do these very bizarre healing tones; high and intense. I was performing at a public concert where a young man was doing a live recording. I came out at the end and asked him how the recording went. He answered, "Well, the first reel went pretty good, but after that, I don't know! I had my headphones on and the volume up really loud, and I heard this really strange sound and all of a sudden, bolts of light were going up my spine. I started seeing lights and something exploded in my head and then I passed out!" He had been listening to these sounds that I was making with the volume cranked way up. Now, he had no picture or expectation, but the actual nature of that sound had an intense effect on his consciousness. So there are certain intrinsic qualities of sound.

The sonic qualities of sound will actually effect human consciousness in fairly predictable ways. But that is not the only way that music effects consciousness and creates a shift. Rhythm will do that. To some degree it entrains or brings your own self into vibration with that rhythm and will shift your energy state to match the intensity of what you are hearing. I think that melody has a major effect. Melody tends to engage the heart and the imagination in a way that is different than rhythm. It is a great evacuator of memory. You could be in a supermarket and find yourself crying without knowing why, and then realize that some Muzak tune has brought up old memories connected with that long forgotten song. Places that want to shift consciousness, like a church, will use hymns or chants over long periods of time because you will come to associate that music with a certain state. Later whenever you hear that music, you will instantly be re-triggered to that state where you first heard it. Just in the same way that certain smells will bring back fully-felt memories.

Repetition of sounds will tend to create an entrainment; like an anchoring within your consciousness. It is like a self-hypnosis.

IS IT HEALING MUSIC?

JL: What do you think about this field of music and the healing arts? As it evolves with all the brain entrainment high-tech elements, to Tibetan bowls and bells, Mongolian overtone chanting, and now Robert Gass' chants from all over the universe... Do you feel 'healing music' is a modality whose time is coming on a commercial basis?

RG: We are dealing here with a movement to some degree. It is pretty hard to separate out the gems from the dross. It is something new. A lot of people are experimenting with different things. It is hard to tell what will prove over time to be of lasting value to people. I have an open mind about it all. I don't know if in ten years whether this will already have been forgotten, or if we will go on to something interesting. It remains to be seen.

I don't take what I do all that seriously. Well, I do and I don't. When I'm in the studio, I take it seriously. It's like playing a game. When I get onto a racquetball court, I'm not against the other person, it is that I want to give it everything that I have. When I am in the studio, I hear something close to perfection in my mind, and I will do anything to create, using all of my mastery and technology, to create that sense of perfection so I can externalize what I hear inside. I take that very seriously; I will work all night to get it. I won't let it go! I really want to create that. So I do take it seriously. But when you ask me the question about the impact of this movement, if it is getting recognized? I don't know. I don't care. I have a great sense of humor about the whole thing.

Numbers of times I have been interviewed, along the lines of, "...As one of the leaders of the New Age, what do you see ahead? What do you hope for the New Age?" Sometimes, I want to answer, "I hope that it dies soon."

JL: So we can just get on with it?

RG: Well, it is just not that important. I'm not all that passionate about the healing music movement, or the New Age movement. I am passionate about life. I'm passionate about, in some small way, making a difference with people whose lives and mine intersect. I'm passionate about the environment. I'm passionate about love. I'm not so passionate about New Age music or music for healing. I mean, I throw myself into it, but...

JL: Wait, you say that you have put out 23 albums at last count?

RG: Well some of them are extinct. Some of them are Acid Rock albums and Rhythm & Blues from the 70's.

JL: Yes, but you're not doing a dozen albums worth of chants from a musicological experiment. All of these chants are callings to higher awareness. Now, it seems to me that you wouldn't be doing one or the other if you were not passionate about it.

RG: (laughing) I like to make music.

JL: Yes, and there are all different kinds of music to be made. You could be doing a revival of Jimi Hendrix.

RG: Well I might. The reason why I am doing all these chants is because this person called me on the telephone and asked me for this one five minute chant. And I thought that it was a stupid idea and a waste of my time, and it tuned out that it wasn't. It is a whimsy to me. Maybe someone else would have called me and asked me to do a Country Western song, and then I would have gotten well-known for that. I just don't have a thing about it.

JL: So what I hear you saying is that it just doesn't matter? It is just the doing of it that is important?

RG: What I notice is that when I sit down and play music, it is increasingly less music that looks and sounds spiritual.

JL: Just music for a good time?

RG: It's just music. Part of what is happening to me is I am thinking less that God or spirit is about words that have a religious sound. To me, that is a trip about religion. To me, spirit is just what's present, its not the thing about it.

SACRED MUSIC

JL: Do you think that music has the ability to help people to transcend? In the past, that was the purpose of Sacred Music. I'm looking for what Sacred Music is about in the year 2000.

RG: Well, there is Sacred Music and there is sacred music.

JL: Let's talk about those distinctions. What was there about the sacred music of the past that used to help people feel closer to God?

RG: To start with, the word sacred means different things to different people. Then, there is something intrinsically in the nature of music itself that brings about a certain state of depth or remembrance. If we want to analyze church music, it was different than the music that was going on outside the church. Outside, the music was lively, playful, Renaissance-type music; it had a different timbre. Inside the church, the music was dense, darker. It was a timbre that people associated with sacred. They were entrained because they heard it in sacred surroundings and they heard it in the context of a mass. So that particular kind of music becomes associated with that kind of experience, which builds with the repetition over time in a service, and over ten and twenty years of having this experience. You put that whole package together and that music creates sacred consciousness for that person.

Is that music intrinsically sacred apart from its culture, or people's association with it? It really depends on what you think sacred means. If you are out sitting in a field and somebody comes by playing a little pipe flute, playing a Renaissance-type tune, and that evokes in you a quality of wondrous delight and life, and you have an experience which you label as sacred, is that music as sacred as a Bach cantata? That is a yes and a no. Yes, it really is. It is not officially Sacred Music, but it is sacred music because it 'sacrilizes' the consciousness in that condition. Maybe for someone else it wouldn't. I know people who walk into a church and hear the music there, and it turns them off. They do not experience being sacrilized by that music. But you and I might go in and hear the same music and go, "ahhhhhhh."

I remember the first time I heard some of this Buddhist stuff. I was so excited, the Tibetan monks and all. I thought, "This is going to be great!" I closed my eyes and then all of a sudden I heard this clanging and what sounded like shouting and screaming. And I thought, "What's this? This isn't sacred music!" I thought that it sounded awful and I have never listened to it again. I found it very disturbing, I didn't find it to be sacred music.

JL: Yet in that culture, in that time and place... If you were sitting in Tibet, you might have transcended right in your seat.

RG: Exactly. So I think that I am challenging this idea of what is sacred music. It is partly an entrainment, its partly an acculturation, its partly a series of associations that make that music, in a certain cultural time and place, sacred.

THE TRIGGERS OF MUSIC

JL: When you think about musical transcendent experiences that you've had, can you identify a common denominator that takes place?

RG: Actually, I have a lot of transcendent experiences with music. I think that what takes place with the music is a triggering. I believe that the transcendent experience already exists within me, it is not some thing that has to be created. There are many states of being which are part of the totality of who I am in this moment. As I identify with one or more parts of my conscious, that is what I experience as being reality. I believe that music creates a transcendent experience by triggering in me that transcendent state of being.

JL: Can you define those musical trigger points?

RG: For me, it is a process of building and release. It is a certain kind of drawing in of tension, then a breakthrough with a burst of energy, and then there is a release after it. Particularly when that building up is happening melodically and energetically. When I hear that, and it is the right kind of melody and the right kind of leaping movement upwards, its the thing that triggers me. Often, I will have a tear or cry for a moment. My consciousness shifts and I come to this state of complete oneness in the moment. And then it passes. But that is not an infrequent experience.

JL: I have experienced that myself as a musician. There have been times where I have listened back to something on tape and it has brought me down to my knees in gratitude for having that creativity pass through me.

RG: In fact, if I don't cry when I hear one of my newly created pieces, I throw it away and go back to work on it more. I am looking for music that effects me that deeply. Sometimes I get embarrassed because I am crying to my own music. But if it doesn't speak to me...

JL: But this is our experience as composers and musicians.

RG: When I talked about those transcendent moments, that was also with listening to the radio. That is not just about my music. It happens all the time listening to music.

JL: When you say listening to the radio, you mean you will hear something, and then out of the blue...

RG: Absolutely! It just touches me so deeply. Music just gets right in. I am very available.

JL: Are there specific artists, on a certain wavelength, that trigger you?

RG: Yes and no. One thing that I find is if I give myself to any music, I enjoy it and it moves me. Often what happens when I am not moved is that I have some prejudice looming, "I don't like that kind of music," sort of thing. But actually, when I get past that, and just open myself to the experience of music, I always love it.

Now are there certain ones that move me deeply, yes. I like Mozart and Bach. To say 'like' understates it a little bit.

JL: What else moves you?

RG: I find I am attracted mostly to acoustic sounds; I listen to very little synthesized music. I find it takes me nowhere. I find it beautiful but soul-less.

JL: I think the reason is that digital music has no harmonics. In the process of creating sound electronically, the air, the breath of the sound, being the overtones, is omitted. It's like cardboard sound.

RG: Now, I have seen people use it in tasteful ways, as a part of other things, that is really quite elegant. But I don't tend to be drawn to it.

TRANSFORMATIONAL CONSULTING

JL: Do you spend most of your time on Spring Hill Music?

RG: No. Actually the majority of my time is spent as president of an international consulting company that does transformational change with large corporations.

JL: What interests you in this work?

RG: A lot of traditional American corporations became uncompetitive in the last ten years. They had a management style and structure that grew out of a different time. As the pace of change picked up, these large systems are like dinosaurs; their nervous system is very far from their brain and sensory apparatus. They have many layers of management between the people who make decisions and the people who are actually the customers. They found that they were no longer competitive in the way that they were doing business. It put them into a crisis over the last 5–10 years. Some were more quick to respond than others. But most corporations have identified that they have to move in consistent directions towards things that promote greater ownership, so that people who work in a place feel more loyalty and willingness to commit to excellence. In terms of levels of hierarchy, a lot of movement towards self-managing teams, breaking down of internal and external boundaries, operating out of a vision, operating out of values. There is a real movement in American corporations in these directions. Some are quite sincere about it, some are doing lip-service and going through the motions. But a lot of them are feeling quite pushed by the competitive environment and they know that they have to make these kinds of changes.

As I look at this change in the workplace, there are things that are consistent for me in the work that I have been doing throughout my life, as a seminar group leader, a musician, etc. This is a leverage point to help make a shift in mainstream America. These companies that I work with have hundreds of thousands of employees. The work we do has a very immediate impact on the quality of life and consciousness of these people. It opens up a greater possibility for their human potential to grow and flourish.

For me, my work in music and my work in organizations are one. I utilize the same principles of harmony, of resonance, of blending our individual energies into a whole in service to a higher vision.[2] ✧

ENDNOTES

1 A catalog of Spring Hill Records is available. See Appendix B.

2 In 1999, Robert published *Chanting; Discovering Spirit in Sound* (NY, Broadway Books, 1999).

Part Three

Resources

Epilogue

I set out to study the profound aspects of sound because I wanted my musical work to generate a powerful impact. But how does one systematically explore a field with no name, no school or curriculum? Even the term *psychoacoustics* makes people nervous. "What are psychoacoustics? The sound that nuts make?" a student quipped recently.

As a writer, I was fortunate to gain access to many soundworkers. I offered editorial exposure to those who would tell me what they'd learned, why and what they did, as well as their vision of the future. These conversations became my college courses; interview subjects became mentors. The work was time and labor intensive. Each conversation consumed 50-100 hours from interview preparation to the actual dialogues, through interminable transcription and edit processes. However, every time I revisit these interviews, I receive something vital and new. Ultimately, the real treasure lies in the comparing, contrasting, and combining of the knowledge of these generous practitioners and their colleagues.

Dr. Jeffrey Thompson uses sound to entrain the brain to access the biological organic intelligence which "...knows how to grow the body from two cells." He is finding methodologies which define the fundamental resonant frequency of the brain to create global realignment of the body's organs.

Vickie Dodd knows that emotions are coded in rhythms. She hears and matches the tempo, emotional content, pitch, and direction with her own voice. "I'm sounding what has been unexpressed, denied, forgotten," she says. Vickie uses sonic bodywork to talk to a client's *well cell* to effectively "...awaken the amnesia of wellness."

Michael Jones has sold more than a million records. The intention of his music is "...to open the heart of the world." In addition to rigorous concert tours, he performs frequently in hospices, schools for the emotionally disturbed, and prisons. Michael plays the piano, he says, in "...partnership, a co-creation" with a higher source, believing "...more than two hands" are on the piano at a time.

Other practitioners of sound healing engage in unique explorations. Janalea Hoffman uses rhythms of 50-60 beats per minute to treat Parkinson's Disease patients. Dr. Molly Scott finds "...the voice at the gate" to be the doorway for psychotherapeutic intervention. Dr. Fred Schwartz uses music in the operating room to reduce the amount of anesthesia–often by half. Jonathan Goldman sees the ancient art of harmonic overtone chanting as a powerful sonic healing and transformational technique. Therese Schroeder-Sheker, sonic angel and scholar, trains harpists to read medical charts and assist the dying in unbinding. What profound work these healers perform!

Tom Kenyon, Robert Gass, Michael Stevens, and Arthur Hull are sonic practitioners who use sound matrixes, chant, Light/Sound Machines, and the infectious camaraderie of drumming. Each specializes in his own domain. Who is to say what these explorations will bring in the future? The similarities *and* differences among them create the synergy that propels soundwork into the 21st century.

The Sonic Alchemists who grace these pages are those I was fortunate enough to meet. Exciting paths are walked by many others:

- Pat Moffit-Cook studies cross-cultural sound healing techniques.[1]
- Bruce BecVar combines modern production techniques with Deepak Chopra's ayurvedic techniques.[2]
- Susan Alexjander explores the DNA strands and finds their musical equivalents.[3]
- Anna Wise works with sound frequencies to stimulate the brain in the most creative approach I have encountered.[4]

- Dr. Valerie Hunt creates recordings of sub-harmonics to supplement the total energy field.[5]
- Dr. Theresa Dale's soundwork correlates musical notes to acupuncture meridians.[6]
- Alexander Doman of *Advanced Brain Technologies* creates innovative and highly sophisticated sound therapy programs for children and adults with learning disabilities and other developmental challenges.[7]
- Dr. Billie Thompson imaginatively and effectively combines the Tomatis Method with *Rubenfeld Synergy* and other modalities.[8]
- Lynn Maass uses sound frequencies to re-educate the brain for those with learning disabilities or chronic conditions.[9]

And the list goes on. These soundworkers are part of the American contingent. However, the emergence of soundwork transcends all geographical boundaries as research blossoms around the world.

As for myself, I entered this exploration as a composer and record producer. After seven years of intensive research, my love of music equals my appreciation of the medium from which music comes–sound. Now when I sit at the piano, one note is as valuable as an entire sonata. I know it is the sound–the vibration–that resonates in me. Music moves me, but it is the sonics of sound that physiologically affect me.

As I finish this epilogue and book, I write into daybreak. With ears covered by headphones, physical fatigue is balanced by the sweet music of Vivaldi. I am using a sonic tool to maximize my productivity and stay awake. *Concentration,* from *The Sound Health Series,*[10] has been created with highly specific psychoacoustic techniques. 'Body Relaxed/Mind Alert' is the ideal state for focus and productivity. The external periodic rhythm is between 50-70 beats per minute. Though my major body pulses respond with soft relaxation, my mind is quite stimulated by the high frequency sounds of flutes and violins. The acoustic instruments are rich with harmonics and the music has been rearranged to create a gentle entrainment effect. Best of all, I was able to produce these recordings because of the knowledge gained from my generous teachers.

The foundation of my work as a *psychoacoustic* composer and producer is now in place. I have had the great fortune to build upon the research of fine soundworkers, some dating back centuries. One of my favorite texts, *On the Sensation of Tone,* was written in 1885.[11] Since Pythagoras, there have been those who recognize the profound in music and sound. Resonance, entrainment, and intention have always been the keys. The marriage of age-old principles and new technologies gives us the ability to be more precise in application.

A major objective of *Sonic Alchemy* is to promote the networking of ideas and the cross-pollenization of research. A progression takes place in the passing of knowledge. I stand on the shoulders of those before me; it is a privilege to be a conduit for their research. As more information is published, we have the opportunity to truly grow this field of soundwork. The Internet allows us to network globally and will thrust the awareness of sonics forward. Sound works well in the digital medium. Who knows how the sound frequencies of DNA will translate on an Intel Pentium chip?[12]

I invite you to utilize the following resources to sculpt your own soundwork. As a music lover, use music and sound with a greater awareness of how it vibrates and nourishes. Create healthy sonic environments in your workplace and home. As a music maker, incorporate this knowledge into composition and production. Combining your gifts of musicianship with the added dimension of psychoacoustics can do great good in the world. If you are a healthcare provider, adapt the principles of entrainment and resonance into your practice. Soundwork is ideal as a complementary modality.

Ultimately, I believe sound cannot be separated from the realm of Spirit. It is a major tributary of the Master Current. I like to think of sound as a sacred *currency.* How we make it and how we use it can enrich us immeasurably. ✧

ENDNOTES

1 Pat Moffit-Cook is the director of The Open Ear Center: 6717 N.E. Marshall Rd., Bainbridge Island, WA 98110. (206) 842-5560. www.openearcenter.com

2 BecVar and Chopra have created a three album set, *The Magic of Healing Music Series,* based on the Ayurvedic doshas, Vata, Pitta, and Kapha.

3 Susan Alexjander: Science & the Arts, P.O. Box 428, Aptos, CA 95001. (831) 335-0339. www.oursounduniverse.com

4 The Anna Wise Center: 530 Third St., San Rafael, CA 94901. (415) 456-2211. www.annawise.com

5 Dr. Valerie Hunt: Malibu Publishing Company, P.O. Box 4234, Malibu, CA 90265. www.bioenergyfields.org

6 Dr. Theresa Dale: The Wellness Center for Research and Education, 13050 San Vicente Blvd, #206, Los Angeles, CA 90049. (310) 656-7117.

7 Alexander Doman, Advanced Brain Technologies: P.O. Box 1088, Ogden, UT 84402. (801) 622-5676. Website: www.advancedbrain.com.

8 Dr. Billie Thompson. www.soundlistening.com

9 Lynn Maass, SoundWorks: 1190 Grand Ave, Suite C, Arroyo Grande, CA. (805) 473-2186. www.brainresources.com

10 *The Sound Health™ Series* is a collection of beautiful, rearranged classical music performed by The Arcangelos Chamber Ensemble. Album titles include: *Concentration, Learning, Thinking, Inspiration, Productivity, Motivation, Relax, and De-Stress.* Produced by Richard Lawrence & Joshua Leeds. Available online at www.sound-remedies.com or by calling (800) 788-0949.

11 Herman Helmholtz, *On the Sensations of Tone.* NY, Dover, 1954.

12 Pentium™ is a registered trademark of Intel Corporation.

Appendix A

CORE PRINCIPLES OF ALFRED TOMATIS

- The ear is like a battery. The primary function of the ear is to convert sound waves to electrical waves that charge the neo-cortex of the brain.
- Sound is a nutrient; we can either *charge* or *discharge* the nervous system by the sounds we take in through both air and bone conduction.
- There is a distinction between *hearing* and *listening*. The two are related but distinct processes. Hearing is passive, listening is active and conscious. This corresponds to the difference between *seeing* and *looking*. Listening and looking are active focusing processes.
- The quality of an individual's listening ability will affect not only spoken and written language development but also alertness, creativity, and the ability to focus. Listening abilities also influence communication thereby shaping social development, confidence and self-image.
- The active process of listening can be re-focused or enhanced by auditory stimulation using musical and vocal sounds rich in high frequencies. This is accomplished through the use of Gregorian Chant and the filtered music of Mozart. Additionally, Tomatis has invented a device known as the *Electronic Ear* which is central to his program.
- The process of listening through the Electronic Ear helps *rehabilitate* the human ear to the ideal listening state. The function of the Electronic Ear is to re-educate, or tonify, the muscles of the middle ear essential to accurate perception of sound, to awaken the intel-

lect and enhance the desire and motivation to listen (not only with the ear, but with the whole body), to place enriched sounds into the voice, and to develop a dominant ear (usually the right ear).

- Communication is a process that begins *in utero*. The unborn child hears as early as the fourth month after conception. Sound literally helps grow the brain and nervous system of the fetus.
- We can only duplicate the sounds that we can hear. This is known as *The Tomatis Effect*. ✧

ENDNOTES

The Author gratefully acknowledges Dr. Ron Minson for his review of this material for accuracy. Dr. Minson is the medical director of The Center for InnerChange in Denver, CO, and is a certified Tomatis practitioner. (See Appendix C for further information.)

Appendix B

Sonic Alchemists Resource Information

Vickie Dodd
Mind/Body Productions
Port Angeles, WA, USA
Tel: (360) 452-5922 Email: sounds@flash.net
Seminars, Books, Music

Robert Gass, Ed.D.
Spring Hill Music
P.O. Box 800, Boulder, CO 80306 USA
Tel: (303) 938-1188 Web: www.springhillmedia.com
Music catalog

Jonathan Goldman
Sound Healers Association
P.O. Box 2240, Boulder, CO 80306 USA
Tel: (303) 443-8181 Web: www.healingsounds.com
Healing Sounds seminars, correspondence courses, Spirit Music tapes and CD's

Janalea Hoffman
Rhythmic Medicine
11445 Craig, Overland Park, KS 66210 USA
Tel: (913) 696-1990 Web: www.rhythmicmedicine.com
Seminars, Books, Music

Arthur Hull
Village Music Circle
108 Coalinga Way, Santa Cruz, CA 95060 USA
Tel: (408) 458-1946 Web: www.drumcircle.com
Seminars, Drums

Michael Jones
Narada Media
4650 N. Port Washington Road, Milwaukee, WI 53212 USA
Tel: (414) 961-8350
Music

Tom Kenyon
Acoustic Brain Research
P.O.Box 98, Orcas, WA 98280 USA
Tel: (360) 376-5781. Email: office@tomkenyon.com Web: www.tomkenyon.com
Seminars, Books, Music

Therese Schroeder-Sheker
Chalice of Repose Project
P.O. Box 169, Mt. Angel, OR 97362 USA Tel: (503) 845-609
Email: corpinfo@chaliceofrepose.org Web: www.chaliceofrepose.org
Seminars, Books, Music, Training programs

Fred Schwartz, M.D.
Transitions Music
1930 Monroe Drive, Atlanta, GA 30324 USA
Tel: (404) 355-4242 Web: www.transitionsmusic.com
Music catalog

Molly Scott, Ed.D.
Creative Resonance Institute
Box U - Warner Hill, Charlemont, MA 01339 USA
Tel: (413) 339-4245 Fax: (413) 339-0144
Seminars

Michael Stevens
Theta Technologies
P.O. Box 130, Fall City, WA 98024 USA
Tel: (800) 395-9148
Light/Sound Machines

Jeffrey Thompson, D.C.
The Center for Neuroacoustic Research
169 Saxony Road, Suite 209, Encinitas, CA 92024 USA
Tel: (760) 942-6749
Email: cnr@neuroacoustic.com Web: www.jeffthompson.com
Seminars, Music, Private sessions

Appendix C

SOUNDWORK RESOURCES

Advanced Brain Technologies (The Listening Program)
Alexander Doman, Director
P.O. Box 1088, Ogden, UT 84402 USA
Tel: (888) 228-1798 Web: www.advancedbrain.com

The American Music Therapy Association
8455 Colesville Road, Suite 1000, Silver Spring, MD 20910 USA
Tel: (301) 589-3300 Web: www.musictherapy.org

Barzak Educational Institute Int'l./OptimaLearning™ Music
Ivan Barzakov, Ph.D. and Pamela Rand, Directors
885 Olive Ave, Suite A, Novato, CA 94945-2455 USA
Tel: (415) 898-0013

BioSonic Sound Healing Enterprises (Tuning Forks)
John Beaulieu, Director
P.O. Box 487, High Falls, New York 12440, USA
Tel: (800) 925-0159 Web: www.biosonics.com

Bonny Foundation (Guided Imagery and Music)
Helen Bonny, Founder
2020 Summons Street, Salina, KS 67401 USA
Tel: (913) 827-1497

Bretforton Hall Clinic (Cymatics)
Peter Guy Manners, M.D., Founder
Vale of Evansham, Worchestershire, England. WRII 5JH.
Evansham 0386-830537

The Center for InnerChange (Tomatis Method, Dynamic Listening Systems)
Ron Minson, M.D., Director
55 Madison Street, Suite 375, Denver, CO 80206 USA
Tel: (303) 320-4411 Web: www.soundmindandbody.com

The Davis Center (Sound Therapies)
Dorinne Davis, Director
98 Rt. 46 W., Budd Lake, NJ 07828 USA
Tel: (973) 347-7662
Email: davis@thedaviscenter.com Web: www.thedaviscenter.com

InnerSense (VibraSound)
Don Estes, Director
12579 Venice Blvd., Los Angeles, CA. 90066 USA
Tel: (310) 828-7714
Email: destes@mindwave.com Web: wwwharmonicresolution.com

International Harp Therapy Program
Christina Tourin, Director
PO Box 333, Mt. Laguna, CA 91948 USA
Tel: (619) 473-0008 Web: www.harprealm.com

International Society for Music in Medicine
Dr. Ralph Spintge, Executive Director
Sportkrankenhaus Hellersen, Paulmannshoher Strasse 17,
D-5880, Ludenscheid, Germany

Kairos Institute of Sound Healing and Acutonics (Tuning Forks)
Donna Carey, Director
157 Pacheco Rd., Box 8, Llano de San Juan, NM 87543 USA
Tel: (505) 587-2689
Email: info@acutonics.com Web: www.acutonics.com

Life Sounds (Accelerated Learning and Music)
Chris Brewer, Director
PO Box 227, Kalispell, MT 59903 USA
Tel: (406) 755-4875 Web: www.musicandlearning.com

LIND (Learning in New Dimensions) Institute
Ole Andersen, Director
P.O. Box 14487, San Francisco, CA 94114 USA
Tel: (415) 864-3396

Lozanov Learning Institute (Accelerated Learning)
Lou Buchsbaum, Director
6325 Woodside Court, Suite 220, Columbia, MD 21046 USA
Tel: (202) 882-4000

Lumina Productions (Cymatics Books & Videos)
Jeff Volk, Director
219 Grant Road, Newmarket, NH 03857 USA
Tel: (603) 659-2929

Mid-Atlantic Institute for Guided Imagery and Music
Carol Bush, Director
Box 4655, Virginia Beach, VA 23454 USA
Tel: (757) 498-0452

The Monroe Institute (Hemi-Sync, Binaural Frequency Programs)
62 Roberts Mountain Road, Faber, VA 22938 USA
Tel: (804) 361-1500 Web: www.monroeinstitute.com

MuSICA (Music and Science Information Computer Archive)
Dr. Norman M. Weinberger, Director
Center for Neurobiology of Learning and Memory
University of California at Irvine, Irvine, CA 92717 USA
Email: mbic@mila.ps.uci.edu Web: www.musica.com

The Music for Healing and Transition Program, Inc. (MHTP)
Melinda Gardiner, Executive Director
22 West End Road, Hillsdale, New York 12529 USA
Email: mhtp@bcn.net Web: www.mhtp.org

Nordoff-Robbins Music Therapy Clinic
New York University
26 Washington Place, New York, NY 10003 USA
Tel: (212) 998-5151 Web: www.nyu.edu/education/music/nrobbins/

Open Ear Center (Publishing, Sound Therapies)
Pat Moffit Cook, Director
6717 NE Marshall Road, Bainbridge Island, WA 98110 USA
Tel: (206) 842-5560 Web: www.openearcenter.com

Pediatric Therapeutics (Sound Therapies)
Sheila Smith Allen, Director
330 Main Street, hatham, NJ 07928 USA
Tel: (973) 635-0202 Email: Ssmiallen@aol.com

Resonant Forte, Inc. (Psychoacoustic music and sound production)
Joshua Leeds, Director
PO Box 150326, San Rafael, CA 94915 USA
Tel: (415) 482-6095 Fax: (415) 482-6034
Email: Joshua.Leeds@thepowerofsound.com Web: www.ResonantForte.com

Resonant Kinesiology Training Program
Susan Gallagher Borg, Director
41 Main Street, Burlington, VT 05401 USA
Tel: (802) 860-2814

Resonant Living, Inc. (Tuning Forks, Healing Sound Devices)
Randy Masters, Director
PO Box 64, Aptos, CA 95001 USA
Tel: (831) 662-2594
Email: resonantliving@yahoo.com Web: www.sacredwindchimes.com

Sound Healers Association
Jonathan Goldman, Founder
P.O. Box 2240, Boulder, CO 80306 USA
Tel: (303) 443-8181 Web: www.healingsounds.com

Sound-Remedies.com (Psychoacoustic Music, Books, and Videos)
Joshua Leeds, Director
PO Box 150326, San Rafael, CA 94915 USA
Tel: (805) 278-9400 Fax: (805) 485-1801
Email: info@sound-remedies.com Web: Sound-Remedies.com

TAKETINA
Reinhard Flatischler, Director
a-1140 Vienna, Muhlbergstre, Vienna, Austria
Tel: 011-43-1-979 50 65 Web: www.taketina.com

Tama-Do Academy of Sound, Color and Movement
Fabien Maman, Director
22937 Arlington Ave., #203, Torrance, CA 90501 USA
(800) 4-TAMA-DO Web: www.tama-do.com

Tomatis Centers worldwide:
Tomatis Développement
22 Boulevard Royal, L- 2449 Luxembourg
Tel: 352.26.27.20, Fax:352.26.27.20.25
Email: info@tomatis-group.com Web: www.tomatis-group.com
Additional Internet information: **www.tomatis.com**

Vox Mundi - The Voice School
Sylvia Nakkach, Director
4053 Harlan St, #202, Emeryville, CA 94608 USA
Tel: (510) 595 0819
E-mail: snakkach@cs.com Web: www.voxmundiproject.com

Appendix D

RECOMMENDED READING

Atwater, F. Holmes. *The Monroe Institute's Hemi-Sync Process: A Theoretical Perspective.* VA: The Monroe Institute, 1988.

Bentov, Itshak. *Stalking the Wild Pendulum: On the Mechanics of Consciousness.* Rochester, VT: Destiny, 1988.

Berendt, Joachim-Ernst. *Nada Brahma: The World is Sound.* VT: Destiny Books, 1987.

Brewer, Chris, and Campbell, Don. *Rhythms of Learning.* NY: Zephyr, 1991.

Browne, Malcolm W. "Ear's Own Sounds May Underlie It's Precision." *New York Times* 9 June 1992: C1.

Campbell, Don. *The Mozart Effect.* NY: Avon Books, 1998.

— *Music: Physician for Times to Come.* IL: Quest Books, 1991.

— *Introduction to the Musical Brain.* TX: MMB, 1983.

Carlson, Neil R. *Physiology of Behavior.* MA: Allyn and Bacon, 1994.

Clynes, Manfred. *Music, Mind, and Brain: The Neuropsychology of Music.* NY: Plenum Press, 1982.

Cushman, A. "Drumming to the Rhythms of Life." *Yoga Journal.* Jan., 1993.

Diallo, Yaya. *The Healing Drum: African Wisdom Teachings.* VT: Destiny, 1989.

Flatischler, Reinhard. *The Forgotten Power of Rhythm.* Mendocino, CA: LifeRhythm, 1992.

— "The Influence of Musical Rhythmicity in Internal Rhythmical Events" *MusicMedicine.* Ed. Ralph Spintge. MO: MMB Music, 1992.; 241-248.

Gardner, Kay. *Sounding the Inner Landscape; Music as Medicine.* Stonington, MN: Caduceus Publications, 1990.

Gass, Robert. *Chanting; Discovering Spirit in Sound.* NY: Broadway Books, 1999.

Gaynor, Mitchell L. *Sounds of Healing.* NY: Broadway Books, 1999.

Goldman, Jonathan. *Healing Sounds.* Rockport, MA: Element, 1992.

— "Sonic Entrainment." *MusicMedicine.* Ed. Ralph Spintge. MO: MMB Music, 1992. 194-208.

— "Sonic Entrainment." *Music: Physician For Times To Come.* Ed. Don Campbell. London: Quest Books, 1991. 217-233.

Guzzetta, Cathie E. "Nursing the Music of the Soul." *Music; Physician for Times to Come.* Ed. Don Campbell. Wheaton, IL: Quest, 1991; 146-166.

Heimrath, Johannes. *The Healing Power of the Gong.* MO: MMB, 1994.

Helmholtz, Hermann. *On the Sensations of Tone.* NY: Dover, 1885.

Hoffman, Janalea. *Rhythmic Medicine; Music with a Purpose.* Leawood, KS: Jamillan Press, 1995.

Hutchinson, Michael. *Mega Brain: New Tools and Techniques for Brain Growth and Mind Expansion.* NY: Ballantine Books, 1987.

— *Mega Brain Power: Transform Your Life with Mind Machines and Brain Nutrients.* NY: Hyperion, 1994.

Jourdain, Robert. *Music, the Brain, and Ecstacy.* NY: Avon Books, 1997.

Kahn, Hazrat Inayat. *The Music of Life.* New Lebanon, NY: Omega Publications, 1983.

Kenyon, Tom. *Brain States.* FL: United States Publishing, 1994.

— *The Hathor Material.* CA: S.E.E. Publications, 1996.

Leeds, Joshua. *The Power of Sound.* VT: Healing Arts Press, 2001.

Le Mee, Katherine. Chant; *The Origins, Form, Practice, and Healing Power of Gregorian Chant.* NY: Bell Tower, 1994.

Leonard, George. *The Silent Pulse; A Search for the Perfect Rhythm that Exists in Each of Us.* NY: Dutton, 1978.

Maxfield, Melinda C. "The Journey of the Drum." *Music and Miracles.* Ed. Don Campbell. Wheaton, IL: Quest Books, 1992. 137-155.

McClellan, Randall. *The Healing Forces of Music.* MA: Element, 1991.

Monroe Institute. *Hemi-Sync.* VA: Monroe Institute, 1989. Monroe, Robert. *Ultimate Journey.* NY: Doubleday, 1994.

Newham, Paul. *The Singing Cure; An Introduction to Voice Movement Therapy.* MA: Shambhala, 1994.

Oster, G. "Auditory Beats in the Brain." *Scientific American* 1973 Vol. 229, 94-102.

Ostrander, Sheila, and E. Schroeder. *Superlearning 2000* NY: Delacorte Press, 1994.

Pohlmann, Ken. "Psycho-What?" *Stereo Review.* Sept. 1989: 117-120.

Redmond, Layne. *When the Drummers were Women.* NY: Harmony, 1997.

Schafer, R. Murray. *The Soundscape.* VT: Destiny, 1977.

Spintge, Ralph. *Music Medicine.* MO: MMB, 1992.

Stockhausen, Karlheinz. *Towards a Cosmic Music.* Dorset, England: Element, 1989.

Tomatis, Dr. Alfred. Interview. *About the Tomatis Method.* Ed. Billie Thompson. Toronto: The Listening Centre Press, 1989. 209-225.

—-*The Conscious Ear.* NY: Station Hill Press, 1991.

—-*The Ear and Language.* Ontario, Canada: Moulin Publishing, 1996.

Weeks, Bradford. *About the Tomatis Method.* Ed. Billie Thompson. Toronto: The Listening Centre Press, 1989. 159-189.

Wise, Anna. *The High Performance Mind; Mastering Brainwaves for Insight, Healing, and Creativity.* NY: Tarcher/Putnam, 1995.

About the Author

Joshua Leeds is a composer, producer, and sound researcher. He is one of few published authorities in the exciting new field of psychoacoustics—the study of the effects of music and sound on the human nervous system. Since 1986 he has produced more than thirty-five recordings, collaborating with leaders in health, psychology, and neurodevelopment. Cocreators include Louise L. Hay, Andrew Weil, M.D., Anna Wise, Dr. Jeffrey Thompson, The Monroe Institute, Advanced Brain Technologies, The Arcangelos Chamber Ensemble, and the Apollo Ensemble.

Since 1991 Joshua has published numerous magazine articles focusing on the therapeutic applications of music and sound. American and European publications include the peer-reviewed *American Journal of Acupuncture, Open Ear Journal, New Age Retailer, Caduceus,* and *Nyt Aspect.* He is the author of *The Power of Sound* (Healing Arts Press, 2001) and *Sonic Alchemy* (InnerSong Press, 1997).

Joshua is the director of Resonant Forte, Inc. Specializing in the creation of audio programs for health, learning, and productivity, Resonant Forte soundtracks are widely distributed in consumer, education, and therapeutic sectors. He is also the founder of the Sound Remedies Catalog, an online resource for psychoacoustically-oriented music, books, and videos (www.sound-remedies.com).

Joshua conducts seminars internationally on the evolving field of psychoacoustics. His emphasis is training musicians, healthcare and education professionals.

Joshua resides in the San Francisco Bay Area.

DISCOGRAPHY ~ RECORDINGS PRODUCED BY JOSHUA LEEDS

2003-05	*The Essential Sound Series* (8 CDs)	Resonant Forte
2002	*Joyful Birth*	Rodale Press
1999	*The Listening Program* [1] (8 CD set)	Advanced Brain Tech
1996-99	*The Sound Health Series* (8 CDs)	Advanced Brain Tech
1998	*Sound Body, Sound Mind Music for Healing* [2]	Upaya (Time/Warner)
1997	*Eight Guided Meditations for Optimum Health* [3]	Upaya (Time/Warner)
1997	*Baroque Garden for Concentration* [4]	The Monroe Institute
1996	*Masterworks for Relaxation* [4]	The Monroe Institute
1991	*Safe Passage* [5]	InnerSong Press
1989	*Rhapsody* [5]	Hay House
1987	*Gift of the Present* [5]	Hay House
1986	*Songs of Affirmation* [5]	Hay House

1 In collaboration with Alex Doman, Ron Minson, M.D., and Lori Riggs

2 In collaboration with Andrew Weil, M.D. and Anna Wise

3 In collaboration with Andrew Weil, M.D.

4 In collaboration with The Monroe Institute

5 In collaboration with Louise L. Hay

Contact Information

For further information about books, recordings, or seminars by Joshua Leeds:

- Mail: PO Box 150326, San Rafael, CA 94915 USA
- Tel: (415) 482-6095 Fax: (415) 482-6034
- Email: Joshua.Leeds@the**power**of**sound**.com
- Websites: www.the**power**of**sound**.com, www.sound-remedies.com, www.ResonantForte.com

THE SOUND REMEDIES CATALOG

The focus of the Sound Remedies Catalog is the emerging field of *soundwork,* broadly defined as the intentional creation and employment of music and sound for specific applications. Sound Remedies contains categorized lists of music and sound programs, as well as resources in the following categories:

- ❑ Children
- ❑ Concentration/Accelerated Learning
- ❑ Healing and Balance
- ❑ Massage/Bodywork
- ❑ Office/Treatment Room Ambience
- ❑ Relaxation/Stress Reduction
- ❑ Sleep
- ❑ Therapeutic Applications
- ❑ Guided Imagery
- ❑ Psychoacoustics
- ❑ Vibroacoustics
- ❑ Binaural Beat Frequencies
- ❑ Tomatis / Sound Stimulation

New programs are constantly being reviewed and added. Categories continue to grow as psychoacoustic programs of high aesthetic value and effective sonic technologies are produced.

Most soundtracks in the catalog have been produced with highly specific methodologies and outcomes in mind. Be it for health, learning, or productivity, these "sonic tools" are designed for the enhancement of human function.

HOW DO I ACCESS THE CATALOG?

The complete Sound Remedies catalog can be viewed online at **www.sound-remedies.com.** Purchases may be made on the secure website or by calling (800) 788-0949 or (805) 278-9400.